The Genesis of Ezra Pound's
C A N T O S

The Genesis of Ezra Pound's

CANTOS

RONALD BUSH

Princeton University Press

Copyright © 1976 by Princeton University Press
Published by Princeton University Press, Princeton, New Jersey
In the United Kingdom: Princeton University Press, Guildford, Surrey
ALL RIGHTS RESERVED

Library of Congress Cataloging in Publication Data will
be found on the last printed page of this book

This book has been composed in Linotype Electra

Printed in the United States of America
by Princeton University Press, Princeton, New Jersey

To Marilyn

CONTENTS

vii

ACKNOWLEDGMENTS

I am grateful to have the opportunity to thank the people who helped make this book. Conversations with John Carroll, Jim McGregor, Bill Quillian, and Steve Salop suggested leads and pointed out many dead ends. John Peck and David Perkins read the manuscript with interest and care, and their encouragement came at a time when it was badly needed. Two editors at Princeton University Press, Jerry Sherwood and Miriam Brokaw, guided the book into print with admirable patience. Andy Rosenbaum and Elizabeth Parry helped read the proof. A grant from the Clark Fund at Harvard paid for some of the preparation costs.

I particularly wish to thank A. Walton Litz. To say that he supervised this work when it was a dissertation gives little idea of how much of his generosity is bound up in it. It is a great pleasure to acknowledge his aid and his kindness.

My greatest debt is acknowledged in the dedication.

Acknowledgments

Pavannes and Divisions. All Rights Reserved.

"Mr. Pound's Cantos," in *New English Weekly* iii, iv (11 May 1933). All Rights Reserved.

"De Gourmont: A Distinction," in *Little Review* 10-11 (Feb.-March 1919). All Rights Reserved.

"Wyndham Lewis," in *The Egoist*, 1914. All Rights Reserved.

"Approach to Paris." *New Age* xiii, 23 (Oct. 2, 1913). All Rights Reserved.

Gaudier-Brzeska. Copyright 1970 by Ezra Pound. All Rights Reserved.

The Selected Letters of Ezra Pound 1907-1941, D. D. Paige, ed. Copyright 1950 by Ezra Pound.

Translations. Copyright 1926, 1954 by Ezra Pound.

Excerpts from the work of T. S. Eliot, including *The Waste Land: A Facsimile and Transcript*, ed. by Valerie Eliot, are reprinted by permission of Harcourt Brace Jovanovich, Inc. and by permission of Mrs. Valerie Eliot and Faber & Faber Ltd.

ABBREVIATIONS

G-B	*Gaudier-Brzeska: A Memoir*. Norfolk: New Directions, 1970.
L	*The Letters of Ezra Pound 1907-1941*, ed. D. D. Paige. New York: Harcourt, Brace & World, Inc., 1950.
LE	*Literary Essays of Ezra Pound*, ed. with an introduction by T. S. Eliot. Norfolk: New Directions, 1968.
Life	Noel Stock, *The Life of Ezra Pound*. New York: Pantheon Books, 1970.
PD 1	*Pavannes and Divisions*. New York: Alfred A. Knopf, 1918.
PD 2	*Pavannes and Divagations*. Norfolk: New Directions, 1958.
P/J	*The Letters of Ezra Pound to James Joyce, with Pound's Essays on Joyce*, ed. with a commentary by Forrest Read, Norfolk: New Directions, 1967.
Selected Prose	*Selected Prose, 1909-1965*, ed. with an introduction by William Cookson. London: Faber and Faber, 1973.
SR	*The Spirit of Romance*. Norfolk: New Directions, 1952.
Translations	*Ezra Pound: Translations*, with an introduction by Hugh Kenner. Norfolk: New Directions, 1963.

A Guide to the Publication History of the *Cantos*
up to and Including 1925's *A Draft of XVI.*
Cantos of Ezra Pound for the Beginning
of a Poem of some Length

NOTE: In the text of this study, reference to these publications will be made according to the *headings* of each entry. For example, Number 1 will appear as *Three Cantos.*

1. *Three Cantos* June-August 1917 (but composed in late 1915)

    These first drafts appeared, respectively, as *Three Cantos I, Three Cantos II,* and *Three Cantos III* in the June, July, and August 1917 numbers of *Poetry.* Along with their immediate revisions in *Lustra,* they are sometimes called the ur-Cantos, and were partially incorporated and partially scrapped when Pound rewrote the beginning of the poem in the summer of 1923. They are reproduced below in Chapter Three.

2. The *Lustra Cantos* October 1917

    The *Lustra Cantos* were superficially revised versions of *Three Cantos,* and appeared as *Three Cantos of a Poem of Some Length* in the American edition of *Lustra* (New York: Alfred A. Knopf, 1917). They were reprinted in *Quia Pauper Amavi* (London: The Ovid Press, 1919), where Pound added marginalia.

3. The *Future Cantos* February-April 1918

    These were chosen excerpts of the *Lustra Cantos* that appeared as "Passages from the Opening Address in a Long Poem," "Images from the Second Canto of a Long Poem," and "An Interpolation taken from the Third Canto of a Long Poem" in the February, March, and April numbers of the London periodical, *The Future.* These excerpts are reproduced in Appendix A.

4. Canto IV October 1919

   Canto IV was published independently by the Ovid Press as *The Fourth Canto* in October 1919. It was reprinted with minor changes in the *Dial* for June 1920, and in *Poems 1918-1921* (New York: Boni and Liveright, 1921). For A *Draft of XVI Cantos*, Pound altered Canto IV slightly more (he added, for instance, the concluding lines — "And we sit here . . . / there in the arena . . ."). The altered version was reprinted in later editions.

5. Cantos V, VI, and VII August 1921

   Cantos V, VI, and VII were first published in the *Dial* for August 1921, and were reprinted with minor changes in *Poems 1918-1921* and in A *Draft of XVI Cantos*. Between A *Draft of XVI Cantos* and A *Draft of XXX Cantos*, Pound considerably altered Canto VI. I have reproduced the original in Appendix B.

6. *The Eighth Canto* (later Canto II) May 1922

   The "Eighth Canto" was published in the *Dial* for May 1922. When Pound revised the beginning of the poem in 1923, he rewrote the Canto's opening and used the rewritten version as Canto II in A *Draft of XVI Cantos*. In subsequent collections, it remained unchanged.

7. The *Malatesta Cantos* (later Cantos VIII, IX, X, and XI) July 1923

   These were published as the "Malatesta Cantos (Cantos IX to XII of a Long Poem)" in the July 1923 *Criterion*. In A *Draft of XVI Cantos*, they were shifted to the position of Cantos VIII to XI.

8. *Transatlantic Review's Two Cantos* January 1924

   Later Canto XIII and the "Baldy Bacon" half of Canto XII, these two Cantos appeared in the first number (January 1924) of Ford's *Transatlantic Review*. Without changing them, Pound moved them to their present position in A *Draft of XVI Cantos*.

9. *A Draft of XVI Cantos* January 1925

   A DRAFT OF XVI. CANTOS of EZRA POUND for the Beginning of a Poem of some Length was published in what Pound called a "dee looks edtn . . . of UN-RIVALLED magnificence" in limited edition by William Bird's Three Mountains Press, with ornamental capitals by Henry Strater. These Cantos were generally the same as the first sixteen Cantos in later editions, with a few exceptions. In addition to the differences in Cantos IV and VI, already mentioned, Canto III did not contain the phrase, "As Poggio has remarked," and ended with a reference to Dante's Casella rather than the present allusion to the story of Ignez da Castro.

The Genesis of Ezra Pound's
C A N T O S

things have ends (or scopes) and beginnings.   To
know what precedes   and what follows

先   後

will assist yr/ comprehension of process

— Canto 77

CHAPTER I

RED HERRINGS

IN January 1925, after a false start and ten years' work, Ezra Pound published A *Draft of XVI Cantos for the Beginning of a Poem of Some Length*. Since 1915, the *Cantos* had shared space on Pound's triangular table with the manuscripts of *Ulysses* and "Gerontion," and had come to incorporate much of what he learned from his contemporaries. Nor did the *Cantos'* evolution end in 1925. Once underway, Pound almost immediately began to alter the manner of the first volume of the *Cantos*, and the poem continued to change over the next forty years. We have only to note the difference between the chronicles of China and John Adams in Cantos LII-LXXI and the personal reverie of the Pisan Cantos to understand how much Pound's succeeding preoccupations could affect the development of the *Cantos*.

And yet, it is rare to read an account of the *Cantos'* organization that acknowledges any development. The reason is not hard to find. In the belated remarks he made about the poem, Pound spoke as if his method had never changed. And even though he explained his procedures in varying and eccentric ways, his remarks were sufficient to mislead several decades of admirers.

At first, Pound hesitated to sanction an authoritative account of the *Cantos*. In 1924, on the eve of the publication of A *Draft of XVI Cantos*, he wrote to R. P. Blackmur that "I do *not* want them commented on, *yet*" (L, p. 190). But the temptation to answer charges of formlessness became too great, and Pound, living in Rapallo, issued two *pronunciamentos*. In 1928 he explained to Yeats that the *Cantos* would eventually "display a structure like that of a Bach fugue."[1]

[1] W. B. Yeats, A *Vision* (New York, 1938), p. 4.

And in the 1933 *New English Weekly* he declared the poem's "ideogramic method."[2] These two formulations, as Eliot said about phrases of his own, had a truly embarrassing success in the world. With their promise of exotic symmetries, they imposed a false set of expectations onto the work and made it nearly impossible to trace the poem's actual genesis. If we are ever to understand the place of the *Cantos* in modern literature, the context of Pound's pronouncements now needs to be restored. Being only critical hindsight in relation to the beginnings of the poem, these statements should no longer be taken as definitive instruction about the *Cantos* as a whole.

Pound's original notion of the *Cantos* can be guessed from hints he left before moving to Italy. In the crevices of his London prose, he described his intention to write a "long imagiste or vorticist poem" (G-B, p. 47), and in the opening of *Three Cantos I* he indicated his desire to write a modernized *Sordello*. The background of Vorticism and the narrative mode of *Sordello*, which will provide the points of departure for the rest of this study, were in 1917 uncomprehended and ignored. Pound made another suggestion, however, which was assimilated by his contemporaries and which ought to supply a corrective to today's prevailing view of the early Cantos' ideogrammic objectivity. In June 1917, *Three Cantos I* addressed Robert Browning, and described the "use" of the *Cantos* and of *Sordello* as the rendering of *"our life, your life, my life extended."* Between June and October 1917, when a revised set of *Three Cantos* was published in the American edition of *Lustra*, Pound discussed the poem with T. S. Eliot[3] and communicated his plan to connect meditation and action. Eliot, we know, in reviews of the next two years informed his readers that the poem's autobiographical status affected its organization. Writing in *To-Day*, Eliot noticed "Pound's recent unfinished epic," and commented:

[2] *The New English Weekly*, III, iv (May 11, 1933), p. 96.

[3] See L, p. 115: "the version [of *Three Cantos*] for the book [*Lustra*] is, I think, much improved. Eliot is the only person who proffered criticism instead of general objection."

"In appearance, it is a rag-bag of Mr. Pound's reading in various languages. . . . And yet the thing has, after one has read it once or twice, a positive coherence; it is an objective and reticent autobiography."[4] A year later, in the *Athenaeum*, Eliot wrote that the *Cantos* showed what "the consummation of Mr. Pound's work could be: a final fusion of all his masks."[5]

What Eliot understood by "reticent autobiography" (a question considered by Chapters Four and Five) may here be summarized as the dramatization of a sensibility in the process of understanding itself. His notion was based on an extension of the narrative techniques of a novel like Joyce's *Portrait* to the writing of poetry. Although Eliot's critical contemporaries were usually not subtle enough to catch his exact meaning, many of them remained reasonably faithful to Pound's intentions. Reviewing the *Cantos*, Maxwell Bodenheim,[6] Babbette Deutsch,[7] Delmore Schwartz,[8] Allen Tate, and R. P. Blackmur, among others, put the unity of

[4] "Ezra Pound," *To-Day*, IV, 19 (September 1918), pp. 6-7.

[5] "The Method of Mr. Pound," *The Athenaeum*, October 24, 1919, p. 1,065.

[6] Bodenheim wrote in "Isolation of Carved Metal" (*The Dial*, LXXII, January 1922, p. 91) that Cantos IV-VII "contain the subconscious matter deposited by years of reading and observation in one man's mind, and in their residence in this subconscious state they have . . . undergone a metamorphosis. . . ."

[7] Babbette Deutsch, in "Ezra Pound's Spars of Knowledge," wrote that "to read the *Cantos* is not so much like listening to good talk . . . it is far rather like over-hearing a soliloquy by a man, who, talking to himself, feels no need to finish a sentence." *The New York Herald Tribune Book Review* (March 26, 1933), p. 4.

[8] Schwartz was more sympathetic. He wrote in "Ezra Pound's Very Useful Labors," *Poetry*, LI, 6 (March 1938), pp. 324-339, that "The Cantos have no plot, although as the poem continues, the repetition of key phrases, characters and situations, makes more and more clear the kind of unity which the *Cantos* do have, a wholeness based on certain obsessions or preoccupations, deriving itself from the character of Pound's mind . . . we have a long poem without a hero . . . or if there is a hero . . . it is, in fact, Pound himself, the taste of Pound, above all his literary taste. . . ."

the poem in the character of Pound's mind. Of these critics, Tate and Blackmur were the most eloquent. Tate, in a review famous for its description of the "conversational form" of the *Cantos*, wrote: "The ostensible subjects of *The Cantos* — ancient, middle, and modern times — are only the materials round which Mr. Pound's mind plays constantly. . . . It is this tone . . . which is the meaning of the Cantos."[9]

Blackmur went further and defined a functional relation between the *Cantos'* speaking voice and the elliptical quality of the subject matter. In "The Masks of Ezra Pound," he explained that the *Cantos* render the voice of an anecdotalist who is searching for the point of familiar stories.[10] By characterizing the historical material of the poem as anecdote rather than narrative, Blackmur implied that the importance of the action per se was secondary to its importance as the reflection of an anterior consciousness.

After Pound went on to emphasize other facets of the poem, the meditative or autobiographical view of the *Cantos* grew unfashionable. Ironically, its last and perhaps most perceptive proponent had little taste for Pound's accomplishment. In the early forties, Yvor Winters discussed the *Cantos'* meditative conventions as evidence in an attack on literary modernism. According to Winters, Pound

> is bent on fusing his impressions into some kind of whole, and he seems to desire a whole which shall not falsify them or violate their essential quality: only one convention is plausible, the convention of remembered impressions, or revery. Thus we get the *Cantos*, poems in which a poet remembers his past experience of all kinds, literary, personal, and imaginative, and moves from recol-

[9] From "Ezra Pound's Golden Ass," *The Nation*, 132, 3440 (June 10, 1931), pp. 632-634. Tate also called the poem a "many voiced monologue."

[10] See R. P. Blackmur, *The Double Agent* (New York, 1935), pp. 48-49. The essay was reprinted from the January-March 1934 *Hound and Horn*.

lection to recollection purely and simply by means of suggestion . . . Pound at maturity, then, sees life primarily as a matter of remembered impressions, and his art is an art of revery: he is a sensibility without a mind, or with as little mind as is well possible.[11]

Donald Davie has called these remarks more applicable to *Three Cantos* than to their revisions,[12] but I do not believe that the Pound who wrote *A Draft of XVI Cantos* would have objected. Winters' phrase "a sensibility without a mind" was not meant as a compliment, and yet it corresponds, as we shall see, to Pound's 1919 admiration for the way Remy de Gourmont differentiated personalities "by the modes of their sensibility, not by sub-degrees of their state of civilization" (LE, p. 340). "Mind," in the sense that Winters used it, meant very little to Pound, who wrote in the same essay that "An 'idea' has little value apart from the modality of the mind which receives it" (LE, p. 341).

§

In the twenties, when the *Cantos'* reviewers were beginning to elaborate Pound's early hints, Pound himself rethought his procedures in musical terms. Heretofore, a technical imitation of music had played only a negligible role in the composition of Cantos I-XVI. In his criticism Pound endorsed Pater's musical paradigm for poetry, but during his first decade in London he wrote about musical structure with the imprecision of an amateur. In a 1915 note to "The Classical Stage of Japan," he admitted: "This looks like a sort of syncopation. I don't know enough about music to consider it musically with any fullness, but it offers to the student of metric most interesting parallels, or if not parallels, sugges-

[11] *In Defense of Reason* (Chicago, 1947), pp. 495-496. Reprinted from *The Anatomy of Nonsense* (1943).

[12] See Donald Davie, *Ezra Pound: Poet As Sculptor* (New York, 1964), p. 78.

7

tions for comparison with sapphics and with some of the troubadour measures. . . ."[13]

When the foundations for the *Cantos* were being laid, then, Pound (as he later said of Yeats) hardly knew "a fugue from a frog." However, from late 1918 to early 1921, Pound reviewed music for *The New Age* under the pseudonym of William Atheling, and in the process developed a knowledge of musical expression. It was during this period that he first met the young violinist, Olga Rudge. And around June 1923, he made friends with a budding composer named George Antheil, who assured him that his (Pound's) musical instincts were sounder than most professionals'.[14] In 1924, Pound published defenses of Antheil in which his descriptions of structure shifted away from phrases derived from Vorticist painting toward a technical musical vocabulary. In an essay entitled "George Antheil," he began to write about "horizontal music"[15] and remarked about Antheil's "analogies to [the work that had been Pound's touchstone for modernist structure] Lewis' 'Timon.' "[16] The essay was revised for book form in *Antheil and the Theory of Harmony* (1924), where Pound crystallized what became the theory of the great bass. In 1928, Wyndham Lewis wrote (only half facetiously) that Pound was "giving up words" and "taking to music."[17] It was in 1928 that Pound explained to Yeats that the *Cantos* would display "a structure like that of a Bach fugue," and in 1929 that he wrote to his father:

> Afraid the whole damn poem is rather obscure, especially in fragments. Have I ever given you outline of main scheme : : : or whatever it is?

[13] "The Classical Stage of Japan: Ernest Fenollosa's Work on the Japanese Noh," ed. by Ezra Pound, *The Drama*, v, 18 (May 1915), p. 229.

[14] See Stock's *Life*, p. 252.

[15] "George Antheil," *The Criterion*, ii, 7 (April 1924), p. 323.

[16] *Ibid.*, p. 331. For the importance of Lewis' "Timon," see below, Chapter Two.

[17] Wyndham Lewis, *Time and Western Man* (Boston, 1957), p. 40.

8

I. Rather like, or unlike subject and response and counter subject in fugue. (L, p. 210)

Given Pound's relatively late education in musical composition, these pronouncements comprise an extremely unlikely description of the *Cantos'* "main scheme" from the beginning. At best Pound's ascription of musical structure to the *Cantos* helps to explain a change in emphasis in Cantos XVII-XXX, written during the mid-twenties. It was in 1928's *A Draft of the Cantos 17-27* that he modified the *Cantos'* Vorticist repetition of design units[18] in a way that reflected his increased appreciation for the qualities of counterpoint and harmony in music.[19] Canto XXV, for example, sounded and developed the theme of Tibullus' *"pone metum, Cerinthe; deus non laedit amantes"* (Put fear aside, Cerinthus. God doesn't harm lovers), playing it off against themes of venality and finally resolving it into an apotheosis (the story of Anchises and Aphrodite). To make sure that his readers were aware of the aesthetic behind these variations, Pound inserted musical references into the epiphany of Anchises, who

> saw the waves taking form as crystal,
> notes as facets of air,
> and the mind there, before them, moving,
> so that notes needed not move.

[18] See below, Chapter Two.

[19] Several writers close to Pound took his cue and explained the riddle of the *Cantos* by means of musical analogies. Yeats wrote that the impressions of the poem were "related like the notes of a symphony," but remained skeptical about Pound's success. (See *The Oxford Book of Modern Verse*, London, 1936, p. xxiv.) Louis Zukofsky, in "American Poetry 1920-1930" (*The Symposium*, January 1930), and "The Cantos of Ezra Pound" (*The Criterion*, April 1931), argued that the *Cantos'* structure resembled not so much a symphony as one of the horizontal melodies that Pound had described in "George Antheil." In "Music Fit for the Odes" (*The Hound and Horn*, January-March 1931), Dudley Fitts cited long passages of the "Antheil" piece and wrote what remains the most satisfying description of the *Cantos'* musical affinities. It was Fitts who first called attention to the lines from Canto XXV cited above.

9

If Pound's pronouncements about the *Cantos'* fugal structure are inappropriate to a consideration of *A Draft of XVI Cantos*, his remarks about the poem's ideogrammic surface are even more so. In his collected and uncollected prose, no programmatic use of the term "ideogram" or "ideograph" appears until 1927. It is true that, in 1915, Pound touted Fenollosa's essay, "The Chinese Written Character as a Medium for Poetry," as "a whole basis of aesthetic" (L, p. 61). However, as Herbert Schneidau noticed,[20] he qualified that statement a year later by writing about "Fenollosa's big essay on verbs, mostly on verbs" (L, p. 82). In 1919, when the "Chinese Character" essay was first printed in the *Little Review*, Pound appended a note (later removed) that made it clear he endorsed the spirit of Fenollosa's remarks about oriental logic, and not their letter: "These precautions should be broadly conceived. It is not so much their letter, as the underlying feeling of objectification and activity that matters."[21] And in *Indiscretions* (1920), Pound suggested that Fenollosa's essay was perhaps a less important poetic tool than the Jamesian novel, to which he was paying tribute: "The sentence being the mirror of man's mind, . . . [we have] long since passed the stage when 'man sees horse' or 'farmer sows rice,' can in simple ideographic record be said to display anything remotely resembling our subjectivity" (PD 2, p. 3).

Finally, in a famous 1921 review of Cocteau's *Poésies*, Pound described Cocteau's poetry as "ideographic" in a tentative and unflattering way that made it difficult to believe he had already appropriated the term for himself. He said of Cocteau's "ideographic representation" that it was "hurrying" and that "it is sometimes incomprehensible [even] if one does read every word and try to parse it in sequence." In contrast, Pound wrote, "I, 'we' wanted and still want a

---

[20] See Herbert Schneidau, *Ezra Pound: The Image and the Real* (Baton Rouge, 1969), pp. 58ff.

[21] *The Little Review*, VI, 8 (December 1919), p. 69.

poetry where the reader must not only read every word, but must read his English as carefully as if it were a Greek that he could not rapidly be sure of comprehending."[22] Considering this ambivalence on Pound's part toward Cocteau's "ideographic" style in 1921, it is highly unlikely that he thought of himself as using such a technique in 1919, when Canto IV was published and the idiom of *A Draft of XVI Cantos* was established.

The first example of what would become Pound's characteristic shorthand use of the term ideogram to mean "heaping together the necessary components of thought"[23] occurred in 1927. In the first number of his own journal, *Exile*, he wrote that Rodker's *Adolphe 1920* was "a definite contribution . . . in that perhaps minor, but certainly far from negligible form whose ideogram has been composed by Longus, Prévost, Benjamin Constant."[24] It seems that by 1927 Pound had picked up the word "ideogram" to redefine once again his intuitive affinity for description by particulars. Like every expression starting with the "image" he adopted for that purpose, the ideogram soon developed its own peculiar connotations. If we are to trust Pound's most famous explanation in the *ABC of Reading*, the disparate elements of an ideogrammic character may be conceptually and emotionally unrelated as long as they overlap in one quality and they combine in a manner that is more spatial or simultaneous than sequential:

> when the Chinaman wanted to make a picture of something more complicated, or of a general idea, how did he go about it?
> He is to define red. How can he do it in a picture that isn't painted in red paint?

[22] Ezra Pound, "Poésies 1917-1920, Jean Cocteau," *The Dial*, LXX, 1 (January 1921), p. 110.
[23] *ABC of Economics* (London, 1933), p. 37.
[24] *The Exile*, ed. by Ezra Pound, No. 1 (Spring 1927), p. 88.

He puts (or his ancestor put) together the abbreviated pictures of

<table>
<tr><td>ROSE</td><td>CHERRY</td></tr>
<tr><td>IRON RUST</td><td>FLAMINGO[25]</td></tr>
</table>

Around 1929, the ideogrammic method became one of the most frequently used phrases in Pound's critical repertory. In 1929's *How To Read*, for instance, he asserted that the first job of the critic was to present his "ideograph of the good" (LE, p. 37). Concurrently, he began to translate his old critical tenets into terms of the ideogram. In 1933's *ABC of Reading*, we can recognize earlier comparisons between the exactitude of science and the procedures of poetry transformed into the following: "By contrast to the method of abstraction, or of defining things in more and still more general terms, Fenollosa emphasizes the method of science, 'which is the method of poetry,' as distinct from that of 'philosophic discussion,' and is the way the Chinese go about it in their ideograph or abbreviated picture writing."[26]

The same process was evident in the "exhibits" at the back of the volume. Below a series of comparative examples first published in 1913, Pound placed this note: "Example of ideogrammic method used by E. P. in *The Serious Artist* in 1913 before having access to the Fenollosa papers."[27]

In *Jefferson and/or Mussolini*, written in 1933, Pound informed his readers that the ideogrammic method was not only the subject but also the form of his criticism: "I am not putting these sentences in monolinear syllogistic arrangement, and I have no intention of using that old form of trickery to fool the reader, any reader, into thinking I have proved anything, or that having read a paragraph of my writing he KNOWS something that he can only *know* by examining a dozen or two dozen facts and putting them all together" (p. 28).

Inevitably, the ideogram had its impact on the *Cantos*.

[25] I cite from the paperback republication. Ezra Pound, *ABC of Reading* (New Directions: New York, 1960), pp. 21-22.
[26] *Ibid.*, p. 20.   [27] *Ibid.*, p. 96.

Parts of "Eleven New Cantos, XXXI-XLI," published in 1934, revealed yet another shift in emphasis, this time toward spatial configurations and away from the expressive movement of an anterior sensibility or of a controlling music. It is easy to see Pound's new emphasis on juxtaposing whole blocks of material in this excerpt from Canto XXXVII:

> "Thou shalt not," said Martin Van Buren, "jail 'em for debt."
> "that an immigrant shd. set out with good banknotes
> and find 'em at the end of his voyage
> but waste paper . . . . if a man have in primeval forest
> set up his cabin, shall rich patroon take it from him?
> High judges? Are, I suppose, subject to passions
> as have affected other great and good men, also
> subject to esprit de corps.
> The Calhouns" remarked Mr. Adams
> "Have flocked to the standard of feminine virtue"
> "Peggy Eaton's own story" (Headline 1932)
> Shall we call in the world to conduct our
> municipal government?

It would be wrong, however, to interpret a change in stress as a genuine new beginning. The ideogrammic method changed the *Cantos* more in theory than in fact. And while the *Cantos'* technique altered slightly, the new theory achieved the prominence of an official program. In a 1933 letter to the *New English Weekly*, Pound made what Blackmur called "a provisional declaration of principles"[28] and announced the *Cantos'* "ideogramic method":

MR. EZRA POUND'S "CANTOS"

Sir, — I am convinced that one should not as a general rule reply to critics or defend a work in process of being written. On the other hand, if one prints fragments of a work one perhaps owes the benevolent reader enough explanation to prevent his wasting time in unnecessary misunderstanding.

[28] Blackmur, p. 59.

The nadir of solemn and elaborate imbecility is reached by Mr. Winter in an American publication where he deplores my "abandonment of logic in the Cantos," presumably because he has never read Fenollosa or my prose criticism and has never heard of the ideogramic method, and thinks logic is limited to a few "forms of logic" which better minds were already finding inadequate to the mental needs of the XIIIth century.

Your reviewer has understood so much and is so far above the American weepers who can't see that there is any main principle of coherence in the poem, that I should like to put him right on one matter.

The poem is not a dualism of past against present. Monism is pretty bad, but dualism (Miltonic puritanism, etc.) is just plain lousy.

The poem should establish an hierarchy of values, not simply: past is good, present is bad, which I certainly do not believe and never have believed.

If the reader wants three categories he can find them rather better in: permanent, recurrent and merely haphazard or casual. (E. Pound)[29]

Pound did not mention how important the voice and the music of the poem had been to him, and the commentators did not afterwards insist. Above all, he declared his intention to vilify any critic who did not see the poem's "ideogramic" logic. To submissive reviewers he tossed two bones: the poem would "establish a hierarchy of values" and it could be divided into categories of "permanent, recurrent and merely haphazard or casual." The latter established the parameters of the next three decades of *Cantos* criticism.

§

The greatest disservice done by Pound's avowal of the ideogrammic method was to distort our perception of the *Cantos* so that a structural device seemed more prominent

[29] *The New English Weekly*, III, iv (May 11, 1933), p. 96.

than the form of the whole. Those who accepted Pound's assertions viewed the *Cantos* as a non-comparable experiment rather than as a long poem belonging to a tradition of long poems. In 1928, Eliot had defended Pound against the charge of objectionable originality, writing that "the poem which is absolutely original is absolutely bad; it is, in the bad sense, 'subjective,' with no relation to the world to which it appeals," but that Pound's poetry possessed a "true originality" which "is merely development."[30] Yet R. P. Blackmur, convinced by Pound that the *Cantos* possessed an original ideogrammic structure, wrote in 1934 that it was a "mistake" to assume "that the *Cantos* make a good part of an ordinary, complex, logically and emotionally arrayed long poem, having as a purpose the increasing realization of a theme. The *Cantos* are not complex, they are complicated."[31]

Under the influence of Pound's instruction, Hugh Kenner disagreed with the normative judgment of Blackmur's statement, but agreed on its substance: "It is usual to search for a subject-matter, a plot, a line of philosophic development, such as it has been Pound's principal achievement to dispense with."[32] Kenner held that all one can say about the development of the poem is that its proportional series of metaphors combine to form patterns of recurrence:

> Pound, quite consciously, never thinks of using two motifs, two blocks of rendering, except as parts, integral parts, of a larger rhythm of juxtaposition and recurrence. This balancing and recurrence of motifs is what holds together single cantos. It also holds together the entire work, the temporarily unfinished condition of which doesn't diminish the structural solidity of the portion existing. . . . Metaphor, conceived in Aristotle's way as a proportion among proportions, becomes in the *Cantos* the principle of major form.[33]

[30] See Eliot's introduction to *Ezra Pound: Selected Poems* (London, 1928), p. 10.
[31] Blackmur, pp. 44-45.
[32] Hugh Kenner, *The Poetry of Ezra Pound* (London, 1951), p. 252.
[33] *Ibid.*, pp. 280-281.

Thus Kenner maintained that the *Cantos* have no final end. In Daniel Pearlman's words, Kenner was not "concerned to reveal a pattern of thematic development that arises out of some inner necessity, or entelechy, which accounts for the elaboration of structure which he endeavors to describe."[34] By denying the *Cantos* "a line of philosophic development," Kenner denied them exactly that *entelechy* which we take to be the sign of an accomplished work of art.

Pound's readers are still waiting for a description of the *Cantos'* major form that will assimilate into one whole the poem's structural idiom, its generic characteristics, and its hierarchy of psychological values. It seems likely that when such a description is realized it will depend less on Pound's experimental method than on certain deep structures of the epic. Pound intended his long poem to be the latest in a line of transformations that began with the way Virgil altered the narrative inflections and the symbolic associations of the *Odyssey's* tale of return. He consciously modeled his work after Dante's *Commedia*, and he did not neglect the many levels of continuity that bind the *Commedia* back to its predecessors. The *Cantos'* inferno,[35] for example, corresponds not only to Dante's *Inferno* but to the presentation of life-killing experience in both the *Odyssey's* Telemacheia and in the Troy and Carthage related incidents at the beginning of the *Aeneid*. Just as Homer, Virgil, and Dante began their epics with characters cut off from the vital forms that sustain spiritual growth, so Pound begins his *Cantos* with an array of similarly arrested figures. As in the case of the *Cantos'* three most famous prototypes, major form grows out of a

[34] Daniel Pearlman, *The Barb of Time: On the Unity of Ezra Pound's Cantos* (New York, 1969), p. 9.

[35] Although Pound insisted that the integrity of Dante's canticles could not be maintained in a modern poem of doubt, he nevertheless allowed a minimum of light to enter the opening section of the *Cantos*. This section, composed of Cantos I to XXX (or perhaps to XLI) may thus fairly be termed the poem's "inferno."

movement from a stifled order of existence to a real order, mythologically indicated as divine, in which the individual, society, and nature are in harmony. The *Cantos'* most thoroughgoing unity is provided by patterns of imagery grounded in the epic's quest for reconciliation with what Pound called the "vital universe" (SR, p. 93). From the beginning, he planned a poem of spiritual education, a modern *Commedia*, and the *Commedia* remains the single best reference for understanding the *Cantos*. That is not to say that Pound wrote a Christian poem. Pound's humanist sense of truth led him to write in *The Spirit of Romance* that "art and humanity, remaining ever the same, gave us basis for comparison of [Shakespeare and Dante]" (SR, p. 157). He saw Dante's epic as a metaphor in the Aristotelian sense of the truth of "nature and the beauty of the world and of the spirit" (SR, p. 163). Pound rejected the *Commedia's* doctrine as "ecclesiastical lumber" (SR, p. 146), but he joined his contemporaries in replacing the authority of the church with the authority of the poetic tradition.

Thus we find in the *Cantos* an understanding based on the terms of earlier poems, but cut off from the foundations upon which those poems rested. According to Daniel Pearlman, "the very core of what the *Cantos* are all about" can be explained by examining man's relation to "the temporal order of nature."[36] Pearlman might with more justice, however, have described that order with a literary phrase like "the golden world," or with Dante's "metaphor" of the divine will. The *Cantos* describe a process of learning to direct the energy of the will so that it is in harmony with the energies of what Canto LXXXI calls the "green world." Awkward as it may seem, the best gloss for the *Cantos'* sense of ordered will is *Paradiso* III: "E'n la sua voluntade è nostra pace — it is the very quality of the blessed state that we keep ourselves

[36] Pearlman, p. 297. Pearlman made the remark in response to George Dekker's *Sailing After Knowledge: The Cantos of Ezra Pound*, from which the phrase "temporal order of nature" was cited.

within the divine will, so that our wills are themselves made one; therefore our rank from height to height through this kingdom, is pleasing to the whole kingdom, as to the King who wills us to His will. *And in His will is our peace.* It is that sea to which all things move. . . ."

A full study of the *Cantos'* epic form would begin with the iconographic ramifications of "that sea to which all things move." It is on that sea that Pound and his characters ride on their "piccioletta barca" (Canto VII, taken from *Paradiso* II), and it is the act of fighting that sea that causes the catastrophes of the *Cantos'* inferno. The poem begins, not accidentally, with the Ulysses of *Inferno* XXVI, whose "mad track" Dante observed from the heights of *Paradiso* XXVII. In the *Cantos*, as in the *Commedia*, the sea of the divine will is the source of both nourishment and disaster:

> The nature of the universe, which holds the centre still and moves all else round it, begins here as from its starting-point, and this heaven has no other *where* but the Divine Mind, in which is kindled the love that turns it and the virtue which it rains down . . . and how time should have its roots in that vessel and in the other [the natural world] its leaves, may now be plain to thee. O covetousness [*cupidigia*] who so plungest mortals in thy depths that none has power to lift his eyes from thy waves! The will blossoms well in men, but the continual rain turns the sound plums to withered. (*Paradiso* XXVII)[37]

If we are to gloss the *Cantos* by the "equations" of the *Commedia*, though, we must be aware that Pound interpreted Dante by modern lights. In 1913 he called Allen Upward's *Divine Mystery* "the most fascinating book on folklore that I have ever opened" (*Selected Prose*, p. 373), and he seems to have used something like Upward's primitivism

[37] Translated by John B. Sinclair in "The *Divine Comedy* of Dante Alighieri" (New York, 1961), Vol. III, pp. 391-393. Unless otherwise indicated, all translations from Dante are from this edition.

to reinterpret the religious, emotional, and psychological system that in Dante stands behind the drawing of the soul toward God. It was through such an anthropological view of Dante's Christianity that in *The Spirit of Romance* Pound traced the "pagan lineage" of the quest for Beatrice:

> The rise of Mariolatry, its pagan lineage, the romance of it, find modes of expression which verge over-easily into the speech and casuistry of Our Lady of Cyprus, as we may see in Arnaut, as we see so splendidly in Guido's "*Una figura della donna miae.*" And there is the consummation of it all in Dante's glorification of Beatrice. There is the inexplicable address to the lady in the masculine. There is the final evolution of Amor by Guido and Dante, a new and paganish god, neither Erôs nor an angel of the Talmud. (SR, pp. 91-92)

Out of Pound's conflation of Dante and contemporary primitivism grew *Three Cantos*, a poem that started to describe a Dantesque journey from misdirected will toward a re-acquisition of archaic man's harmony with the vital universe. The poem was to be a ritual awakening of ancient truths. Although it began in a modern inferno, Pound altered Dante's linear progression by adapting the repetitive strategies of ancient ritual and ritual drama. He even found a precedent for this experiment in Fenollosa's remarks about the Japanese Noh cycles, which Pound edited at the same time he began *Three Cantos*. Fenollosa had written that the Noh plays gather "the Shinto god dance, the lyric form of court poetry, the country farces, and a full range of epic incident" (*Translations*, p. 278). In his notes, Pound added that the Noh cycle "presents, or symbolizes, a complete diagram of life and recurrence" (*Translations*, p. 222). *Three Cantos* proclaimed itself a "meditative/Semi-dramatic, semi-epic story," and went on, not gratuitously, to allude to Dante and the Noh drama in quick succession. Pound's fusion of Dante's epic and the Noh's "diagram of life and recurrence" was connected in his mind with early comparisons between the *Commedia* and European mystery cycles,[38] and remained constant throughout the *Cantos*.

There is, then, no simple solution to the problem of what the *Cantos* are about. In the remainder of this study, I propose to outline some of the intricate and sometimes surprising ways in which Pound's literary and intellectual preoccupations combined between 1912 and 1925 to produce the germ of the *Cantos* and the poem's first fruit. I will begin with the problem of poetic organization.

[38] Cf. *The Spirit of Romance*, p. 154: "The *Commedia* is, in fact, a great mystery play, or better, a cycle of mystery plays."

CHAPTER II

A FIRST SET OF STRUCTURAL TERMS

THE structural method of the *Cantos* started in an intuition and changed gradually as Pound progressed from one stage of composition to the next. To argue whether the formal assumptions of the poem are *imagiste* or Vorticist or ideogrammic or something else is ultimately futile, a little like arguing whether a recently deceased friend should be described as he was at twenty or thirty-five or sixty. In the following discussion of the Vorticist background of *Three Cantos*, therefore, I do not propose a new aesthetic basis for the entire poem. I merely wish to establish a structural framework more appropriate to the first stage of the *Cantos* than the ideogrammic formulation which has traditionally been applied.

In 1912, when Pound was enunciating the principles of *imagisme*, structure did not strike him as a fundamental problem. The imagist poem presented a single moment of intensity, "an intellectual and emotional complex in an instant of time" (LE, p. 4), and as such did not need the guiding control structure provides. The thrust of Pound's 1913 "A Few Don'ts by an Imagiste" was for the poetic novice to pare his work down to its essence. He wrote in that essay that "It is better to present one Image in a lifetime than to produce voluminous works" (LE, p. 4), and two years later, in the same vein, that "A Chinaman said long ago that if a man can't say what he has to say in twelve lines he had better keep quiet" (G-B, p. 88). He characterized his quintessentially imagistic poem, "In a Station of the Metro," as a *hokku*, a " 'one image poem' " and described it as "a form of super-position, that is to say, it is one idea set on top of another" (G-B, p. 89). The traditional structures of western verse worked against such spareness by insisting that the poet pad his message to fill out a received form. In 1912, Pound would acknowledge the necessity of form only with considerable redefinition: "*Form.*–I think there is a 'fluid' as well as a 'solid' content, that some poems may have form as a tree has form, some as water poured into a vase. That most symmetrical forms have certain uses. That a vast number of subjects cannot be precisely, and therefore not properly rendered in symmetrical forms."[1]

As much as Pound seemed to dislike traditional forms, however, he could avoid their necessity only as long as his experimental verse remained miniature. A longer piece would demand the clarifying pressure of structure in order to be comprehensible. For reasons both public and private he could not sustain the brevity of *hokku*-like verse for an indefinite period. For one thing, even the most enlightened portion of his literary audience regarded two-line poems with something less than seriousness. Harold Monro, the editor of *Poetry and Drama* and one of Pound's early patrons, wrote in an article entitled "The Imagists Discussed" that the representative imagist poem "can be said in the one minute before lunch" and that imagist verse was "petty poetry; it is minutely small: it seems intended to be. Such images should appear by the dozen in poetry. Such reticence denotes either poverty of imagination or needlessly excessive restraint."[2]

Pound might have been able to shrug off this kind of criticism, though it came from a well-disposed source, but for a certain internal uneasiness. He had grown up, like Keats a hundred years before him, with the conviction that a man cannot be a great poet unless he master the long poem. Whitman stood as an example and a challenge, and Pound had been planning an epic poem of one kind or other ever since his undergraduate days at Hamilton.[3] There are indica-

---

[1] From 1912's *Prolegomena*, first printed in *Poetry Review*, I, 2 (February 1912), pp. 72-76. Reprinted in LE, pp. 8-12.

[2] *The Egoist*, II, 5 (May 1, 1915), p. 79.

[3] See Stock's *Life*, p. 19.

tions that during his *imagiste* period he was frequently bothered by the contradictions between his practice and aspiration. In a 1914 note in *The Fortnightly Review* he wrote, "I am often asked whether there can be a long imagiste or vorticist poem,"[4] and in *Drama* (1915) he repeated the question: " 'Could one do a long Imagiste poem, or even a long poem in vers libre?' "[5] In both cases we can prudently assume that the question was "often asked" by none other than Pound himself. As the projected epic became more of a reality, he began to rethink his commitment to imagism. He was determined to retain his *"imagiste"* principles, but was equally determined to expand his subject and scope. His solution was to emphasize the image not as the end-all of a poem but as the starting point, one unit out of which a structure might be built. Many years later, he chronicled his change in emphasis in the following note: "The defect of earlier imagist propaganda was not in misstatement but in incomplete statement. The diluters took the handiest and easiest meaning, and thought only of the STATIONARY image. If you can't think of imagism or phanopoeia as including the moving image, you will have to make a really needless division of fixed image and praxis or action."[6]

[4] The note was printed at the end of "Vorticism" in *The Fortnightly Review*, xcvi (N.S.), 573 (September 1, 1914), pp. 461-471, and "Vorticism" was reprinted in *Gaudier-Brzeska*, pp. 81-94.

[5] In a note to "The Classical Stage of Japan," *The Drama*, v, 18 (May 1915), pp. 199-247. The note occurs on p. 224 and was reprinted in *Noh, or Accomplishment* in its original 1917 publication and in its republication in *Translations*, where the note appears on p. 237. In both "Vorticism" and "The Classical Stage," Pound answered his question in the affirmative and pointed to the example of the Japanese Noh plays, which he saw as imagist performances of some length. For a discussion of the impact of the Noh drama on the *Cantos*, see below, Chapter Three.

[6] *ABC of Reading*, p. 52. Both Hugh Kenner (see *The Poetry of Ezra Pound*, London: 1951, Chapter Seven ff.) and Herbert Schneidau (see *Ezra Pound: The Image and the Real*, Baton Rouge: 1969, pp. 56-63) make this passage an important part of their understanding of the way the *Cantos* work.

It is not necessary, however, to rely on one of Pound's twenty-year-old memories for our understanding of developments after imagism. In 1915, the year that *Imagisme* was finally eclipsed by Vorticism and the year that *Three Cantos* were written, Pound outlined a shift in his poetics away from an endorsement of a simple super-position of images toward an affirmation of complex structure. "As for Imagisme," published in *The New Age* for January 28, 1915, sketched out the manner in which he believed the imagist aesthetic could be amplified. After reaffirming his sense of the genesis and nature of the image ("energy creates pattern . . . emotional force gives the image"), he went on to explain that a single image was only the building block of an artistic whole: "Intense emotion causes pattern to arise in the mind. . . . Perhaps I should say, not pattern, but pattern-units, or units of design. . . . The difference between the pattern-unit and the picture is one of complexity. The pattern-unit is so simple that one can bear having it repeated several or many times. When it becomes so complex that repetition would be useless, then it is a picture, an 'arrangement of forms.' "

One could at this point look ahead nine months to *Three Canto II*'s manifold repetition of images or pattern-units expressing "drear waste," and allow Pound's theory and practice to explain each other. However, I wish to postpone such a discussion until the next chapter, for I believe we would do better to more precisely define his sense of such key words as "pattern-unit" and "design" before applying them to *Three Cantos*. The meaning of these terms cannot be separated from the contemporary context that produced them, a context that involved a transition in Pound's aesthetic principles from Pater, Yeats, and aestheticism to Lewis and continental modernism.

§§

During 1914-1915, the period when *Three Cantos* were planned and written, Pound was intrigued by the relation between literature and the other arts. It is true that in all of his Vorticist propaganda, he was careful to indicate that the different arts worked through different media: "Every concept, every emotion presents itself to the vivid consciousness in some primary form. It belongs to the art of this form. If sound, to music; if formed words, to literature; the image, to poetry; form, to design; colour in position, to painting; form or design in three planes, to sculpture; movement, to the dance or to the rhythm of music or of verses."[7]

But, usually, he would also assert that the formal arrangements of the arts were generalizable. Vorticism meant an attitude toward structure and aesthetics that transcended any single medium. He wrote in September 1914 that "What I have said of one vorticist art [that it is interesting only as an arrangement of forms] can be transposed for another vorticist art" (G-B, p. 88), and later that the term Vorticism had come about because he and the others "wished a designation that would be equally applicable to a certain basis for all the arts" (G-B, p. 81). Pound initially imagined the generalized Vorticist aesthetic, the "general basis for all the arts" in musical terms. He wrote that the Vorticist possessed a "musical conception of form, that is to say the understanding that you can use form as a musician uses sound. . . ."[8]

The technical considerations of musical composition had little meaning for Pound during this period, and during his early years in London he almost never referred in his criticism to individual musical works or particular musical constructions.[9] The musical analogies he used in his prose around

[7] "Vortex: Pound," *Blast*, No. 1, p. 154. Reprinted in G-B, p. 81.

[8] "Affirmations . . . Vorticism," *The New Age*, XVI, 11 (January 11, 1915), p. 278.

[9] I am speaking about Pound's remarks concerning musical structure, and not about his awareness of local musical effects. He was, of course, familiar with the immediate applications of, say, cadence to poetry. Pound did occasionally make very general remarks, under the influence of Dolmetsch, on the structural qualities of Bach or Mozart, and some of those remarks are alluded to below. He was attracted to the plucked sounds of Dolmetsch's revived instruments and to the

1915 were acquired at second hand, through the mediation of his critical predecessors. Pound's generalizations about the musical nature of the arts reflected a half-century of conceiving literature in terms of the purer art of music. In *Blast* No. 1, he (mis)quoted Pater's statement that "All arts constantly aspire to the condition of music," and claimed Pater as the earliest "ancestor" of Vorticism (p. 154).

Pound's "inheritance," of course, included the whole of Pater's criticism. In "An Essay on Style," Pater explained that the condition of music meant a unity of matter and form: "If music be the ideal of all art whatever, precisely because in music it is impossible to distinguish the form from the substance or matter, the subject from the expression, then, literature, by finding its specific excellence in the absolute correspondence of the term to its import, will be but fulfilling the condition of all artistic quality in things everywhere, of all good art."[10] Pater's idealization of a literature of musical "expression" diluted the notion of organic unity he had acquired from Coleridge. He found the Coleridgean theory of composition, with its stress on the organic tightness of a work organized around a single germ of insight, to be constricting. Pater called it "one-sided," and explained that

---

polyphonic patterns of early music because they corresponded to the hard qualities he had already applauded in poetry and sculpture. He imposed on early music the same terminology (e.g. "pattern-units") derived from Vorticist artwork that he had imposed on his own poetry. Therefore, I would argue that statements like "early music starts with the mystery of pattern" (LE, p. 434) were formulated according to notions previously held about the visual arts, and that Pound's references to polyphonic structure were applications of an already formulated aesthetic rather than critical starting points.

Pound usually invoked Bach or (in the most general descriptions) Bach's practices as a kind of shorthand endorsement of a precision that had been too long out of fashion. His allusions to Bach, far from being personal touchstones, can be traced through the writings of Dolmetsch to a neo-classical movement in music at the time that used Bach as a standard counter-example to Romantic music, and, in the process, helped to revive Bach's popularity.

[10] Walter Pater, *Appreciations* (London, 1889), p. 37.

it did not allow for the way an artist displays his "dexterity" by raising each individual part of his work "to the higher degree of expressiveness."[11] In comparison, a musical arrangement of parts permitted the artist to make every part of a work expressive not just of the controlling design of the whole, but of the full and manifold emotional potentiality of that part.

Pater's modification of Coleridge appropriated for poetry a greater opportunity for suggestive overtone, but at the price of relaxed architectural rigour. As David de Laura has remarked, "the drift of Pater's reiterated reflections on form and matter, thought and word, is atomic, fractionary, a matter of this or that expressive unit."[12] And Pater's diffusion of the Romantic focus was a large part of the "inheritance" involved in Pound's "musical conception" of forms in relation.

W. B. Yeats provided the transition from Pater to Pound. In "The Symbolism of Poetry," Yeats wrote about the emotional excellencies of music—its aspiration, via an accent on expression over content, toward an unconditional formal harmony; and its consequent immediacy of spiritual communication:

> All sounds, all colours, all forms, either because of their preordained energies or because of long association, evoke indefinable and yet precise emotions, or, as I prefer to think, call down among us certain disembodied powers, whose footsteps over our hearts we call emotions; and when sound, and colour, and form are in a musical relation, a beautiful relation to one another, they become, as it were, one sound, one colour, one form, and evoke an emotion that is made out of their distinct evocations and yet is one emotion. The same relation exists between all portions of every work of art, whether it be an epic or a song, and the more perfect it is, and the more various and numerous the

[11] Pater, *Appreciations*, pp. 80-81.
[12] David J. de Laura, *Hebrew and Hellene´ in Victorian England: Newman, Arnold and Pater* (Austin, 1969), p. 332.

elements that have flowed into its perfection, the more powerful will be the emotion, the power, the god it calls among us. Because an emotion does not exist, or does not become perceptible and active among us, till it has found expression, in colour or in sound or in form, or in all of these, and because no two modulations or arrangements of these evoke the same emotion, poets and painters and musicians . . . are continually making and unmaking mankind.[13]

Elaborating Pater's principles, Yeats set up an explicit equation between the notes of music and the colors of painting or the elements of poetry, and generalized the relations between elements as "musical arrangement." He reinforced Pater's dilution of organic unity by characterizing the structure of a work as a river into whose "perfection" elements have "flowed." In addition, he contended that each particular "modulation" or "arrangement" of form is inimitable, and that each new arrangement influences perception ("make mankind"). He extended the spiritual authority of musical form by writing that musical arrangements in the arts call "gods . . . among us."

Pound's early essays repeated Yeats's axioms, sometimes without even changing Yeats's phraseology. We have seen that in Pound's Vorticist propaganda he referred to the musical arrangements of colors in painting and of images in poetry, and that he insisted in *Prolegomena* that the form of some poems is "fluid," like "water poured into a vase." In *Prolegomena*, he also restated Yeats's contention that each arrangement of forms is inimitable. "I believe," he wrote, "in an 'absolute rhythm,' a rhythm, that is, in poetry which corresponds exactly to the emotion or shade of emotion to be expressed." Finally, Pound accepted Yeats's spiritualization of form. As late as 1914, he was still using "mood," the Yeatsian term for the revelation of a timeless spiritual verity,

[13] W. B. Yeats, *Essays and Introductions* (London, 1961), pp. 156-157.

to describe Vorticist art: "great works of art [are] lords over fact, over race-long recurrent moods, and over tomorrow" (G-B, p. 92).[14]

The nuances of a musical conception of structure handed down by his poetic "ancestors" colored Pound's assimilation of twentieth-century art. Indeed, the very terms he first used to criticize the Vorticists caused him to put a high value on lyric manner, and made it difficult for him to come to terms with modern painting's new obduracy. Perhaps most important of all, the stress that Pater and then Yeats put on the fluid structures of musical composition established Pound's life-long uneasiness with tight structures of any kind, mechanical or organic. The loose structural idiom of the *Cantos* was from the beginning more a product of late Victorian criticism than of a revolutionary modern sensibility. In order to discern the precise mixture of that structural idiom, however, we must trace the interaction of Pound's late Victorian principles with the very different actualities of the modern painting he confronted in 1913-1914. Out of that interaction came the critical terminology that Pound formulated in *As for Imagisme* and then applied in *Three Cantos*.

§

While Pound was working his way towards a twentieth-century art, Wyndham Lewis had already arrived. Pound once wrote that "there would have been no [Vorticist] movement without Lewis,"[15] and later that "W[yndham] L[ewis] certainly *made* vorticism. To him alone we owe the existence of BLAST."[16] Lewis was not only the leading practitioner of

[14] For a history of the Yeatsian origin of Pound's use of "mood," see Thomas Jackson's *The Early Poetry of Ezra Pound* (Cambridge, 1968), p. 52.

[15] *Pavannes and Divisions*, p. 246.

[16] In a 1956 letter to Gladys Hynes, cited by William C. Wees in "Pound's Vorticism: Some New Evidence and Further Comments," *Wisconsin Studies in Contemporary Literature*, VII (1966), pp. 211-216.

modernism in England but also its outstanding theorist, and as such he provides a yardstick with which to measure the idiosyncrasy of Pound's Vorticist criticism.

Lewis had been studying art in Paris for nine years when Roger Fry's exhibit, "Manet and the Post-Impressionists," startled the London art world. By November 1910, Lewis had absorbed the impact of Matisse and the Fauves, had assimilated Picasso's "analytic" cubism, and was beginning to work on what he believed was a post-Cubist visual idiom. By 1912, the year of Fry's second post-impressionist show, Lewis had composed his designs for the text of Shakespeare's *Timon of Athens*. *Timon*, which William Wees has described as the integration of "mask-like faces, stylized limbs, truncated bodies, arcs, lines, and wedges, with overlapping and intersecting black and white planes, to produce abstract designs with representational details,"[17] proclaimed Lewis' maturity and struck Pound as a masterpiece. Its style seems to have been descended from an early cubist work like Picasso's 1907 *Nu à la Draperie*, in which for the first time intersecting planes were used to define a form. Picasso, however, was concerned with the delineation of volumes and an overall effect of classically balanced repose. In *Timon*, Lewis disdained both the illusion of volume and the effect of repose to attain an organization of linear design with which he could express violent drama. Its system of interlocking and rhythmic lines (I have reproduced two of the compositions below) is reminiscent of a Futurist painting like *Nude Descending a Staircase*, but even that comparison is not adequate.

[17] William C. Wees, *Vorticism and the English Avant-Garde* (Toronto, 1972), p. 140. My treatment of Vorticism owes a great deal to Wees's book, not least the possibility of treating the movement with a brevity that would have been impossible without it. The reader interested in a full discussion is encouraged to consult not only *Vorticism and the English Avant-Garde* but Walter Michel's *Wyndham Lewis: Paintings and Drawings* (Berkeley and Los Angeles, 1971), which has an introductory essay by Hugh Kenner.

Lewis in his aesthetic criticism differentiated his work both from the Picasso of 1912-1914 (whose style was in transition from analytic cubism to the synthetic cubism of a collage like 1913's *Violin, Bottle and Glass*) and from the Futurists. In the pages of *Blast* Nos. 1 and 2, he explained that his aesthetic was more radically modern than the Cubists', more classically organized than the Futurists'. Cubism, Lewis wrote, was only the most recent phase of "naturalism," whose crystalline compositions were devoted to a "scientific" veracity that was irrelevant or hostile to art. Since the Cubists, children of Cézanne, were interested only in natural forms, they had no feeling for composition, which alone could rescue painting from the "facile and sententious formulas" of the past.[18] The Cubists, especially Picasso, founded their invention on the posed model, or the posed Nature-Morte, and used these models as frequently as the Impressionists.

According to Lewis, it is the business of painting to embody not nature but life. "Nature," he wrote, "is no more inexhaustible, fresh, welling up with invention, etc., than life is to the average man of forty, with his groove, his disillusion, and his little round of habitual distractions." The life of art, on the other hand, is an energized organization as interesting as nature. "It is no EQUIVALENT for Life, but ANOTHER Life, as NECESSARY to existence. . . ." As for the Futurists, Lewis was willing to praise them in so far as they "rejected the POSED MODEL," the imitative and static side of Cubism, and substituted "the hurly-burly and exuberance of actual life." His paintings made use of rhythmic lines, a Futurist idiom, but his theory explicitly rejected Futurist rationale. To Lewis, the moving-picture pretensions of Marinetti were absurdly "impressionist and scientific," and prevented the Futurists from attaining the true artist's deliberateness and control.

Lewis' Vorticist insistence on the priority of composition over representation was in part based on Kandinsky and the

[18] Unless otherwise indicated, the Lewis citations come from *Blast*.

Expressionists, who had opened the way toward judging a picture solely on pictorial grounds. In *Blast* No. 1, Lewis' colleague Edward Wadsworth translated large chunks of Kandinsky in a review of 1912's *Ueber das Geistige in der Kunst* ("Concerning the Spiritual in Art").[19] Wadsworth was especially alive to Kandinsky's comparisons of painting to music, and stressed musical analogy when he summed up Kandinsky's arguments: "The constructive tendencies of painting Herr Kandinsky divides into two groups—(1) sim-

---

[19] I include a selection of passages:

"Form alone, even if it is quite abstract and geometrical, has its inner timbre. . . ."

"It is easy to notice here that some colours are accentuated in value by some forms and weakened by others. In any case bright colours vibrate more strongly in pointed, angular forms (e.g. a yellow triangle). Those that have a tendency to deepen will increase this effect in round forms (e.g. a blue circle). It is naturally clear on the other hand that the unsuitability of the form to the colour must not be regarded as something 'inharmonious,' but on the contrary as a new possibility, and consequently harmony."

". . . the Timbre of the Organic is heard in the form it chooses, even if it is quite suppressed. On this account the choice of the real object is important. In the two-fold Timbre (spiritual chord) of both component parts of the form the organic can support the abstract (by means of concord or discord) or it can be disturbing to it. The object can create only an accident Timbre, which, if substituted by another, calls forth no essential difference in fundamental timbre. . . ."

"The flexibility of the single form . . . its direction in the picture (movement), the preponderance of the corporeal over the abstract in this single form on the one hand, and on the other the combination of forms which create the big shape of the whole picture: further, the principles of concord and discord in all the aforesaid parts, i.e., the juxtaposition of the single forms, the interpenetration of one form with another, the distortion, the binding and tearing apart of the individual forms, the same treatment of the groups of forms, of the combination of the mysterious with the definite, the rythmic with the non-rythmic on the same plane, the abstract forms with the purely geometrical (simple or complicated) and the less definitely geometrical, the same treatment of the combination of the boundary lines of the forms from one another (heavy or light), etc.—all these are the elements which create the possibility of a purely aesthetic counterpoint and which will lead up to this counterpoint."

Wyndham Lewis from "Timon of Athens," Plate 98.
The Herbert F. Johnson Museum of Art, Cornell University

Wyndham Lewis from "Timon of Athens," Plate 100.
The Herbert F. Johnson Museum of Art, Cornell University

ple composition of a more or less obviously geometrical character, which he calls 'melodic composition,' and which has been more generally employed by western artists (Duccio, Ravenna mosaics, Cezanne), and (2) complicated rythmic composition which he calls 'symphonic,' and which is the characteristic medium of oriental art and of Kandinsky himself."

Lewis shared some of Wadsworth's enthusiasm (he called Kandinsky "the only PURELY abstract painter in Europe"), but he believed that in some ways Kandinsky was already as outdated as Picasso. Lewis especially disliked the spiritualized connotations of Kandinsky's very nineteenth-century (and very German) devotion to music. He wrote that "Kandinsky, docile to the intuitive fluctuations of his soul, and anxious to render his hand and mind elastic and receptive, follows this unreal entity into its cloud-world, out of the material and solid universe. He allows the Bach-like will that resides in each good artist to be made war on by the slovenly and wandering Spirit." Lewis was eager to stress the artist's task of imposing definite shape on his vision, and he deprecated Kandinsky's work as "ethereal, lyrical, and cloud-like." He objected to Kandinsky's willingness to exclude certain "powerful and definite forms" merely because they occurred in nature.

It is perhaps this last objection that gives us our clearest view of Lewis' values. Whatever his arguments with representational art, he was temperamentally unable to let abstractionism slide into aestheticism. He wrote that "my soul has gone to live in my eyes," but added that his eyes "will never forget that red is the colour of blood." The true artist, in other words, uses iconography as well as arrangement to make an imaginative statement that interprets nature though it does not reproduce it. In *Timon*, Lewis' conviction that art should be more than emotional harmony and his temperamental bellicosity combined to produce a series of compositions in which "arrangements" of stark, clean, spear-like forms are *animated* by elements of narrative and drama.

35

Lewis often used the figure of a machine to convey the vitality and directedness of design. He held that, like a machine or the human body, a well-designed work of art harnesses large amounts of energy to perform its aesthetic function efficiently. He derided Picasso's compositions as mere "masonry," constructed to pose more than to work. "Picasso's structures," he wrote, "are not energetic ones, in the sense that they are very static dwelling houses." A machine-like painting, on the other hand, is a living thing. Its lines and masses imply force and action. Moreover, the artist of the twentieth century who patterns his work after the dynamics of a machine is only continuing a long-established tradition. "Artists have always represented men as more beautiful, more symmetrically muscular, with more commanding countenances than they usually, in nature, possess. And in our time it is natural that an artist should wish to endow his 'Bonhomme' when he makes one in the grip of an heroic emotion, with something of the fatality, grandeur, and efficiency of a machine." Thus, whereas the artist of the Renaissance idealized man's perfect, Vitruvian proportions and desired to portray him in classically peaceful works of art, Lewis the modernist idealizes man's efficiency, power, and activity, and wishes to portray him in compositions that capture the conflicting antagonisms and energies of the machine.

Unlike the Futurists, however, who admired merely the power and motion of the machine, Lewis emphasized the perfect design and craftsmanship it required to control conflicting energies for long periods of time: "All revolutionary painting to-day has in common the rigid reflections of steel and stone in the spirit of the artist; that desire for stability as though a machine were being built to fly or kill with. . . ."[20] In so far as it represented man's harnessing of energy through craft, the machine became the most characteristic emblem of the Vorticist movement, more significant, as we shall see, than the vortex itself. T. E. Hulme, who was closer than

[20] "The Cubist Room," *The Egoist* I, 1 (January 1, 1914), p. 9.

Pound to the rest of the movement and in some ways a more representative spokesman, took up the metaphor of machine-as-organized-energy in the peroration of his most important essay, "Modern Art and its Philosophy." Hulme wrote that the destiny of the moderns was to "attempt to create in art, structures whose organisation, such as it is, is very like that of machinery."[21] Lewis, who was not on the best of terms with Hulme, nevertheless later grudgingly admitted "All the best things Hulme said about the theory of art were said about my art. . . . We happened, that is all, to be made for each other, as critic and 'creator.' What he said should be done, I *did*. Or it would be more exact to say that I did it, and he said it."[22]

§

In December 1913, Ezra Pound wrote William Carlos Williams of his long-awaited success in forming a revolutionary movement that would launch the twentieth-century renaissance: "We are getting our little gang together after five years of waiting" (L, p. 27). Wyndham Lewis remembered Pound's membership differently: "Ezra Pound attached himself to the Blast group. That group was composed of people all very 'extremist' in their views. . . . What struck them principally about Pound was that his fire-eating propagandistic utterances were not accompanied by any very experimental efforts in his particular medium . . . this certain discrepancy between what Pound said . . . and what he did, was striking enough to impress itself on anybody. . . . Pound supplied the Chinese Crackers, and a trayful of mild jokes, for our paper."[23]

Whatever the reality, it must be admitted that Pound received more than he gave. Consider, for example, the way the two figures defended the Vorticist movement. As Lewis

[21] *Speculations* (London, 1936), p. 105.
[22] *Blasting and Bombardiering* (Berkeley and Los Angeles, 1967), p. 100.
[23] *Time and Western Man* (Boston, 1957), p. 39.

wryly suggests, Pound was second to none in his vociferous-
ness. And yet, compared to the absorption in recent developments of twentieth-century art that Lewis displayed in the
remarks just considered, Pound's criticism indicated that
he was still living in the world of Pater rather than Picasso.
In "Vortex: Pound," his speaking platform in *Blast* No. 1,
Pound gave his own "ancestry" for Vorticism: Pater, Whistler, Picasso, and Kandinsky. Picasso seems to have been included almost as an afterthought.

But Pater, whose considerable "inheritance" we have ex-
amined, appeared in the premiere position as the author of
[*sic*] "All arts approach the conditions of music." And it was
their "condition of music" that attracted Pound to the work
and criticism of the other two. He delighted in Kandinsky's
Ueber das Geistige in der Kunst, and, in "Vorticism" (September 1914) he wrote that his autobiographical account of
modern art would be unnecessary were he able to rely on his
readers' having read the German treatise (G-B, p. 86). In
"Vorticism," Pound also quoted admiringly from "The Red
Rag," Whistler's account of the musical quality of his own
paintings,[24] and asserted that it was Whistler who had let
in "cubism, and Kandinsky, and the lot of us" (G-B, p. 85).
He used Whistler's statement that "You are interested in

[24] See G-B, p. 85. The argument to which Pound refers goes as
follows:

"Why should not I call my work 'symphonies,' 'arrangements,'
'harmonies,' and 'nocturnes'? . . . My picture of a 'Harmony in Grey
and Gold' is an illustration of my meaning . . . combination of grey
and gold is the basis of the picture. Now this is precisely what my
friends cannot grasp. They say, 'Why not call it "Trotty Veck," and
sell it for a round harmony of golden guineas?' . . . As music is the
poetry of sound, so is painting the poetry of sight, and the subject
matter has nothing to do with the harmony of sound or of colour.

"The great musicians knew this. Beethoven and the rest wrote music
—simply music; symphony in this key, concerto or sonata in that. On
F or G they constructed celestial harmonies—as harmonies—as combinations, evolved from the chords of F or G and their minor cor-
relatives." James M. Whistler, *The Gentle Art of Making Enemies*
(New York, 1890), pp. 126-127.

a certain painting because it is an arrangement of lines and colours" first in "Vortex: Pound," and then for the opening of "Vorticism": "It is no more ridiculous that a person should receive or convey an emotion by means of an arrangement of shapes, or planes, or colours, than that they should receive or convey such emotion by an arrangement of musical notes." (G-B, p. 81)

In fact, the broad assertions of late Victorian criticism (then two artistic generations old) exerted so powerful a hold over Pound's aesthetic that in the 1913-1914 accounts of Vorticism he never got past them to consider the particular characteristics of the paintings at hand. When we consider the following, we realize that Pound's terms are so general that they might be describing any number of things other than their ostensible subject, the work of Edward Wadsworth:

> Mr. Wadsworth's work gives me pleasure, sometimes like the pleasure I have received from Chinese and Japanese prints and painting; for example, I derive such pleasure from Mr. Wadsworth's "Khaki." Sometimes his work gives me a pleasure which I can only compare to the pleasure I have in music, in music as it was in Mozart's time. If an outsider wishes swiftly to understand this new work, he can do worse than approach it in the spirit wherein he approaches music.[25]

In 1914, Pound sometimes attempted a more precise description of the structural idiom of Lewis and Wadsworth, but his vocabulary could not get beyond a few terms loosely drawn from musical forms. For example, he used the musical-literary term "motif" to describe Lewis' compositional units (G-B, pp. 92-93), and gropingly referred to Wadsworth's patterns as both "motifs" and "notes in a fugue."[26] Aware of the deficiency of his descriptions, Pound wrote in March

[25] G-B, p. 93. Reprinted from "Vorticism" (September 1914).
[26] See "Edward Wadsworth, Vorticist," *The Egoist*, I, 16 (August 15, 1914), pp. 306-307.

1914 that it was difficult to write about the new painting because "it is perhaps so close to one's poetic habit of creation that prose is ill got to fit it."[27] It would be more accurate to say that Pound so closely associated the painting with his own "poetic habit" and aesthetics that he could not perceive its differences or find terms to describe them. As we have seen, though, Lewis seems to have had no problem differentiating Pound's 1914 habits from his own.

The very different emblems that Pound and Lewis chose to represent the new movement in 1914 furnish a striking illustration of the distance between their structural orientation. Lewis' "machine" communicated conscious engineering and the stability and permanence that were the results of energy firmly harnessed imposed construction. On the other hand, Pound's "vortex," although it was probably his most important contribution to the *Blast* circle, was one more of his "fluid" forms. In "Vortex: Pound," he wrote that one can think of vorticist man "as DIRECTING a certain *fluid force* against circumstance, as CONCEIVING instead of merely observing and reflecting" (my italics). And in "Vorticism" he redefined the "image" as "a radiant node or cluster; it is what I can, and must perforce, call a VORTEX, from which, and through which, ideas are constantly rushing" (G-B, p. 92). Admittedly, the fluid form of the vortex was precisely defined. In *The New Age* Pound wrote, "if you clap a strong magnet beneath a plateful of iron filings, the energies of the magnet will proceed to organise form . . . the design in the magnetised iron filings expresses a confluence of energy."[28] And yet, the confluence of energy within the vortex, unlike the force-lines of a machine, had no segmented parts or joints, did not easily call up the considerations of planned architecture with which Lewis presumably designed *Timon*. As Herbert Schneidau has remarked, the

[27] "Exhibition at the Goupil Gallery," *The Egoist*, I, 6 (March 16, 1914), p. 109.
[28] "Affirmations . . . Vorticism," *The New Age*, XVI, 11 (January 14, 1915), p. 277.

fluid force of a vortex, rather than being externally shaped by an imposed structure, "illustrated form created and maintained by constant force. The form is self-contained, coterminus with the force that creates it, and is independent of its medium."[29]

It is clear that Pound's conceptualization of the vortex had structural affinities with his view of the imagist poem, "an intellectual and emotional complex in an instant of time." And so, even while Lewis had achieved a notion of art as crafted form, Pound still seemed to be working in terms of the fluid structures of Paterian musical expression. The vortex, though it seemed to be a blow for precision and against muzziness, was in fact an unstructured and exceedingly difficult model with which to plan the articulation of "a poem of some length."

§§

Some time in late 1914, Pound's conceptualization of Vorticist painting changed. The change was subtle, but left clear traces in the articles entitled "Affirmations" he wrote for the new year. In those articles, he began to generate a provisional vocabulary to deal with the segmentation of Lewis' and Wadsworth's work. It is true that his old musical notions of formal arrangement remained, along with some of the concomitant terminology. But along with them he used certain phrases in a way that suggested he had stopped rigidly imposing his old aesthetics on the paintings in front of him, and had started making terms that would fit the paintings. Tentatively, he began to acknowledge that Lewis and Wadsworth did not "arrange" their compositions out of a number of disparate elements, but built them with a few units that were designed to repeat and interact.

From the start, Pound had been aware that the Vorticists took considerable care about the small forms out of which

[29] Herbert Schneidau, "Vorticism and the Career of Ezra Pound," *Modern Philology*, 65.3 (February 1968), p. 222.

their paintings were made. In his first review of Lewis in June 1914, he reproduced two little block designs that Lewis himself had singled out, and wrote: "If you cannot see the control and skill and power in these two designs, God help you."[30] In the same article Pound commented on the organization of Lewis' *Timon* ("a type emotion . . . delivered . . . in lines and masses and planes"), but did not remark on any special relation between Lewis' miniature designs and his structural arrangements. Three months later, Pound once again described *Timon*, and once again indicated that he thought of Lewis' designs and his organization as separate achievements: "I believe that Mr. Wyndham Lewis is a very great master of design; that he has brought into our art new units of design *and* new manners of organisation"[31] (my emphasis). When he attempted to describe the articulation of the design, Pound could do nothing more than fall back on his old musical vocabulary: "If you ask me what his 'Timon' means, I can reply by asking you what the old play means. For me, his designs are a creation on the same *motif*."[32] Lewis' designs and organization were integrally related, but, in order to make sense of that relation, the poet first needed to consider Lewis' work in terms that were not colored by Pater's aesthetic.

Pound's first departure was hardly visible, no more than a slight variation on old terms. In "Affirmations . . . Vorticism" (January 1915), he recited the now traditional obeisances toward Pater and Whistler. He told his readers that "organisation of form and colour is 'expression'; just as musical arrangement of notes by Mozart is expression," and he spoke of the "motives" of form that the Vorticist artist, with his "musical conception of form" was wont to use. Then, in an almost imperceptible movement, he varied his formula. He called Lewis "a more significant artist than Kandinsky."

[30] "Wyndham Lewis," *The Egoist*, I, 12 (June 15, 1914), p. 233.
[31] From the *Fortnightly Review* "Vorticism" piece. Reprinted in G-B, pp. 92-93.
[32] *Ibid.*, p. 93.

And, to describe the patterns in a work by Edward Wadsworth, he used the word "form-motif," a word that called attention to its novelty by an awkward hyphenation:

> They say Cezanne began taking "impressions of form."
> That is not the same thing as conceiving the forms about
> one as a source of "form-motifs," which motifs one can
> use later at one's pleasure in more highly developed compositions.
>
> It is possible that this search for form-motif will lead
> us to some synthesis of western life comparable to the
> synthesis of oriental life which we find in Chinese and
> Japanese painting. This lies with the future. Perhaps there
> is some adumbration of it in Mr. Wadsworth's "Harbour
> of Flushing."[33]

To a follower of Pound's prose it was obvious that he had made the first step in perceiving Vorticism not just as one part of the movement that began with Whistler, but (in Lewis' frame) as a unique experiment. "Form-motif," although it had been improvised out of an old habit of musical notation, was a term that took its resonance from the present actuality of Wadsworth's designs.

What had been tentative in "Affirmations . . . Vorticism" was soon a touchstone of Pound's criticism. "Affirmations [IV] . . . As For Imagisme," a landmark in Pound's eyes, called attention to his reformulation:

> The term "Imagisme" has given rise to a certain amount
> of discussion. . . . I can only say what I meant by the word
> when I made it. Moreover, I cannot guarantee that my
> thoughts about it will remain absolutely stationary. I spend
> the greater part of my time meditating the arts, and I
> should find this very dull if it were not possible for me
> occasionally to solve some corner of the mystery, or, at
> least to formulate more clearly my own thoughts as to
> the nature of some mystery or equation.

[33] "Affirmations . . . Vorticism," *The New Age*, XVI, 11 (January 14, 1915), p. 278.

Pound pointed back to "Affirmations . . . Vorticism" ("In the second article in this series . . ."), and amplified. He reaffirmed his sense of the origin of the image ("energy creates pattern . . . emotional force gives the image"), and then he announced his self-conscious formulation of a new term: "I am using this term 'pattern-unit,' because I want to get away from the confusion between 'pattern' and 'applied decoration.' " The pattern-unit would refer primarily to the "vorticist picture":

> Intense emotion causes pattern to arise in the mind—perhaps I should say, not pattern, but pattern-units, or units of design. . . . By pattern-unit or vorticist picture I mean the single jet. The difference between the pattern-unit and the picture is one of complexity. The pattern-unit is so simple that one can bear having it repeated several or many times. When it becomes so complex that repetition would be useless, then it is a picture. . . .

The "image," Pound wrote, should be regarded as a pattern-unit, which, verbalized, would have its "suitable or cognate rhythm form and . . . timbre-form."[34]

Although the term itself appeared in slightly different avatars from essay to essay, Pound's conceptualization of "pattern-unit" remained constant for the rest of the decade. In his sixth "Affirmation," "Analysis of this Decade," Pound used the expression "radicals in design" to describe the units of Wadsworth's wood-blocks.[35] In late 1915, he called the units of Lewis' work "form-units" (G-B, p. 26). As late as 1919 Pound still described Lewis as "a man known chiefly as a revolutionary inventor of forms, what his adherents [i.e., Pound] termed 'forms in combination.' "[36] The new phrases,

[34] All the citations in this paragraph are from "Affirmations . . . As for Imagisme," *The New Age*, xvi, 13 (January 28, 1915), pp. 349-350.

[35] "Affirmations VI . . . Analysis of this Decade," *The New Age*, xvi, 15 (February 11, 1915), p. 411.

[36] "Wyndham Lewis at the Goupil," *The New Age*, xxiv, 16 (February 20, 1919), pp. 263-264.

"units of design," "pattern-units," "radicals in design," "forms in combination" comprised a critical vocabulary that had one sure foot in the twentieth century. Unlike an expression like "motive," "pattern-unit" had certain overtones that could be explained only by its derivation from Lewis and Wadsworth. A "pattern-unit" was a well-formed entity possessed of the hard, geometric beauty of twentieth-century graphics. To an observer of Vorticist composition, the meaning of Pound's "radicals in design" was clear. He had perceived that a "picture" like *Timon's* "The Creditors" (reproduced above) did not, Kandinsky-like, balance shape against disparate shape, but instead repeated a few units that had been designed to intensify their singleness as they combined in rhythmic waves. "Radicals in design," unlike notes in arrangement, did not surrender the shapeliness of their integrity to an encompassing pattern. Though they resembled *leitmotifs* in that their impact changed from repetition to repetition, a "radical" did not maintain the Wagnerian leitmotif's pretext of being an incidental detail in a more important narrative structure. "Radicals" were so essential a part of their "design" that one could not conceive of the whole independent of its parts.

&

Pound called Lewis' portfolio, *Timon of Athens*, "a great work . . . the most articulate expression of my own decade" (G-B, p. 93). As he had already admitted to spending six months "restless for a meaning . . . in a wilderness of doubt" trying to "come to some deeper understanding"[37] of the portfolio, he did not make the statement casually. The depth of Pound's response to *Timon* tells us a good deal about the background of his new terminology, and suggests that Lewis' masterpiece was an important influence on the writing of his projected long poem.

"The pattern-unit," Pound had written, "is so simple that

[37] "Wyndham Lewis," *The Egoist* I, 12 (June 15, 1914), p. 233.

one can bear having it repeated many times. When it becomes so complex that repetition would be useless, then it is a picture." It was the complexity of *Timon* that he immediately admired, and, with the aid of his recently minted terms, he lifted *Timon* to a stature above Vorticist sculpture: "In painting one can have a much greater complexity, a much greater number of form units than in sculpture . . . in, say, one of the more complex designs of Lewis' 'Timon' " (G-B, p. 26). However, it is evident that Pound's admiration extended beyond a formalist appreciation of *Timon's* organization. He respected Lewis' attempt to bring life as well as shape to his compositions, and he wrote that "Mr. Lewis's painting is nearly always emotional" (G-B, p. 93).

From the start, Pound was aware of *Timon's* sense of movement, its elements of conflict and drama. Before "As For Imagisme," he wrote that in *Timon* Lewis was declaring "that the intelligent god is incarnate in the universe, in struggle with the endless inertia,"[38] and an appreciation for *Timon's* expression of "struggle" remained latent in his reformulated critical descriptions. It was *Timon's* description of struggle that he had in mind when, in an "Affirmation" after *As For Imagisme*, he praised Lewis' "sense of dynamics" (G-B, p. 116). And it was their element of "dynamic" movement that made Lewis' "forms in combination" so attractive. Pound saw narrative potentiality in Lewis' method, and it seems that he grouped *Timon* along with his own planned experimental poetic narrative. At least, we find him in 1919 describing *Timon* in a manner tantalizingly similar to the encyclopedic inferno of the *Cantos*, then already in progress: " 'Timon,' " he wrote, suggested "a complete possible world of violent or impassive forms," and, along with Lewis' war paintings, *Timon* made Lewis "appear as a narrative painter with an apparently unlimited subject-matter, a capacity for suggesting unlimited subject-matter."[39]

[38] *Ibid.*, p. 234.
[39] "Wyndham Lewis at the Goupil," *The New Age* xxiv, 16 (February 20, 1919), p. 264.

That Pound may have chosen *Timon* as one model for his own attempt at a major "modern" narrative composition is a probability reinforced by the fact that recognizable features of the *Cantos* first appeared in descriptions of Lewis' work. In the 1914 essay, "Wyndham Lewis," Pound described *Timon* with explicit reference to his own literary aspirations:

> I daresay one's own art seems always the hardest. One feels that Mr. Lewis has expressed this struggle ["the struggle of driving the shaft of intelligence into the dull mass of mankind"]. One feels that in literature it is almost impossible to express it for our generation. One has such trivial symbols arrayed against one, there is only "The Times" and all that it implies, and the "Century Magazine" and its likes and all that they imply, and the host of other periodicals and the states of mind represented in them. It is so hard to arrange one's mass and opposition. Labour and anarchy can find their opponents in "capital" and "government." But the mind aching for something that it can honour under the name of "civilisation," the mind, seeing that state afar off but clearly, can only flap about pettishly striking at the host of trivial substitutes presented to it. One's very contentions are all in the nature of hurricanes in the traditional teapot.
>
> The really vigorous mind might erect "The Times," which is of no importance, into a symbol of the state of mind which "The Times" represents, which is a loathsome state of mind, a malebolge of obtuseness.
>
> And having done so, some aesthete left over from the nineties would rebuke one for one's lack of aloofness.

Unarguably, by the time he wrote the above, a germ of the "Hell" Cantos was formed in Pound's mind. It seems that here in 1914 he was thinking of *Timon* as a trail-blazer that expressed his own themes in a modern manner.[40] At any rate,

---

[40] What makes the passage interesting even beyond the light it throws on the development of the *Cantos* is its last sentence: "And

that is what I make of "One feels Mr. Lewis has expressed this struggle. One feels that in literature it is almost impossible for our generation."

In June 1914, Pound felt that a literary analogue to *Timon* was "almost impossible for our generation." Six months later in "As for Imagisme," however, he began the process of translating some of *Timon*'s structural principles into usable terms. Six months after that, in September 1915, he began the composition of *Three Cantos*. It was, I believe, the aid of his new critical terminology that enabled him to start constructing an answer to his old question, "Can one do a long Imagiste poem?" Images that function in a long poem like the "forms in combination" in Lewis' *Timon* could be developed without obscuring their individual impact. Because such images would be designed to make a pattern of their own when repeated "in combination," they would have no further need of an imposed narrative structure. In the light of *Timon* and his structural description of it, the planned *Cantos* metamorphosed in Pound's mind from a musically organized work resembling a Wagnerian opera to something recognizably different. Although (as we shall see) *Three Cantos* retained their share of late Victorian fluid form, dream-like transitions, and words used as *leitmotifs*, they also displayed structural features that could only be reflections of Pound's Vorticist criticism. Their incidents were facet-like groupings designed to interlock and "repeat." They possessed a very *Timon*-like "sense of dynamics," an inexorable movement toward a receding center. They displayed a narrative expansiveness in which a few incidents were made, like *Timon*, to suggest "unlimited subject-matter." I do not

having done so, some aesthete left over from the nineties would rebuke one for one's lack of aloofness." Pound, it seems, in 1914 not only was able to imagine the turn away from the nineties that the *Cantos* would involve, but he was also uncomfortably aware that a part of himself—the "aesthete" part he later attempted to exorcise in "Hugh Selwyn Mauberley"—would be made extremely uncomfortable by the change.

think it would be inaccurate, therefore, to describe Pound's structural method during the first stage of composing the *Cantos* as more "Vorticist" than ideogrammic. And so, in the remainder of this study, I have chosen one of his Vorticist descriptions, "radicals in design," to describe the structure of the early Cantos.

§

One more influence of Vorticism on the *Cantos* remains to be considered. I have in mind the change in Pound's, poetic decorum as his toleration of ugliness in poetry broadened. Several commentators have touched the surface of this subject by pointing to the increasing sarcasm of Pound's "Vorticist" verse. Wees, for example, noticed that "A new Poundian persona—a combined *enfant terrible* and social satirist—appeared as early as April, 1913,"[41] and concluded, "In early 1914, as Pound began to address himself to the social and cultural conditions of his day, he gave up the Imagists' cool, decorous tone."[42] Wees, however, does not account for the aesthetic significance of such a transition. The imagist's "cool, decorous tone" was descended in a straight line from the aesthete's desire to portray a world more beautiful and more intense than life.

By 1913, many forces aside from "the social and cultural conditions" of the day had made such a principle aesthetically as well as culturally untenable. In *Blast* No. 1, Edward Wadsworth translated Kandinsky to the effect that harmony was not a function of the beauty of individual forms or even of the smooth relation between forms, but depended on interesting dissonance. "The insuitability of form to colour," Kandinsky wrote, "must not be regarded as something 'inharmonious,' but on the contrary a new possibility, and consequently harmony." Picasso, by the year (1912) of Kandinsky's pronouncement, had put into practice an analogous

---

[41] Wees, *Vorticism*, p. 128.
[42] *Ibid.*, p. 127.

but more advanced form of the same perception. Picasso's 1912 collages incorporated materials from the mundane world in a deliberate attempt to expand the decorum of painting. Probably more than anything else, Picasso's work finally destroyed the artistic respectability of decorous gracefulness. Certainly Wyndham Lewis, although he disapproved of certain things about Kandinsky and Picasso, accepted their new decorum as one of the givens of modern art. Lewis, in fact, made the characteristic boast that he would beat them at their own game, and wrote in a section of *Blast* No. 1 entitled "Orchestra of Media":

> The surfaces of cheap manufactured goods, woods, steel, glass, etc., already appreciated for themselves, and their possibilities realised, have finished the days of fine paint.
>
> Even if painting remains intact, it will be much more supple and extended, containing all the elements of discord and "ugliness" consequent on the attack against traditional harmony.
>
> The possibilities of colour, exploitation of discords, odious combinations, etc., have been little exploited.
>
> A painter like Matisse has always been harmonious, with a scale of colour pleasantly Chinese.
>
> Kandinsky at his best is much more original and bitter. But there are fields of discord untouched.

In 1914-1915, Pound's criticism unhesitatingly followed Lewis' lead. In the very first of his defenses of the movement, Pound wrote that "The modern artist wishes dung to stay dung, earth to stay earth, and out of this he wishes to grow one or two flowers, which shall be something emphatically *not* dung, *not* earth."[43] Later, he even dropped the flower imagery: "you will never awaken a general or popular art sense so long as you rely solely on the pretty. . . . Our respect

[43] "The New Sculpture," *The Egoist*, 1, 4 (February 16, 1914), p. 68.

is not for the subject-matter, but for the creative power of the artist . . . in Rodin's 'La Vieille Healmière,' the 'beauty' of the work depends in no appreciable degree on the subject, which is 'hideous' " (G-B, pp. 97-98). Pound concluded his memoir *Gaudier-Brzeska* with the warning that the artist cannot be "forbidden any element" (G-B, p. 125), and he celebrated the way Vorticist composition was able to give the most mundane materials a new life: "These new men have made me see form, have made me more conscious of the appearance of the sky where it juts down between houses, of the bright pattern of sunlight which the bath water throws up on the ceiling, of the great 'V's' of light that dart through the chinks over the curtain rings. . . ." (G-B, p. 126).

Out of these convictions, the *Cantos* would develop an inclusivity that helped to redefine modern verse. However, as Lewis observed, in 1914 there was a "certain discrepancy between what Pound said . . . and what he did." As we shall see, 1915's *Three Cantos* contained hardly a trace of painting's new "ugliness." Shimmering images and a slightly irregular narrative tone set *Three Cantos'* dominant "timbre." Whatever attempt Pound made before 1919 to incorporate this new decorum into his poetry was limited to the satiric pieces that were collected in *Ripostes* and *Lustra*. And it is instructive to note that Pound considered those pieces to be minor work. In 1914, he had made it clear that he did not consider "sketches" to be significant art:

> On the other hand, no artist can possibly get a vortex into every poem or picture he does. One would like to do so, but it is beyond one. Certain things seem to demand metrical expression, or expression in a rhythm more agitated than the rhythms acceptable to prose, and these subjects, though they do not contain a vortex, may have some interest, an interest as "criticism of life" or of art. It is natural to express these things, and a vorticist or imagiste writer may be justified in presenting a certain amount of work which is not vorticism or imagisme, just as he might

be justified in printing a purely didactic prose article. *Unfinished sketches and drawings* have a similar interest; they are trials and attempts toward a vortex. (G-B, p. 94, my emphasis)

In the appendix to 1920's collected poems (*Umbra*), Pound made a definitive classification of his work, and labelled all of his satires "sketches," setting them off from the "Seafarer," "Cathay," and "Homage to Sextus Propertius," which he called "major personae."[44] Chapter Five will reconsider the question of decorum and discover what catalysts were required before Pound could apply Vorticist "ugliness" to the *Cantos*.

[44] *Umbra, The Early Poems of Ezra Pound* (London, 1920), p. 128.

CHAPTER III

THE GROWTH OF *THREE CANTOS*

Three Cantos

I

Hang it all, there can be but one *Sordello!*
But say I want to, say I take your whole bag
    of tricks,
Let in your quirks and tweeks, and say the
    thing's an art-form,
Your *Sordello*, and that the modern world
Needs such a rag-bag to stuff all its thought in;
Say that I dump my catch, shiny and silvery
As fresh sardines flapping and slipping on the
    marginal cobbles?
(I stand before the booth, the speech; but the
    truth
Is inside this discourse — this booth is full
    of the marrow of wisdom.)
Give up th' intaglio method.

                   Tower by tower
Red-brown the rounded bases, and the plan
Follows the builder's whim. Beaucaire's slim
    gray
Leaps from the stubby base of Altaforte —
Mohammed's windows, for the Alcazar
Has such a garden, split by a tame small
    stream.
The moat is ten yards wide, the inner court-
    yard

53

Half a-swim with mire.
Trunk hose?
                    There are not. The rough men swarm out
In robes that are half Roman, half like the
        Knave of Hearts;
And I discern your story:
                            Peire Cardinal
Was half forerunner of Dante. Arnaut's that
        trick
Of the unfinished address,
And half your dates are out, you mix your eras;
For that great font Sordello sat beside —
'Tis an immortal passage, but the font? —
Is some two centuries outside the picture.
Does it matter?
                    Not in the least. Ghosts move about me
Patched with histories. You had your business:
To set out so much thought, so much emotion;
To paint, more real than any dead Sordello,
The half or third of your intensest life
And call that third *Sordello*;
And you'll say, "No, not your life,
He never showed himself."
Is't worth the evasion, what were the use
Of setting figures up and breathing life
        upon them,
Were 't not *our* life, your life, my life,
        extended?
I walk Verona. (I am here in England.)
I see Can Grande. (Can see whom you will.)
                    You had one whole man?
And I have many fragments, less worth?
        Less worth?
Ah, had you quite my age, quite such a
        beastly and cantankerous age?
You had some basis, had some set belief.
Am I let preach? Has it a place in music?

54

                    I walk the airy street,
See the small cobbles flare with the poppy
        spoil.
'Tis your "great day," the Corpus Domini,
And all my chosen and peninsular village
Has made one glorious blaze of all its lanes —
Oh, before I was up — with poppy flowers.
Mid-June: some old god eats the smoke, 'tis
        not the saints;
And up and out to the half-ruined chapel —
Not the old place at the height of the rocks,
But that splay, barn-like church the Renais-
        sance
Had never quite got into trim again.
As well begin here. Began our Catullus:
"Home to sweet rest, and to the waves' deep
        laughter,"
The laugh they wake amid the border rushes.
This is our home, the trees are full of laughter,
And the storms laugh loud, breaking the
        riven waves
On "north-most rocks"; and here the sunlight
Glints on the shaken waters, and the rain
Comes forth with delicate tread, walking from Isola Garda —
                    Lo soleils plovil,
As Arnaut had it in th' inextricable song.
The very sun rains and a spatter of fire
Darts from the "Lydian" ripples; *"locus undae,"*
        as Catullus, *"Lydiae,"*
And the place is full of spirits.
Not *lemures,* not dark and shadowy ghosts,
But the ancient living, wood-white,
Smooth as the inner bark, and firm of aspect,
And all agleam with colors — no, not agleam,
But colored like the lake and like the olive
        leaves,

Glaukopos, clothed like the poppies, wearing
      golden greaves,
Light on the air.
Are they Etruscan gods?
The air is solid sunlight, *apricus*,
Sun-fed we dwell there (we in England now);
It's your way of talk, we can be where we will
      be,
Sirmio serves my will better than your Asolo
Which I have never seen.
                    Your "palace step"?
My stone seat was the Dogana's curb,
And there were not "those girls," there was
      one flare, one face.
'Twas all I ever saw, but it was real. . . .
And I can no more say what shape it was . . .
But she was young, too young.
                True, it was Venice,
And at Florian's and under the north arcade
I have seen other faces, and had my rolls for
      breakfast, for that matter;
So, for what it's worth, I have the background.
             And you had a background,
Watched "the soul," Sordello's soul,
And saw it lap up life, and swell and burst —
"Into the empyrean?"
So you worked out new form, the meditative,
Semi-dramatic, semi-epic story,
And we will say: What's left for me to do?
Whom shall I conjure up; who's my Sordello,
My pre-Daun Chaucer, pre-Boccacio,
           As you have done pre-Dante?
Whom shall I hang my shimmering garment on;
Who wear my feathery mantle, *hagoromo*;
Whom set to dazzle the serious future ages?
Not Arnaut, not De Born, not Uc St. Circ who
      has writ out the stories.

Or shall I do your trick, the showman's booth,
    Bob Browning,
Turned at my will into the Agora,
Or into the old theatre at Arles,
And set the lot, my visions, to confounding
The wits that have survived your damn'd
    Sordello?
(Or sulk and leave the word to novelists?)
What a hodge-podge you have made there! —
Zanze and *swanzig*, of all opprobrious rhymes!
And you turn off whenever it suits your fancy,
Now at Verona, now with the early Christians,
Or now a-gabbling of the "Tyrrhene whelk."
"The lyre should animate but not mislead the
    pen" —
That's Wordsworth, Mr. Browning. (What a phrase! —
That lyre, that pen, that bleating sheep, Will
    Wordsworth!)
That should have taught you avoid speech figura-
    tive
            And set out your matter
As I do, in straight simple phrases:
            Gods float in the azure air,
Bright gods, and Tuscan, back before dew was shed,
It is a world like Puvis'?
            Never so pale, my friend,
'Tis the first light — not half light — Panisks
And oak-girls and the Maenads
Have all the wood. Our olive Sirmio
Lies in its burnished mirror, and the Mounts
    Balde and Riva
Are alive with song, and all the leaves are
    full of voices.
"*Non è fuggito.*"
            "It is not gone." Metastasio
Is right — we have that world about us,

And the clouds bow above the lake, and there are
      folk upon them
Going their windy ways, moving by Riva,
By the western shore, far as Lonato,
And the water is full of silvery almond-white
      swimmers,
The silvery water glazes the up-turned nipple.
How shall we start hence, how begin the progress?
Pace naif Ficinus, say when Hotep-Hotep
Was a king in Egypt —
    When Atlas sat down with his astrolabe,
      He, brother to Prometheus, physicist —
              Say it was Moses' birth-year?
Exult with Shang in squatness? The sea-monster
Bulges the squarish bronzes.
(Confucius later taught the world good manners,
Started with himself, built out perfection.)
            With Egypt!
Daub out in blue of scarabs, and with that greeny
      turquoise?
Or with China, O *Virgilio mio*, and gray gradual
      steps
Lead up beneath flat sprays of heavy cedars,
Temple of teak wood, and the gilt-brown arches
Triple in tier, banners woven by wall,
Fine screens depicted, sea waves curled high,
Small boats with gods upon them,
Bright flame above the river! Kwannon
Footing a boat that's but one lotus petal,
With some proud four-spread genius
Leading along, one hand upraised for gladness,
Saying, "Tis she, his friend, the mighty goddess!
      Paean!
Sing hymns ye reeds,
        and all ye roots and herons and swans be
      glad,
Ye gardens of the nymphs put forth your flowers."

What have I of this life,
   Or even of Guido?
    Sweet lie! — Was I there truly?
Did I knew Or San Michele?
   Let's believe it.
Believe the tomb he leapt was Julia Laeta's?
Friend, I do not even — when he led that street
   charge —
I do not even know which sword he'd with him.
Sweet lie, "I lived!" Sweet lie, "I lived beside
   him."
And now it's all but truth and memory,
Dimmed only by the attritions of long time.

"But we forget not."
     No, take it all for lies.
I have but smelt this life, a whiff of it —
The box of scented wood
Recalls cathedrals. And shall I claim;
Confuse my own phantastikon,
Or say the filmy shell that circumscribes me
Contains the actual sun;
     confuse the thing I see
With actual gods behind me?
      Are they gods behind me?
How many worlds we have! If Botticelli
Brings her ashore on that great cockle-shell —
His Venus (Simonetta?),
And Spring and Aufidus fill all the air
With their clear-outlined blossoms?
World enough. Behold, I say, she comes
"Apparelled like the spring, Graces her subjects,"
(That's from *Pericles*).
Oh, we have worlds enough, and brave *décors*,
And from these like we guess a soul for man
And build him full of aery populations.

59

Mantegna a sterner line, and the new world
    about us:
Barred lights, great flares, new form, Picasso
    or Lewis.
If for a year man write to paint, and not to
    music —
O Casella!

II

    Leave Casella.
Send out your thought upon the Mantuan palace —
Drear waste, great halls,
Silk tatters still in the frame, Gonzaga's
    splendor
Alight with phantoms! What have we of them,
Or much or little?
Where do we come upon the ancient people?
"All that I know is that a certain star" —
All that I know of one, Joios, Tolosan,
Is that in middle May, going along
A scarce discerned path, turning aside,
In level poplar lands, he found a flower, and
    wept.
"*Y a la primera flor*," he wrote,
"*Qu'ieu trobei, tornei em plor.*"
There's the one stave, and all the rest forgotten.
I've lost the copy I had of it in Paris,
Out of the blue and gilded manuscript
Decked out with Couci's rabbits,
And the pictures, twined with the capitals,
Purporting to be Arnaut and the authors.
Joios we have. By such a margent stream,
He strayed in the field, wept for a flare of
    color,
When Coeur de Lion was before Chalus.

Or there's En Arnaut's score of songs, two tunes;
The rose-leaf casts her dew on the ringing
glass,
Dolmetsch will build our age in witching music.
Viols da Gamba, tabors, tympanons:

"Yin-yo laps in the reeds, my guest departs,
The maple leaves blot up their shadows,
The sky is full of autumn,
We drink our parting in saki.
Out of the night comes troubling lute music,
And we cry out, asking the singer's name,
And get this answer:
" 'Many a one
Brought me rich presents; my hair was full of
jade,
And my slashed skirts, drenched in expensive
dyes,
Were dipped in crimson, sprinkled with rare
wines.
I was well taught my arts at Ga-ma-rio,
And then one year I faded out and married.'
The lute-bowl hid her face.
"We heard her weeping."

Society, her sparrows, Venus' sparrows, and
Catullus
Hung on the phrase (played with it as Mallarmé
Played for a fan, "*Rêveuse pour que je plonge,*");
Wrote out his crib from Sappho:
"God's peer that man is in my sight —
Yea, and the very gods are under him,
Who sits opposite thee, facing thee, near thee,
Gazing his fill and hearing thee,
And thou smilest. Woe to me, with
Quenched senses, for when I look upon thee,
Lesbia,

There is nothing above me
And my tongue is heavy, and along my veins
Runs the slow fire, and resonant
Thunders surge in behind my ears,
And the night is thrust down upon me."

That was the way of love, *flamma dimanat.*
And in a year, "I love her as a father";
And scarce a year, "Your words are written in
  water";
And in ten moons, "*Caelius, Lesbia illa* —
That Lesbia, Caelius, our Lesbia, that Lesbia
Whom Catullus once loved more
Than his own soul and all his friends,
Is now the drab of every lousy Roman."
So much for him who puts his trust in woman.
So the murk opens.
     Dordoigne! When I was there,
There came a centaur, spying the land,
And there were nymphs behind him.
Or going on the road by Salisbury
Procession on procession —
For that road was full of peoples,
Ancient in various days, long years between them.
Ply over ply of life still wraps the earth here.
Catch at Dordoigne.
     Viscount St. Antoni
In the warm damp of spring,
Feeling the night air full of subtle hands,
Plucks at a viol, singing:
     "As the rose —
Si com, si com" — they all begin "*si com.*"
"For as the rose in trellis
Winds in and through and over,
So is your beauty in my heart, that is bound
  through and over.
So lay Queen Venus in her house of glass,

62

The pool of worth thou art,
Flood-land of pleasure."

But the Viscount Pena
Went making war into an hostile country
Where he was wounded:
"The news held him dead."
St. Antoni in favor, and the lady
Ready to hold his hands —
This last report upset the whole convention.
She rushes off to church, sets up a gross of
        candles,
Pays masses for the soul of Viscount Pena.

Thus St. Circ has the story:
"That sire Raimon Jordans, of land near Caortz,
Lord of St. Antoni, loved this Viscountess of
        Pena
'Gentle' and 'highly prized.'
And he was good at arms and *bos trobaire*,
And they were taken with love beyond all
        measure,"
And then her husband was reported dead,
"And at this news she had great grief and sorrow,"
And gave the church such wax for his recovery,
That he recovered, and
"At this news she had great grief and teen,"
And fell to moping, dismissed St. Antoni;
"Thus was there more than one in deep distress."

So ends that novel. And the blue Dordoigne
Stretches between white cliffs,
Pale as the background of a Leonardo.
"As rose in trellis, that is bound over and
        over,"
A wasted song?
No Elis, Lady of Montfort,
Wife of William à Gordon, heard of the song,

Sent him her mild advances.
                    Gordon? Or Gourdon
Juts into the sky
                    Like a thin spire,
Blue night's pulled down around it
Like tent flaps, or sails close hauled. When
        I was there,
La noche de San Juan, a score of players
Were walking about the streets in masquerade,
With pikes and paper helmets, and the booths,
Were scattered align, the rag ends of the fair.
False arms! True arms? You think a tale of
        lances . . .
A flood of people storming about Spain!
                    My cid rode up to Burgos,
Up to the studded gate between two towers,
Beat with his lance butt.
                    A girl child of nine,
Comes to a little shrine-like platform in the
        wall,
Lisps out the words, a-whisper, the King's writ:
"Let no man speak to Diaz or give him help or
        food
On pain of death, his eyes torn out,
His heart upon a pike, his goods sequestered."
He from Bivar, cleaned out,
From empty perches of dispersed hawks,
From empty presses,
Came riding with his company up the great
        hill —
"Afe Minaya!" —
                    to Burgos in the spring,
And thence to fighting, to down-throw of Moors,
And to Valencia rode he, by the beard! —
Muy velida.
                    Of onrush of lances,
Of splintered staves, riven and broken casques,

64

Dismantled castles, of painted shields split up,
Blazons hacked off, piled men and bloody rivers;
Then "sombre light upon reflecting armor"
And portents in the wind, when De las Nieblas
Set out to sea-fight,
"Y *dar neuva lumbre las armas y hierros.*"
Full many a fathomed sea-change in the eyes
That sought with him the salt sea victories.
Another gate?
        And Kumasaka's ghost come back to tell
The honor of the youth who'd slain him.
Another gate.
        The kernelled walls of Toro, *las almenas*;
Afield, a king come in an unjust cause.
Atween the chinks aloft flashes the armored
    figure,
Muy linda, a woman, Helen, a star,
Lights the king's features . . .
                "No use, my liege —
She is your highness' sister," breaks in Ancures;
"*Mal fuego s'enciende!*"
Such are the gestes of war "told over and over."
And Ignez?
           Was a queen's tire-woman,
Court sinecure, the court of Portugal;
And the young prince loved her — Pedro,
Later called the cruel. And other courtiers were
    jealous.
Two of them stabbed her with the king's conni-
    vance,
And he, the prince, kept quiet a space of years —
           Uncommon the quiet.
And he came to reign, and had his will upon the
    dagger-players,
And held his court, a wedding ceremonial —
He and her dug-up corpse in cerements
Crowned with the crown and splendor of Portugal.

A quiet evening and a decorous procession;
Who winked at murder kisses the dead hand,
Does leal homage,
"Que depois de ser morta foy Rainha."
Dig up Camoens, hear out his resonant bombast:
                           "That among the flowers,
As once was Proserpine,
Gatheredst thy soul's light fruit and every
          blindness,
Thy Enna the flary mead-land of Mondego,
Long art thou sung by maidens in Mondego."
What have we now of her, his *"linda Ignez"*?
Houtmans in jail for debt in Lisbon — how
          long after? —
Contrives a company, the Dutch eat Portugal,
Follow her ship's tracks, Roemer Vischer's
          daughters,
Talking some Greek, dally with glass engraving;
Vondel, the Eglantine, Dutch Renaissance —
The old tale out of fashion, daggers gone;
And Gaby wears Braganza on her throat —
Commuted, say, another public pearl
Tied to a public gullet. Ah, *mon rêve,*
It happened; and now go think —
Another crown, thrown to another dancer, brings
          you to modern times?

    I knew a man, but where 'twas is no matter:
Born on a farm, he hankered after painting;
His father kept him at work;
No luck — he married and got four sons;
Three died, the fourth he sent to Paris —
Ten years of Julian's and the ateliers,
Ten years of life, his pictures in the salons,
Name coming in the press.
                           And when I knew him,
Back once again, in middle Indiana,

Acting as usher in the theatre,
Painting the local drug-shop and soda bars,
The local doctor's fancy for the mantel-piece;
Sheep — jabbing the wool upon their flea-bit
    backs —
The local doctor's ewe-ish pastoral;
Adoring Puvis, giving his family back
What they had spent for him, talking Italian
    cities,
Local excellence at Perugia,
                        dreaming his renaissance,
Take my Sordello!

III

   Another's a half-cracked fellow — John Heydon,
Worker of miracles, dealer in levitation,
In thoughts upon pure form, in alchemy,
Seer of pretty visions ("servant of God and
        secretary of nature");
Full of a plaintive charm, like Botticelli's,
With half-transparent forms, lacking the vigor
        of gods.
Thus Heydon, in a trance, at Bulverton,
Had such a sight:
Decked all in green, with sleeves of yellow
        silk
Slit to the elbow, slashed with various purples.
Her eyes were green as glass, her foot was leaf-
        like.
She was adorned with choicest emeralds,
And promised him the way of holy wisdom.
"Pretty green bank," began the half-lost poem.
Take the old way, say I met John Heydon,
Sought out the place,
Lay on the bank, was "plungèd deep in swevyn;"

And saw the company — Layamon, Chaucer —
Pass each in his appropriate robes;
Conversed with each, observed the varying
    fashion.
And then comes Heydon.
                "I have seen John Heydon."
Let us hear John Heydon!
              "*Omniformis
Omnis intellectus est*" — thus he begins, by
    spouting half of Psellus.
(Then comes a note, my assiduous commentator:
Not Psellus *De Daemonibus*, but Porphyry's *Chances*,
In the thirteenth chapter, that "every intellect
    is omniform.")
Magnifico Lorenzo used the dodge,
Says that he met Ficino
In some Wordsworthian, false-pastoral manner,
And that they walked along, stopped at a well-
    head,
And heard deep platitudes about contentment
From some old codger with an endless beard.
"A daemon is not a particular intellect,
But is a substance differed from intellect,"
Breaks in Ficino,
"Placed in the latitude or locus of souls" —
That's out of Proclus, take your pick of them.
Valla, more earth and sounder rhetoric —
Prefacing praise to his Pope Nicholas:
"A man of parts, skilled in the subtlest sciences;
A patron of the arts, of poetry; and of a fine
    discernment."
Then comes a catalogue, his jewels of conversa-
    tion.
No, you've not read your *Elegantiae* —
A dull book? — shook the church.
The prefaces, cut clear and hard:
"Know then the Roman speech, a sacrament,"

Spread for the nations, eucharist of wisdom,
Bread of the liberal arts.
                         Ha! Sir Blancatz,
Sordello would have your heart to give to all
      the princes;
Valla, the heart of Rome,
Sustaining speech, set out before the people.
"*Nec bonus Christianus ac bonus*
                       Tullianus."
Marius, De Bellay, wept for the buildings,
Baldassar Castiglione saw Raphael
"Lead back the soul into its dead, waste
      dwelling,"
Corpore laniato; and Lorenzo Valla,
"Broken in middle life? bent to submission? —
Took a fat living from the Papacy"
(That's in Villari, but Burckhardt's statement
      is different) —
"More than the Roman city, the Roman speech"
(Holds fast its part among the ever-living).
"Not by the eagles only was Rome measured."
"Wherever the Roman speech was, there was Rome,"
Wherever the speech crept, there was mastery
Spoke with the law's voice while your Greek
      logicians . . .
More Greeks than one! Doughty's "divine
      Homeros"
Came before sophistry. Justinopolitan
Uncatalogued Andreas Divus,
Gave him in Latin, 1538 in my edition, the rest
      uncertain,
Caught up his cadence, word and syllable:
"Down to the ships we went, set mast and sail,
Black keel and beasts for bloody sacrifice,
Weeping we went."
I've strained my ear for *-ensa, -ombra,* and
      -ensa

And cracked my wit on delicate canzoni —
                    Here's but rough meaning:
"And then went down to the ship, set keel to
          breakers,
Forth on the godly sea;
We set up mast and sail on the swarthy ship,
Sheep bore we aboard her, and our bodies also
Heavy with weeping. And winds from sternward
Bore us out onward with bellying canvas —
Circe's this craft, the trim-coifed goddess.
Then sat we amidships, wind jamming the tiller.
Thus with stretched sail
                    We went over sea till day's end:
Sun to his slumber, shadows o'er all the ocean.
Came we then to the bounds of deepest water,
To the Kimmerian lands and peopled cities
Covered with close-webbed mist, unpiercèd ever
With glitter of sun-rays,
Nor with stars stretched, nor looking back from
          heaven,
Swartest night stretched over wretched men there.
Thither we in that ship, unladed sheep there,
The ocean flowing backward, came we through to
          the place
Aforesaid by Circe.
Here did they rites, Perimedes and Eurylochus,
And drawing sword from my hip
I dug the ell-squre pitkin, poured we libations
          unto each the dead,
First mead and then sweet wine,
Water mixed with white flour.
Then prayed I many a prayer to the sickly
          death's-heads
As set in Ithaca, sterile bulls of the best,
For sacrifice, heaping the pyre with goods.
Sheep, to Tiresias only,
Black, and a bell sheep;

70

Dark blood flowed in the fosse.
Souls out of Erebus, cadaverous dead
Of brides, of youths, and of many passing old,
Virgins tender, souls stained with recent tears,
Many men mauled with bronze lance-heads,
Battle spoil, bearing yet dreary arms:
These many crowded about me,
With shouting, pallor upon me, cried to my men
    for more beasts;
Slaughtered the herds — sheep slain of bronze,
Poured ointment, cried to the gods,
To Pluto the strong, and praised Proserpine.
Unsheathed the narrow steel,
I sat to keep off the impetuous, impotent dead
Till I should hear Tiresias.
But first Elpenor came, our friend Elpenor,
Unburied, cast on the wide earth —
Limbs that we left in the house of Circe,
Unwept, unwrapped in sepulchre, since toils urged
    other,
Pitiful spirit — and I cried in hurried speech:
'Elpenor, how art thou come to this dark coast?
Cam'st thou afoot, outstripping seamen?' And
    he in heavy speech:
'Ill fate and abundant wine! I slept in Circe's
    ingle,
Going down the long ladder unguarded, I fell
    against the buttress,
Shattered the nape-nerve, the soul sought Avernus.
But thou, O King, I bid remember me, unwept,
    unburied!
Heap up mine arms, be tomb by the sea-board, and
    inscribed,
A man of no fortune and with a name to come;
And set my oar up, that I swung 'mid fellows.'
Came then another ghost, whom I beat off, Anticlea,
And then Tiresias, Theban,

71

Holding his golden wand, knew me and spoke first:
'Man of ill hour, why come a second time,
Leaving the sunlight, facing the sunless dead
    and this joyless region?
Stand from the fosse, move back, leave me my
    bloody bever,
And I will speak you true speeches.'
                        "And I stepped back,
Sheathing the yellow sword. Dark blood he drank
    then
And spoke: 'Lustrous Odysseus, shalt
Return through spiteful Neptune, over dark seas,
Lose all companions.' Foretold me the ways and
    the signs.
Came then Anticlea, to whom I answered:
'Fate drives me on through these deeps; I sought
    Tiresias.'
I told her news of Troy, and thrice her shadow
                Faded in my embrace.
Then had I news of many faded women —
Tyro, Alcmena, Chloris —
Heard out their tales by that dark fosse, and
    sailed
By sirens and thence outward and away,
And unto Circe buried Elpenor's corpse."

Lie quiet, Divus.
                In Officina Wechli, Paris,
M. D. three X's, Eight, with Aldus on the Frogs,
And a certain Cretan's
                Hymni Deorum:
(The thin clear Tuscan stuff
    Gives way before the florid mellow phrase.)
Take we the Goddess, Venus:
                  Venerandam,
Aurean coronam habentem, pulchram,
Cypri munimenta sortita est, maritime,

Light on the foam, breathed on by zephyrs,
And air-tending hours. Mirthful, *orichalci,*
   with golden
Girdles and breast bands.
               Thou with dark eye-lids,
Bearing the golden bough of Argicida.

Northrop Frye, writing about *Paradise Lost,* differentiated the epic poem from long poems that are simply narrative ("the more stories . . . [a narrative poet] tells, the more successful he is") or simply encyclopedic. The epic, according to Frye, is "a poem that derived its structure from the epic traditions of Homer and Virgil and still had the quality of universal knowledge which belonged to the encyclopedic poem." That is, the epic structure as it has been passed down from the *Odyssey* to the *Aeneid* to *Paradise Lost* remains uniquely able to evoke enduring patterns of human experience. Frye contends that three structural elements account for much of the epic's archetypal validity. First, the action is split "neatly in two" between the wanderings of a hero and a comedy of reintegration. Second, the epic begins *in medias res* with its hero at the furthest point from home (in *Paradise Lost* from a spiritual home) and in the middle of a cyclical action of desolation, quest, and renewal. Third, the epic hero is presented in need of supernatural guidance for his return, and is forced to negotiate between two types of guidance — divine and demonic revelation. The divine is given unmysteriously in broad daylight and illuminates a present situation. The demonic, which at first appears to be more useful, is gotten by dark and sometimes forbidden ritual, illuminates the future rather than the present, and ultimately proves misleading.[1]

Pound out of deference to certain intellectual fashions of his youth at first preferred to call the *Cantos* a "long poem"

---

[1] See the first essay ("The Story of All Things") in Frye's *Five Essays on Milton's Epics* (London, 1965).

rather than an epic.[2] The symbolists had branded the epic
outdated because of its prolonged narrative continuity,[3] and
Pound was reluctant to disagree. Nevertheless, he sensed the
vitality of what Frye calls "the story of all things," and returned again and again for support to the epics of the past.
Noel Stock describes unpublished correspondence circa 1909
between Pound and his mother in which Pound was already
relating the American poet to traditional considerations of
epic structure:

> there was an exchange of letters about the conditions
> necessary for an epic and his own duties as an American
> poet. The conditions necessary for an epic, he told her,
> were (1) a beautiful tradition, (2) a unity in the outline
> of that tradition, as was to be found in the *Odyssey*, (3)
> a Hero, mythical or historical, and (4) a 'damn long time
> for the story to lose its garish detail and get encrusted
> with a bunch of beautiful lies.' Dante, he thought,
> escaped these necessities by dipping into a multitude
> of traditions and unifying them 'by their connection with
> himself.' . . . An epic in the real sense, he said, was the
> speech of a nation through the mouth of one man.
> Whitman had let America speak through him. . . . (*Life*,
> p. 76)

The same year Pound wrote in "What I feel about Walt
Whitman" that Whitman was to America what "Dante is
to Italy," and that his own "birth-right" encompassed both
(*Selected Prose*, pp. 115-116). In 1910's *The Spirit of Romance*, although he fashionably wrote that it would be "un-
profitable" to compare "the tremendous lyric of the sub-

---

[2] In 1924 he wrote that A *Draft of XVI Cantos* "ain't an epic. It's
part of a long poem" (L, p. 189).

[3] Norman Foerster, in *The Fortunes of Epic Poetry: A Study in
English and American Criticism 1750-1950* (New York, 1962), describes the reaction against epic in the prose of Wilde, Johnson, Pater,
Symons and Symonds. Foerster's book is an invaluable aid for recog-
nizing the conventional tincture of many of Pound's statements.

jective Dante" to an epic (SR, p. 153), he went on himself
to compare it to the poems of Milton, Wordsworth, Shelley,
and Whitman (see SR, pp. 154-157). Years later, his symbolist reticence gone, he would openly affirm that the *Divine
Comedy* was an interiorization of the epic histories of Homer
and Virgil. The "crime and punishment motif," he wrote in
a 1934 review of Binyon's englished *Inferno*, "binds through
from Homer to Virgil to Dante" (LE, pp. 212-213). Back
in 1910 he had written that the journey to the underworld
was "a confirmed literary habit of the race" (SR, p. 161).
Beginning with 1915's *Three Cantos*, he reconfirmed that
habit with new composition.

As Pound conceived his "long poem" in 1915, it would
have to be both epic and modern. That is, although it might
partake of "a unity in the outline" of "a beautiful tradition,"
it would have to meet post-symbolist standards of accept-
ability. Part of that problem, as we have seen, could be solved
by making the poem *Timon*-like and "Vorticist" — constructing it out of a pattern of "radicals in design." In 1915, however, Pound had been too long a dramatic poet to be fully
content with achieving merely a Vorticist surface. He was
then more interested in dramatic technique than in structure,
and he attempted to model *Three Cantos* after the most
sophisticated example of dramatic narration he could discover. Though he had formerly mentioned Whitman as the
end of the epic tradition, the example he finally settled on
was Browning. Pound wrote to his father in 1915 that "If you
like the 'Perigord' you would probably like Browning's *Sordello*. . . . You'll have to read it sometime as my big long
endless poem that I am now struggling with, starts off with
a barrelfull of allusions to *Sordello* which will intrigue you
if you haven't read the other. . . . A great work and worth
the trouble of hacking it out. I began to get it on about the
6th reading. . . ."[4]

[4] An unpublished letter in the Paige collection at Yale, cited by
Myles Slatin, "A History of Pound's Cantos I-XVI, 1915-1925,"
American Literature, xxxv, 2 (May 1963), p. 185.

Three Cantos I did indeed start off "with a barrelfull of allusions to *Sordello*":

> Hang it all, there can be but one *Sordello*!
>   But say I want to, say I take your whole
>   bag of tricks,
>   Let in your quirks and tweeks, and say the
>   thing's an art-form,
> Your *Sordello*, and that the modern world
> Needs such a rag-bag to stuff all its thought
>   in;
> Say I dump my catch, shiny and silvery
> As fresh sardines flapping and slipping on
>   the marginal cobbles?
> (I stand before the booth, the speech; but
>   the truth
> Is inside this discourse — this booth is full
>   of the marrow of wisdom.)

Pound here was not, as he was in 1908's "Mesmerism," gently chiding an admirable but slightly clumsy predecessor. *Three Cantos I*'s tribute to Browning is serious, and the last lines of this citation are the clearest statement in Pound's canon about the narrative procedure of the *Cantos*. In 1915, Pound had noticed what Browning's academic readers would not perceive for another forty years: *Sordello* is a poem whose narrator affects the objective viewpoint of a man describing the events in a diorama booth beside him. He pretends to have nothing to do with the images projected in the booth. But in fact the "meaning" or truth of *Sordello* does not reside in the narrator's simple account of the show (his "speech"); it lies in his meditation upon a story that resembles the story of his own life. *Sordello*'s truth is very much "inside this discourse" — that is, inside the question-and-answer of narrator and projected image. In 1915, Pound took over Browning's "booth," and in his *Cantos* portrayed a narrator recounting the images of his mind for the purposes of establishing just such a discourse.

Pound's contention that *Sordello* represented the advance

guard of narrative technique can be traced to Browning's own claims. *Sordello* announced itself as an attempt to modernize Dante (to "launch once more/that lustre" — 1, 365-366), and the poem provided its own account of the evolution of narrative art. In Book V, Sordello, in the process of renouncing his poetic vocation, recapitulates the history of literature to date and is given a vision of future achievements. He tells us that the poet's task has always been to communicate an ordered vision of the soul, and that the poet's power has increased from the time man first dissociated the conditions of the soul from the appearances of action. Sordello's review of narrative art goes on to explain how spiritual reality was formalized by the device of myth in ancient times, by a pageant of vices and virtues in the middle ages, and by an array of generalized moral types in the Renaissance.[5] The highest form of narrative (of which Sordello is allowed only a glimpse) consists, according to the poem, of the dramatization of uncharacterized emotional states:

> "I circumvent
> "A few, my masque contented, and to these
> "Offer unveil the last of mysteries —
> "Man's inmost life shall have yet freer play:
> "Once more I cast external things away,
> "And natures composite, so decompose
> "That" . . . Why, he writes *Sordello*!
>
> (v, 614-620)

By designating the new art of narrative with only the name of his own work,[6] Browning indicated he had more in mind

---

[5] Dante, in Browning's analysis, could convey moral discriminations but was unable to render the human conditions from which those discriminations had been drawn. Masquerading as just another witness to his narrative, Dante allowed his judgments, his moral "shading," to obscure the human record, and consequently deprived his readers of the opportunity of making their own moral dissociations. *Sordello* called a work like the *Commedia* an "elemental masque" in which prominent light and shade "suppress/All ordinary hues that softening blend/Such natures with the level" (v, 583-588).

[6] Marginalia in the 1863 edition labeled it "synthesist" as opposed to "epoist" and "analyst." Pound, however, retained Browning's first

than a Wordsworthian spiritual history. Apparently, he already regarded Wordsworth as an ancestor, for in Book II he differentiated three different kinds of the new Romantic narrative. Once a poet has seen "somewhat of man's state," Browning wrote, there are three ways he can depict it. Poets "can say they have so seen." Or, if they are "better," they can say "what it was they saw." But for Browning and his followers, the poetic task must be more, must be to "Impart the gift of seeing to the rest." These poets are called at 1, 928 the "Makers-see," and they convey to their readers the circumstances that make each man's spiritual vision peculiar to himself. Poetry, for Browning, must not only dramatize emotional experience; it must also communicate to its audience (and thus *make* them *see*) how experience is grounded in the conditions of an individual life.

Thus *Sordello* was written not as history but as dramatized history. By making the narrator a character in his own story, Browning makes us understand how a storyteller uses the events of another poet's life for building blocks so that he can construct a satisfactory expression of himself. Thus, one recent critic has written that "We are not seeing into the life of objects but into the creative consciousness, framer of its own world. The poem's subject is the speaker's consciousness."[7] Another reminds us that "It must never be forgotten that Sordello . . . is a projection, resurrected from the past into . . . 'present' contemplation . . . the Speaker . . . seeks an understanding of the phantom whom he has himself created from hints, 'facts' of a vague history drawn from the dim past."[8] In *Three Cantos I*, Pound put it this way:

> You had your business:
> To set out so much thought, so much emotion;

---

designation. He ended *Three Cantos II* with "take my Sordello" and offered his readers both a predecessor and a genre.

[7] W. David Shaw, *The Dialectical Temper: The Rhetorical Art of Robert Browning* (Ithaca, 1968), p. 24.

[8] R. Colombus and C. Kemper, "Sordello and the Speaker: A Problem in Identity," *Victorian Poetry*, 11, 4 (autumn 1964), p. 254.

To paint, more real than any dead Sordello,
The half or third of your intensest life
And call that third *Sordello;*[9]

The methods Browning used to construct his dramatized history are relevant to an understanding of *Three Cantos*. The most important of those methods was a paratactic presentation of events.[10] Browning believed that his story could not be presented in a traditional manner. In Book II of *Sordello*, the poem's hero, under recognizably nineteenth-century conditions, vainly tries to resuscitate poetry, using traditional poetic forms. Afterwards the narrator observes that, although Sordello had cast aside clichéd usages and "slow rewrought" his language, "welding words into the crude mass from the new speech round him," the result was only "fond essay." The age was not propitious, and Sordello's creations fell to pieces:

> Piece after piece that armour broke away,
> Because perceptions whole, like that he sought
> To clothe, reject so pure work of thought
> As language: thought may take perception's
>   place
> But hardly co-exist in any case,
> Being its mere presentment — of the whole
> By parts, the simultaneous and the sole
> By the successive and the many.
>
> (II, 588-595)

[9] N.B. Pound did *not* write: "call that third [the character] Sordello." He wrote "And call that third [the poem] *Sordello.*" (And he meant it, because he authorized the italics to be reprinted in the *Lustra Cantos*.) That is, he did not make the simplistic judgment that Browning recreated his own poetic development in the person of a character, but realized that the character and everything else in the poem is subsidiary to the consciousness of the narrator.

[10] For a discussion of the multiple levels of paratactic or "simultaneous" constructions in *Sordello*, see Michael Mason, "The Importance of Sordello," in *The Major Victorian Poets: Reconsiderations*, ed. by Isabel Armstrong (Lincoln, 1969), pp. 125-152 (especially pp. 135-136).

Sordello founders on the rock of an insurmountable nine-teenth-century problem. "Perceptions whole" — a complete vision of life — once could be communicated through continuous narrative by a Spenser or a Dante, whose language relied on a system of symbolic correspondences to connect values with action. But the language available to modern poets had lost its symbolic precision in becoming a pure "work of [scientific] thought." It could communicate "the successive and the many" relative truths of the modern world, but in it the status of the imagination had been reduced to that of the imaginary. Thus the shapeliness of traditional poetic forms was no longer available. The modern poet was forced to fragment narrative unity in order to accommodate a maze of incoherent, competing, relative truths, all purporting to be the scientific successors to an older, religiously based system of ordered beliefs.

Browning's solution to this problem in contemporary poetics was *Sordello*'s infamously confusing use of parataxis. For Browning, in order to be authentically modern, a poem must forego narrative continuity and render the fragmentation of a modern consciousness. His solution was taken over by Pound, who in *Three Cantos I* imitated *Sordello*'s form and wrote that "the modern world/Needs such a rag-bag to stuff all its thought in."

Browning helped to dramatize *Sordello*'s speaker by other, more superficial techniques, and those techniques also left their imprint on *Three Cantos*. For example, Browning made *Sordello*'s narrator play a role so obtrusive that the reader could not forget him. Between the poem's "story" and its audience strutted a director who (like his Hollywood counterpart) was part poet, part con-man. Browning's self-caricature is the prototype for Pound's "Old Ez." On the surface, he appears to be a clownishly arrogant lecturer.[11] "Pointing,

---

[11] Daniel Stempel, in "Browning's *Sordello*: The Art of the Makers-See," *PMLA*, 80, pp. 554-561, identifies the narrator as a diorama lecturer of a particular nineteenth-century variety. Stempel provides much useful background and intelligently discusses the role of the narrator in *Sordello*.

pole in hand" (1, 30), this ungainly charlatan uses vulgarly colloquial diction to interject a series of smirking comments. He abuses his readers, he wise-cracks about his characters, and he even (in Book III) steps completely outside his story-telling to remark upon the difficulty of *Sordello*. Meanwhile, of course, he is reminding us that *Sordello* is only a story, and that we must constantly look past the story to the nature of the "creative consciousness" behind it. In *Three Cantos*, Pound picked up some of this charlatan's mannerisms ("Then comes a note, my assiduous readers") in order to accomplish the same narrative purpose.

The reverse side of *Sordello*'s con-man is a serious poet, and on the reverse side of his vulgar chatter we discover the shorthand notation with which one poet speaks to another. Much of the remaining difficulty in *Sordello* comes from Browning's conception of the poem as a communication from one poet to "a few" selected colleagues. In Book V, Sordello learns that the poets of the future will effect a kind of "brother's speech":

> "How I rose,
> "And how have you advanced! since evermore
> "Yourselves effect what I was fain before
> "Effect, what I supplied yourselves suggest,
> "What I leave bare yourselves can now invest.
> "How we attain to talk as brothers talk,
> "In half-words, call things by half-names,
>   no balk
> "From discontinuing old aids. Today
> "Takes in account the work of Yesterday:
> "Has not the world a Past now, its adept
> "Consults ere he dispense with or accept
> "New aids? a single touch more may enhance,
> "A touch less turn to insignificance
> "Those structures' symmetry the past has
>   strewed
> "The world with, once so bare. Leave the mere
>   rude

"Explicit details! 'tis but brother's speech
"We need, speech where an accent's change gives
          each
"The other's soul — no speech to understand
"By former audience: need was then to expand,
"Expatiate — hardly were we brothers! true —
"Nor I lament my small remove from you,
"Nor reconstruct what stands already. Ends
"Accomplished turn to means; my art intends
"New structure from the ancient; as they
          changed
"The spoils of every clime at Venice, ranged
"The horned and snouted Libyan god, upright
"As in his desert, by some simple bright
"Clay cinerary pitcher — Thebes as Rome,
"Athens as Byzant rifled, till their Dome
"From earth's reputed consummations razed
"A seal, the all-transmuting Triad blazed
"Above. Ah, whose that fortune? Ne'ertheless
"E'en he must stoop contented to express
"No tithe of what's to say — the vehicle
"Never sufficient

                                    (v, 620-654)

This is "makers-see" poetry carried to its logical extreme.
The readers whom Browning would "make see" are fellow
writers. In narrative poetry of this sophistication, nuances are
conveyed by "an accent's change" — that is, by minor variations on traditional usages. We need no laborious explanation
to understand the influence of this conception on *Three
Cantos* and all of Pound's work. Calling things by their half-
names, allusively using the works of Yesterday to bespeak
a tradition, varying an inheritance by an accent's change —
all these are characteristics we have learned to associate with
the school of Pound and Eliot. The lines beginning "Ends/
Accomplished turn to means" could be used as an epigraph
to modernist poetry.

Sordello, then, and the Cantos modeled after it, intend to be a new kind of narrative poetry — a poetry that portrays not just an action but an authentically modern dramatization of the way an action acquires significance within an individual intelligence. Browning carefully chose the "story" of *Sordello* to fit the caricature of himself he presented as the poem's narrator. *Sordello's* speaker is the type of a poet seeking a modern poetic identity, and the "plot" he projects recounts a series of tentative postures assumed by a developing fellow poet. We at first assume that the Sordello in the story is an honest portrait of a twelfth-century troubadour, but it does not take long before we realize he is no such thing. The narrator requires the image of a poet like himself, and the Sordello in his story acts much less like a Troubadour than like one of Shelley's protagonists. *Sordello's* line of development, such as it is, centers around the narrator's increasing success at coming to terms with images of his older, failed poetic "selves." The various poetic and intellectual phases through which Sordello passes during the poem are representative of the artistic stages of Browning's youth. *Sordello's* development culminates when, through the depiction of his Shelleyan hero's necessary collapse, the narrator decides (very much as in Browning's essay on Shelley) that visionary poetry is no longer tenable.[12]

If *Sordello* revealed any reservations on Browning's part about his experimental narrative form, they concerned the

[12] The "discourse" between Browning's narrator and protagonist is a distorted reflection of the development of the *Purgatorio*. As Francis Fergusson has pointed out, in the *Purgatorio* the spiritual awareness of Dante the protagonist increases until he reaches the level of insight Dante the narrator has all along displayed. (See Francis Fergusson, *Dante's Comedy of the Mind* [Princeton, 1953], *passim.*) *Sordello* is less an imitation *Purgatorio* than a modern *Inferno* in which a narrator puzzles through the problems of time and belief and discovers his former self in the plight of an infernal crisis. Compare Joyce, who (in *Ulysses*) discovers Stephen in a nightmare from which he is trying to awake. Joyce (and Pound in his *Cantos*) explores an inferno much larger than Browning's circle of poets.

limitations of the poem's *bildungsroman* plot. During the "palace steps" digression at the end of Book III, Browning's narrator complains about the uncomfortable restrictions that any coherent story imposes on an author's imagination. He declares that any "lay" is "but an episode/In the bard's life," and compares each story to a port of call which the sailor must leave to continue his "Eastward . . . voyage."[13] Whatever its virtues, then, *Sordello* was still too circumscribed a form to contain the range of personalities and temperaments Browning would later explore in individual dramatic monologues.

In the extended exordium at the beginning of *Three Cantos*, Pound developed Browning's "palace step" discontentments into plans for a post-*Sordello* long poem. "Your 'palace step'?" Pound wrote, "My stone seat was the Dogana's curb." And again, "You had one whole man?/And I have many fragments." And most instructively:

> So you worked out new form, the meditative,
> Semi-dramatic, semi-epic story,
> And we will say: What's left for me to do?
> Whom shall I conjure up; who's my Sordello,
> My pre-Daun Chaucer, pre-Boccacio,
> As you have done pre-Dante?

Taken together, these cryptic remarks announced in "brother's speech" that Pound would take Browning's "new form" on the "Eastward" voyage through many times and cultures that *Sordello* never made. *Three Cantos* would be the next phase in narrative poetry. It would apply Browning's "meditative,/Semi-dramatic, semi-epic" method to "many fragments" rather than to one life. By indicating his desire to "conjure

---

[13] See *Sordello*, III, 614-677. One thinks of this statement of Pound's, written between the 1912 *New Age* publication of his *Patria Mia* series and the 1913 book-length manuscript: "With the real artist there is always a residue, there is always something in the man which does not get into his work. There is always some reason why the man is always more worth knowing than his books are." (*Patria Mia* [Chicago, 1950], p. 40.)

up" a "pre-Boccacio" as his narrator's poetic counterpart, Pound declared his poem would include many tales instead of one, and would provide a kaleidoscope of incidents instead of "one whole man" for his narrator to meditate upon. That declaration was never rescinded. Once Pound made it, however, he was faced with several structural problems. Though a series of Boccaccio-like (or Ovidian)[14] tales could be built like "radicals in design" to reflect prismatically many permutations of the same moment of struggle, Pound had no "story" or "biography" to help him decide which "radicals" to choose and what order to put them in. Very likely he had already conceived the *Cantos* as a "hierarchy of values"[15] in which each "radical" in the hierarchy would be elevated (as he in 1914 had intended to elevate the *Times*) from a fact to a "symbol of a state of mind."[16] However, for this progress of mental states he would still need principles of selection and organization.

Pound decided (probably long before 1915) to choose the "story of all things" for his organizing "plot." His narrative stance obtained from Browning, he took the rudiments of a structure from the epic tradition. As Dante had made his peripatetic protagonist a composite of Odysseus and Aeneas, so Pound compounded Dante and absorbed the poet quester into the narrator of *Three Cantos*. Like Dante in the *Commedia*, the speaker of the *Cantos* is *in medias res* — as far as he can be away from his spiritual home, and traveling through desolate lands. The "radicals" Pound's poet-narrator as first projects are images of himself — shipwrecked souls existing in what Pound later said was intended as the poem's "dark forest."[17] To parallel Browning's *Sordello*, the most

---

[14] Jim McGregor reminds me that Ovid's *Metamorphoses* (Pound's "sacred book") provided the primary structural model for both Chaucer and Boccaccio. Is is possible that the *Cantos'* invisible patterns of intention might also be imitations of schemata (see Brooks Otis, *Ovid as an Epic Poet* [London, 1966]) in Ovid?

[15] See above, Chapter One, p. 14.

[16] See above, Chapter Two, p. 47.

[17] *Impact* (Chicago, 1960), p. 15.

important "radical" was a portrait of the young Pound, whom I shall (not without precedent) call E. P. Sordello had been alienated in Browning's poem from traditional poetic forms, traditional language, and the traditional place of a poet in society. In *Three Cantos*, E. P. sits on the Dogana's steps in much the same situation. He is a young poet and would-be Odysseus stymied in Venice with his Calypso — a puerile vision of a nine-year-old girl. (In fact a parody of Dante's Beatrice, the girl whom Dante first saw at the age of nine.) E. P. portrays the state in which the *Cantos'* questing narrator long ago began his journey. He is like Aeneas — sitting in a ruined city and about to set sail for another city that will be the spiritual completion of the first.

Pound was aware that there would have to be a certain arbitrariness in the selection of the other "radicals" of misfortune for the poem's inferno, and he was determined that uncertainty about the selection should not get in the way of the poem's development. As late as 1922, he wrote that "The first 11 cantos are preparation of the palette. I *have to* get down all the colours or elements I want for the poem. Some perhaps too enigmatically and abbreviatedly. I hope, heaven help me, to bring them into some sort of design and architecture later" (L, p. 180).

Nevertheless, even when he wrote *Three Cantos*, Pound seems to have had some idea of what "colours" he preferred. When the poem's exordium ends and the narrator enters the dark forest of "drear waste" in earnest, he finds a series of figures who share certain recognizable characteristics. All of them — the lute girl, mooning Catullus, Viscount St. Antoni, the Cid, Camoens' Pedro, John Heydon, Ficino, and Odysseus — are stranded in mid-life, dreaming of their renascence. They are all led by desire for a small number of traditionally sacred objects (love, honor, beauty, fame), and they are all imprisoned by intelligences inadequate to perceive the true object from its meretricious imitation. They anticipate other figures in later Cantos (Malatesta, Niccolo

86

d'Este), and share their melancholy fate. The unhappy lovers are in the dark about love. The displaced knights cannot recognize honorable action. The confused poet-narrator wants to write a poem transfused with divine light in an age when the gods are hidden and poetry is discouraged at every turn. The best he can manage, we discover in Canto V, is "Topaz . . . and three sorts of blue; but on the barb of time."

The first Cantos, then, confront us with a sequence of floundering characters and a narrator's consciousness that the characters exist in an inferno. The narrator by convention cannot know the nature of paradise and must follow his characters in their progress. Readers sometimes fail to recognize the infernal plight of the figures who populate the early Cantos as they fail to see why Dante places Ulysses, Capaneus, Latini, and Farinata in Hell. Dante and Pound refuse to reduce the stature of such figures by blackening them. They were great men who were damned because of their misdirected virtù, and the narrator approaches them with respect. Only as the reader comes to understand the reality of peace and virtue in the *Commedia* and the *Cantos* does his response to figures such as Latini and Malatesta change from identification to pity.

i: *Understanding the Primitive Vision*

The germ of Pound's epic was nourished by his preoccupations of 1913-1915. I have already talked about the influence of Lewis and Wadsworth on Pound's conception of structure. To these, we must add the late 1913 acquisition of the Fenollosa materials (especially the "Noh"), the interests shared with Yeats during three winters at Stone Cottage, discussions about primitive art with Henri Gaudier-Brzeska, Pound's continued curiosity about the Middle Ages, several trips to Provence, an enthusiasm for Allen Upward, and the influence of Remy de Gourmont. As a tree's form depends both on its genetic pattern and on its nourishment, so Pound's epic filled out with materials that were at hand. In the following sections, I would like to consider the most important of those materials.

About 1913-1914, Pound was much involved with certain people who wanted to redefine art so that it would include the energies of the primitive. The primitivism of the early twentieth century had been colored by Nietzsche, Frazer, Picasso, and the discovery of the cave paintings. It not only recognized the need to allow for the spontaneous or "natural" in man, but it went on to take account of the darkness of both man and nature. Twentieth-century primitivism began to include the extra-human forces that man never would be able to domesticate, and primitive art was seen for the first time not as simply unskilled art but as expression of the power and energy in the archaic mind — the mind that was being explained by, among others, Freud, Jung, Frazer, Jane Harrison, and Lawrence. Some artists, such as Marinetti, believed that art, in order to accommodate the primitive, would have to be fluid, inchoate. Others believed that archaic man related power to elemental shapes, and that so-called primitive art achieved its power not by its lack of constraint but by harnessing the energies of the pure forms of geometry that underlie more sophisticated forms, as bone and muscle underlie flesh. It was with this second group that Pound formed his alliance.

The most convenient way to begin reconstructing Pound's primitivist perspective is to double back to certain Vorticist documents. Vorticism had not only absorbed the aesthetic innovations of Cubism and Expressionism, but it also had absorbed their primitivist bias, and Pound assimilated both when he embraced the movement. It would, in fact, not be inaccurate to say that he accepted Vorticist primitivism even faster than he did its disturbingly new concepts of structure and decorum. Certainly, after Pound's long association with Yeats and Yeats's theories of spiritualism, he was ripe for the appeal of the archaic.[18]

[18] On the influence of Yeats's mysticism, see Thomas H. Jackson, *The Early Poetry of Ezra Pound* (Cambridge, 1968), Chapter Two.

Perhaps the earliest and most central document of Vorticist primitivism was T. E. Hulme's 1914 essay, "Modern Art and Its Philosophy." Hulme had returned in 1913 from a trip to Berlin with an enthusiasm for Wilhelm Worringer's exposition of the value of primitive abstractions.[19] In "Modern Art and Its Philosophy," Hulme espoused archaic or "geometric" art because it avoided the Romantic view that divinity and nature answered to man's feelings, and because it expressed in hard, unrepresentative forms "the superhuman abstract idea of the divine."[20] Critics have commented on the influence of Hulme's call for a new hardness in modern sensibility,[21] but few have noticed the details of his immediate effect on Pound. Reviewing Hulme's "almost wholly unintelligible lecture on cubism and new art" in *The Egoist*, Pound slid over Hulme's call for hardness and emphasized the lecture's treatment of archaic values.[22] His review contrasted the effeteness of Greek sculpture with the archaic power of Greek tragedy, a form that reminded the ancients "of chaos and death and the then inexplicable forces of destiny and nothingness and beyond." He commented that Hulme and another speaker had expressed the opinion that art should involve "something beyond man, something important enough to be fed with the blood of hecatombs," and added that "The introduction of Djinns, tribal gods, fetiches, etc. into the arts is therefore a happy presage." Finally, Pound ended his essay with a credo about modern art, and he stressed not its Cubist aesthetic but its reliance on primitive vitality:

> We turn back, we artists, to the powers of the air, to the djinns who were our allies aforetime, to the spirits

[19] See William Wees, *Vorticism and the English Avant-Garde* (Toronto, 1972), pp. 78-85.

[20] The essay was published in *Speculations: Essays on Humanism and the Philosophy of Art*, ed. by Herbert Read (London, 1936), pp. 75-109.

[21] See Wees, p. 84, and Monroe K. Spears, *Dionysus and the City: Modernism in Twentieth-Century Poetry* (New York, 1970), p. 15.

[22] "The New Sculpture," *The Egoist*, I, 4 (February 19, 1914), pp. 67-68.

of our ancestors. It is by them that we have ruled and shall rule, and by their connivance that we shall mount again into our hierarchy. . . .

Modern civilisation has bred a race with brains like those of rabbits and we who are the heirs of the witch-doctor and the voodoo, we artists who have been so long the despised are about to take over control.

And the public will do well to resent these "new" kinds of art.

The *Blast* group, then, did not disavow tradition when they took up primitivism. They merely extended the tradition to include the masterpieces of the archaic period. Pound explained:

> The vorticist has not this curious tic for destroying past glories. . . . We do not desire to evade comparison with the past. We prefer that the comparison be made by some intelligent person whose idea of "the tradition" is not limited by the conventional taste of four or five centuries and one continent. (G-B, p. 90)

For the first number of *Blast*, Gaudier-Brzeska wrote a history of sculpture, *Vortex*, which thumbed its nose at the classical tradition and skipped from the primitive to the twentieth century. He began his history with the cave paintings in the Dordogne caverns, which utilized the "driving power" of "life in the absolute." He catalogued the several geometric forms by which major primitive cultures had come to figure the absolute. In Egypt, according to Gaudier-Brzeska, the outer world was perceived in terms of towering divinity and so the prevailing form was vertical. The Greeks diluted their Egyptian heritage by replacing an image of the divinity with images of themselves. "The absence of direct energy lasted for a thousand years." (Until the gothic.) The moderns, the inheritors of tradition, have refused to copy the effete Greeks and have returned to the power of the elements themselves. "WE the moderns: Epstein, Brancusi, Archipenko, Dunikowski, Modigliani, and myself, through the incessant struggle in the complex city . . . we have mastered the elements . . . we have made a combination of all the possible shaped masses — concentrating them to express our abstract thoughts of conscious superiority."

At about the same time that the Vorticists were incorporating primitive elements into art and sculpture, Ernest Fenollosa and Allen Upward helped to suggest how primitive power entered into language, and pointed the way to a poetry that could once again reflect more than human energies. Like Gaudier-Brzeska, Fenollosa saw the true roots of tradition in the primitive, and regarded the classical Greeks as the great diluters. "The sentence-form," he wrote in *The Chinese Written Character* essay, "was forced upon primitive men by nature itself. It was not we who made it; it was a reflection of the temporal order in causation. All truth has to be expressed in sentences because all truth is the *transference of power*" (p. 12).[23] He went on to say that the laws of predication and the use of the copula (the tree *is* green) were later developments that cut men off from natural energy. "All nations have written their strongest and most vivid literature before they invented a grammar" (p. 16). The energy of the primitive, Fenollosa claimed, entered language through the power of transitive verbs. He added that the copula, "is," by which we conceive the mode of things as petrified solidity, was actually a verb whose original energy had been smothered. "There is in reality no such verb as a pure copula, no such original conception: our very word *exist* means 'to stand forth,' to show oneself by a definite act. 'Is' comes from the Aryan root *as*, to breathe. 'Be' is from *bhu*, to grow" (p. 15).

Allen Upward today is more obscure than Fenollosa, but he was no less important to Pound. Upward met Pound at

[23] My references are to the paperback republication, *The Chinese Written Character as a Medium for Poetry*, ed. by Ezra Pound (San Francisco, 1950).

Yeats's soirées during 1911, and was part of Yeats's occult circle.[24] For our purposes, his significance lies in the way he was able to coordinate suggestive etymology with a conception of a fluid universe. In *The New Word* (1910), Upward expressed his doubts about a standard textbook definition of the universe, which ran: "The Universe is made up of Matter and Power" (p. 109). The muddle-headed latinists, according to him, got their sense of matter all wrong. "No one but a schoolmaster writing a scholastic treatise in technical terms would dream of using the word matter in the sense of substance. For everybody else, and for the schoolmaster himself in his waking hours, it means very much what mat means, a knot, or knotwork, a tangle or net" (p. 114). Upward explained that it all would have been clear had we by-passed Latin and consulted the true source of knowledge about the world, primitive language, specifically "the old mother-tongue [gothic] of the White race" (p. 112). We then would have learned: "The word *noti* gives us the clew to mat and matter. On the one hand it merges into *knot* . . . on the other hand it merges into the French *natte*, and so into net and mat. For a mat, as it seems needful to point out to philologists, is a net in which the holes are smaller, and the knots closer together" (p. 113).

Upward concluded that matter is a knot of energy, and that the textbook doubled the necessary number of universal components. The atom is a knot, a vortex, and the opposing schools of materialists and idealists choose to see one aspect or the other, and not the antecedent form. One great idealist conceived of religion as a cross because he sensed the relationship: "The Cross is a rude picture of a knot. As such it is the sign of Matter; and the Man on the cross signifies the

---

[24] See Herbert Schneidau, "Pound and Yeats: The Question of Symbolism," *ELH*, XXXII, 2 (June 1965), p. 226. Schneidau provides a fuller discussion of Upward, Mead, the *Quest* circle and the "fluid universe" in his *Ezra Pound: The Image and the Real* (Baton Rouge, 1969), pp. 118ff.

thought that Matter is Evil" (p. 194). For Upward, a more precise image was that of the waterspout, in which energy of the wind interpenetrates the swirling matter of water. He called his image a "whirl-swirl." For him, the waterspout symbolized man's relation to the universe. It presented Man and God as two interpenetrating strengths, two pulses which take on shape when they join and could not exist without one another. We see the whirl-swirl in an illusory skin as a ball, but in reality it is a magic crystal:

> Consider this idea. Consider this inner strength, coming and going, turning and returning, millions of beats in every tick of secular time, while, throbbing through the network woven by their meeting, the overstrength comes and goes faster than flashes in a diamond.
>
> It is no longer a mere word. It is a magic crystal, and by looking long into it, you will see wonderful meanings come and go. It will change colour like an opal while you gaze, reflecting the thoughts in your own mind. It is a most chameleon-like ball. It has this deeper magic that it will show you, not only the thoughts you knew about before, but other thoughts you did not know of, old, drowned thoughts, hereditary thoughts; it will awaken the slumbering ancestral ghosts that haunt the brain; you will remember things you used to know and feel long, long ago.
> (pp. 200-201)

In 1914, when Pound reviewed *The New Word*, he said that "what Mr. Upward says will be believed in another twenty or fifty or a hundred years, just as a lot of Voltaire's quiet thrusts are now a part of our gospel."[25] His review especially commended Upward's etymological insights into myth. Pound quoted a passage in which Upward derived the meaning of "glaukopis" (one of the epithets of Athene in the *Odyssey*), and the full passage is worth our attention:

[25] "Alan Upward Serious," *The New Age*, XIV, 25 (April 23, 1914), pp. 779-780.

That old talk about the Gods, which is called mythology, is confused in many ways, partly because all language is confused . . . [primitive man's] language is tangled and twisted beyond our power wholly to unravel, because it was beyond their power; because it began as a tangle when man's mind was still a blur, and he saw men as trees walking. . . . How hard the old cloistered scholarship, to which the Nobels of a bygone age gave their endowments, has toiled to understand the word *glaukopis*, given to the goddess Athene. Did it mean blue-eyed, or gray-eyed, or — by the aid of Sanskrit — merely glare-eyed? And all the time they had not only the word *glaux* staring them in the face, as the Athenian name for owl, and the name of ox-eyed Hera to guide them, but they had the owl itself cut at the foot of every statue of Athene, and stamped on every coin of Athens, to tell them that she was the owl-eyed goddess, the lightning that blinks like an owl. For what is characteristic of the owl's eyes is not that they glare, but that they suddenly leave off glaring, like lighthouses whose light is shut off. We may see the shutter of the lightning in that mask that overhangs Athene's brow, and hear its click in the word *glaukos*. And the leafage of the olive, whose writhen trunk bears, as it were, the lightning's brand, does not glare, but glitters, the pale under face of the leaves alternating with the dark upper face, and so the olive is Athene's tree, and is called *glaukos*. Why need we carry owls to Oxford? (*The New Word*, pp. 238-39)

For Upward, such a derivation demonstrated that primitive perception of nature was more sensitive than our own. He believed, however, that it was still possible for modern man to put himself into the shoes of his ancestors and understand what they experienced. His derivation of "glaukopis" was just one example of a special kind of etymological "understanding":

understanding is one of those words that explain themselves. Like the Swedish *forsta*, which is still found in some parts of England as forestand, it tells its own story. A picture of Leighton's shows it to the eye. A man is teaching a boy the use of the bow. He leans over the boy from behind, grasping the boy's hands in his, and guiding them while the bow is drawn. That boy is *understanding* how to draw a bow. (p. 66)

Upward desired to "understand" the origins of once living beliefs, and he used etymology as a treasure-house of clues to aid him in making sense of the dry facts of history and anthropology.

Upward's next book, *The Divine Mystery*, was written in 1913 to approach the myths behind religion with many of the same techniques he had used in *The New Word*. Joyce later acknowledged it as a possible "running marginal comment on Circe,"[26] and Pound in 1913 paid it an extraordinary tribute. Reviewing *The Divine Mystery* in *The New Freewoman*, he singled out this passage:

> I was sitting like Abraham in my tent door in the heat of the day, outside a Pagan city of Africa, when the lord of the thunder appeared before me, going on his way into the town to call down thunder from heaven upon it.
>
> He had on his wizard's robe, hung round with magical shells that rattled as he moved; and there walked behind him a young man carrying a lute. I gave the musician a piece of silver, and he danced before me the dance that draws down the thunder. After which he went his way into the town; and the people were gathered together in the courtyard of the king's house; and he danced before them all. Then it thundered for the first time in many days; and the king gave the thunder-maker a black goat — the immemorial reward of the performing god.
>
> So begins the history of the Divine Man, and such is his rude nativity. The secret of genius is sensitiveness. The Genius of the Thunder who revealed himself to me could

---

[26] *Letters of James Joyce*, ed. by Stuart Gilbert (New York, 1957), p. 156.

not call the thunder, but he could be called by it. He was more quick than other men to feel the changes of the atmosphere; perhaps he had rendered his nervous system more sensitive still by fasting or mental abstraction; and he had learned to read his own symptoms as we read a barometer. So, when he felt the storm gathering round his head, he put on his symbolical vestment, and marched forth to be its Word, the archetype of all Heroes in all Mysteries.

Pound then commented: "So begins the most fascinating book on folk-lore that I have ever opened. . . . He has never forgotten the very real man inside the event or the history. It is this which distinguishes him from all the encyclopaedists who have written endlessly upon corn gods, etc."[27]

One cannot say that Upward had any significant part in initiating Pound's speculations on myth, spirit, energy, and etymology since Pound's poetry had always been preoccupied with such matters. But Upward seems to have served Pound, as Vico served Joyce, as an example of a common-sensical man acquainted with science and philology who nevertheless reinforced poetic intuitions about the vital universe. To Pound's Yeatsian beliefs, Upward added pseudo-scientific metaphors and convinced Pound that ecstasy could be depicted in a straightforward manner. Pound's famous 1915 description of myth owed as much to Upward as it did to Yeats:

The first myths arose when a man walked sheer into "nonsense," that is to say, when some very vivid and undeniable adventure befell him, and he told someone else who called him a liar. Thereupon, after bitter experience, perceiving that no one could understand what he meant when he said that he "turned into a tree" he made a myth — a work of art that is — an impersonal or objective story woven out of his own emotion, as the nearest equation he

[27] "The Divine Mystery," *The New Freewoman*, I, 11 (November 15, 1913), pp. 207-208.

was capable of putting into words. That story, perhaps, then gave rise to a weaker copy of his emotion in others, until there arose a cult, a company of people who could understand each other's nonsense about the gods. (LE, p. 431)

We can trace Upward's influence on Pound as early as the seminal 1912 essay, "Psychology and the Troubadours." We have seen that in his review of *The Divine Mystery*, Pound quoted Upward to the effect that the divine hero was a sensitive man who "had rendered his nervous system more sensitive still by fasting or mental abstraction; and . . . had learned to read his own symptoms as we read a barometer." Apparently, Upward discussed the subject with Pound some time in 1912, for we find Upward's electrical-charge metaphors and his conception of induced sensitivity to natural forces in Pound's essay. In "Psychology and the Troubadours," Pound speculated on the *dulce stil nuovo*, and reasoned that the Tuscan intimacy with the vital universe may have resulted from Trecento conditions that served to increase psychological sensitivity. Trecento poetry, he wrote, developed love as one path toward creating an electrical polarity within the nervous system:

There are at least two paths . . . the one ascetic, the other for want of a better term "chivalric." In the first the monk, or whoever he may be, develops, at infinite trouble and expense, the secondary pole within himself, produces his charged surface which registers the beauties, celestial or otherwise, by "contemplation." In the second, which I must say seems more in accord with *"mens sana in corpore sano"* the charged surface is produced between the predominant natural poles of two human mechanisms.

Sex is, that is to say, of a double function and purpose, reproductive and educational; or, as we see in the realm of fluid force, one sort of vibration produces at different intensities, heat and light. (SR, p. 94)

The electric current gives light where it meets resistance. I suggest that the living conditions of Provence gave the necessary restraint, produced the tension sufficient for the results. . . . (SR, p. 97)

Pound retained the kernel of these remarks in his central "Medievalism" essay, which may date from the same period but was probably written much later:[28]

> The Tuscan demands harmony in something more than the plastic. . . . There is the residue of perception, perception of something which requires a human being to produce it. . . .
> And dealing with it is not anti-life. . . . The senses at first seem to project for a few yards beyond the body. Effect of a decent climate where a man leaves his nerve-set open, or allows it to tune in to its ambiance, rather than struggling, as a northern race has to for self preservation, to guard the body. . . .
> He declines, after a time, to limit reception to his solar plexus. The whole thing has nothing to do with taboos and bigotries. . . . The conception of the body as perfect instrument of the increasing intelligence pervades. (LE, pp. 151-152)

> We appear to have lost the radiant world where one thought cuts through another with clean edge, a world of moving energies . . . magnetisms that take form, that are seen, or that border the visible, the matter of Dante's *paradiso*, the glass under water. . . . (LE, p. 154)

In *The New Word*, Upward declared that man stood in the same relation to nature as water to the downswirling wind within a water spout. If man properly perceived this relation, according to Upward, he would know that his psychic energy must be counter-exerted in phase with the pulse of down-swirling nature. When he did so, he would

[28] See Donald Gallup, A *Bibliography of Ezra Pound*, London, 1963, entry C710.

have access to "old, drowned thoughts, hereditary thoughts
... things you used to know and feel long, long ago" (p. 201).
In "Psychology and the Troubadours," Pound also took over
this Upwardian conception of a counter-assertive consciousness and called it "close on the vital universe":

> Let us consider the body as pure mechanism. Our kin-
> ship to the ox we have constantly thrust upon us; but be-
> neath this is our kinship to the vital universe, to the tree
> and the living rock, and, because this is less obvious — and
> possibly more interesting — we forget it.
>
> We have about us the universe of fluid force, and below
> us the germinal universe of wood alive, of stone alive. Man
> is — the sensitive physical part of him — a mechanism, for
> the purpose of our further discussion a mechanism rather
> like an electric appliance. . . . As to his consciousness, the
> consciousness of some seems to rest, or to have its center
> more properly, in what the Greek psychologists called the
> *phantastikon*. Their minds are, that is, circumvolved about
> them like soap-bubbles reflecting sundry patches of the
> macrocosmos. And with certain others the consciousness
> is "germinal." Their thoughts are in them as the thought
> of the tree is in the seed . . . these minds . . . affect mind
> about them, and transmute it as the seed the earth. And
> this latter sort of mind is close on the vital universe. . . .
> (SR, pp. 92-93)

Pound took Upward's universe of fluid forces and made his
own interpretation of the way man's swirl outward interpenetrates nature. Pound's "germinal" consciousness is an
artist's active mind which wills interpenetration of the world
by feeling. In his writing, the artist's unswirling creative
imagination became the means by which the downswirling
energies of the gods became manifest. Man did not express
God by trying to mirror him, but by struggling to create new
forms.

The most important primitive tenet of "Psychology and
the Troubadours" was that great art is always a ritual lead-

ing to awareness of what Upward called the "hereditary thoughts" of myth. Pound wrote that "chivalric love" is "a religion" (SR, p. 87), and added that "Provençal song is never wholly disjunct from pagan rites of May Day" (SR, p. 90). More importantly, he wrote that the canzone, which culminated with Dante, is "good art as the high mass is good art . . . [it] is a ritual. It must be conceived and approached as ritual. It has its purpose and its effect" (SR, p. 89). Pound, of course, thought of the *Commedia* along with Dante's canzoni as a spiritual education. In *The Spirit of Romance* he wrote that the *Commedia's* divisions were to be conceived as "mental states" (SR, p. 128). "Hell is the state of man . . . who has lost 'the good of the intelligence' " (SR, p. 129), whereas Paradise is the state of man whose intelligence is most in tune with God.

We have seen that Upward was a source of Pound's notion of divinity and it is not impossible that Upward also colored the way he read Dante's epic. Upward, after all, had written that his "sensitive" was the "archetype of all Heroes in all Mysteries," and *The Divine Mystery* chronicled the history of man's religion as a journey from darkness to light. In his review, Pound wrote: "The first half of the book is planned . . . on the slow recognition of the sun. That is to say, primitive man turns from his worship of the dead, and of the earth and of various fears, to a worship of life-giving Helios." If Upward was in fact influencing Pound to see a modern *Commedia* as a ritual journey through history, then the importance of Helios in the *Cantos* (especially in Canto XV) becomes more understandable. Like *The Divine Mystery*, the *Cantos* recount an increasing ritual perception of the light, beginning with the Nekyia (an archaic "worship of the dead"), and ending with the sun visions of *Thrones*.

The imprint of Upward on *Three Cantos* was explicit and pervasive. In *Three Cantos I*, Pound took Upward's *aperçus* about the word "glaukopis" and used both the word and Upward's method to introduce his major theme — modern man's blindness to the spirits of nature. He presents himself at Sirmio, the home of Catullus:

This is our home, the trees are full of laughter,
And the storms laugh loud, breaking the riven
       waves
On "north-most rocks"; and here the sunlight
Glints on the shaken waters, and the rain
Comes forth with delicate tread, walking from Isola Garda —
      Lo soleils plovil,
As Arnaut had it in th' inextricable song.
The very sun rains and a spatter of fire
Darts from the "Lydian" ripples; *"locus undae,"*
      as Catullus, *"Lydiae,"*
And the place is full of spirits.
Not *lemures,* not dark and shadowy ghosts,
But the ancient living, wood-white,
Smooth as the inner bark, and firm of aspect,
And all agleam with colors — no, not agleam,
But colored like the lake and like the olive
      leaves,
Glaukopos, clothed like the poppies, wearing
      golden greaves,
Light on the air.
Are they Etruscan gods?
The air is solid sunlight, *apricus,*
Sun-fed we dwell there (we in England now);
It's your way of talk, we can be where we will be,
Sirmio serves my will better than your Asolo
Which I have never seen.

"The place is full of spirits," but their forms are inaccessible because we have lost "the good of the intelligence." However, through the power of glimpses (natural and etymological) into the primitive reality, the spirits begin to come clear. We are not told of the presence of Athene, but we are presented with her manifestations: "colored like the lake

101

and like the olive leaves, Glaukopos." Thus, Pound presents her hidden in a nugget and discoverable only by "understanding" her as the ancients, in their rituals, had understood her. "Glaukopos" is a real remnant of her presence. The reader is expected to ponder strange words as he ponders the unusually detailed settings. We find the same technique in Canto II, where Dionysus appears, a "wine red glow in the shallows" before Acoetes wills him a shape, and where Athene and Apollo make unidentified appearances:

> Olive grey in the near,
>> far, smoke grey of the rock-slide,
> Salmon-pink wings of the fish-hawk
>> cast grey shadows in water,
> The tower like a one-eyed grey goose
>> cranes up out of the olive-grove

The *Cantos* work by the ritual repetition of such divine manifestations until the reader has "understood" them well enough to be told the gods' names. It is not until Canto XXI that we are told the "tower" of Canto II is "Phoibus, turris eburnea," the tower of Apollo. Even in Canto XXI, the explanation is darkened by the nugget of Latin, but there are reinforcements for the perceptive: "In the crisp air, / the discontinuous gods; / Pallas, young owl in the cup of her hand, / And, by night, the stag runs, and the leopard, / Owl-eye amid pine boughs." Eliot noticed that Dante habitually presented an image without naming it, and allowed the reader gradually to sense its power. Pound, partly because of Upward, hid the *Cantos*' divinities in rocks and strange words, given but unexplained.

ii: *Yeats and the Noh*

During the winters of 1913-1914 and 1914-1915, which preceded the composition of *Three Cantos*, Pound stayed with Yeats at Stone Cottage in Sussex. Beforehand, he wrote his mother that "My stay in Stone Cottage will not be in the least profitable. I detest the country. Yeats will amuse me part of the time and bore me to death with psychical research the rest. I regard the visit as a duty to posterity" (L, p. 25). But, despite his affected disinterest in Yeats's "psychical research," during the time of his visits Pound became involved in several of Yeats's poetic projects. According to Noel Stock, it was Pound who "chose, or helped to choose" the title *Responsibilities* for the collection of Yeats's 1913-1914 poems (*Life*, p. 160). And when we remember that it was in *Responsibilities* that Yeats began to experiment with unexplained parallels between contemporary, historical, and mythological figures, Pound's involvement takes on some interest. Poems like "To a Wealthy Man . . . ," "To a Shade," and "The Grey Rock," with their use both of the past and of mythology to put modern culture in perspective, strongly resemble certain aspects of *Three Cantos*. Especially "The Grey Rock," in which the tragic members of the Rhymers club are juxtaposed in a narrator's meditation with a story about the immortals of Gaelic legend.

The experimental juxtapositions of these poems seem to have grown out of Yeats's habit of correlating legends that Pound described in '*Noh*' *or Accomplishment*. "All through the winter of 1914-5," he wrote, "I watched Mr. Yeats correlating folk-lore (which Lady Gregory had collected in Irish cottages) and data of occult writers, with the habits of charlatans of Bond Street" (*Translations*, p. 236). Whatever he thought of Yeats's occultism and his symbolism, Pound apparently felt some respect for the meditative use of mythical correlations in *Responsibilities*. He wrote about the volume that "Mr. Yeats is a romanticist, symbolist, occultist, now for better or worse, now and for always. That does not matter. What does matter is that he is the only one left who has sufficient intensity of temperament to turn these modes into art."[29]

Pound was especially taken with "The Grey Rock." According to Charles Norman, it was Pound who persuaded

[29] "Mr. Yeats's New Book," *Poetry*, ix, 3 (December 1916), p. 151.

Harriet Monroe to give *Poetry*'s first annual award to the poem.[30] And, in a review of *Responsibilities* for the May 1914 issue of *Poetry*, Pound made one comment that tied "The Grey Rock" to *Sordello*: "I have said that *The Grey Rock* was obscure; perhaps I should not have said so, but I think it demands unusually close attention. It is an obscure, at least, as *Sordello*, but I can not close without registering my admiration for it all the same" (LE, p. 381). Immersed in the paratactic obscurities of *Sordello*, Pound evidently saw "The Grey Rock" as an analogous experiment. His "admiration" for the poem indicates that it had at least a peripheral influence on the modernized *Sordello* that he was then beginning to plan. It is my guess that *Three Cantos* owed some of the ease with which they shifted from story to story to the conversational transitions of "The Grey Rock."

Pound and Yeats cooperated on a second project at Stone Cottage whose formal impact on *Three Cantos* was even greater than that of "The Grey Rock." In 1913, after Pound acquired the Fenollosa papers, he and Yeats began the task of translating and editing samples of Japanese Noh drama. And, although Pound later deprecated the Noh because of its "softness,"[31] during 1913-1916 his translations had an extremely close relation to the writing of *Three Cantos*. From September 1914 to April 1916, he five times suggested a connection between the Noh plays and his projected long poem.[32] And in the lengthy explanations that he appended to his translations of the Noh during 1914 and 1915 (later col-

---

[30] Charles Norman, *Ezra Pound* (New York, 1960), p. 132.

[31] In March 1917 Pound wrote Joyce that he did not like the Noh translations "so well as the Chinese stuff in Lustra" (P/J, p. 102), and in June 1918 he wrote John Quinn that he found them "unsatisfactory. I daresay it's all that could be done with the material . . . it's all too damn soft" (L, p. 137). Schneidau, in his article "The Question of Symbolism," tries to use this evidence to prove that Pound had probably relinquished the plays to Yeats as early as 1914, but Slatin and the evidence I cite below make his argument questionable.

[32] See Slatin, pp. 183-186.

lected in 1916's *'Noh' or Accomplishment*),[33] he continued many of the preoccupations about myth, ritual, and religious art that appeared in "Psychology and the Troubadors." It appears likely that the Noh cycle, with its ritually oriented sequence of separate but interrelated plays, helped to shape Pound's idea of how the *Cantos* might be both a "primitive" and a modern poem.

Pound had written in *The Spirit of Romance* that the patterns of repetition and convolution of difficult Trecento canzoni had a ritual "purpose and effect," and "make their revelations to those who were already expert" (SR, p. 89). He conceived of all ritual as a cyclical return to the clues of divine presence until revelation transformed an initiate's understanding of those clues, and he wrote in that sense of Dante's *Commedia* as "a great mystery play, or better, a cycle of mystery plays" (SR, p. 154). The *Commedia*, he wrote, was one of those works that "are keys or pass-words admitting one to a deeper knowledge," and apparently the poem's cyclical action was for him part of that initiation.

The Noh cycle appealed to Pound because of its similarity to his ritual conception of Dante, and because its ritual roots were not hidden like Dante's in a superimposed linear "plot." Like the Cantos of the epic he was planning, he wrote that certain Noh plays "are only 'formed' and intelligible" when considered as part of the Ban-Gumi, the full Noh programme (*Translations*, p. 216). That program was a quasi-religious ceremony performed on certain occasions of state. He described the cycle as a "service," and he recounted the service in phrases very close to the ones he would later use about his own *Cantos*: "The Noh service presents, or symbolizes, a complete diagram of life and recur-

[33] Part III of *'Noh' or Accomplishment* was only an expanded version of a manuscript first published in the *Quarterly Review* (Volume CCI, pp. 450-477) for October 1914; and Parts I and II of *'Noh' or Accomplishment* were expanded versions of an article that appeared in *Drama* (Volume 18, pp. 199-247) for May 1915.

rence" (*Translations*, pp. 221-222). Moreover, Pound was attracted to the way the Noh cycle was able to encompass more material than even Dante's "cycle of mystery plays." He quoted Fenollosa on the way the "Noh" service self-consciously amalgamated various layers of earlier Japanese art:

> It was not until the fourth period of Japanese culture, that is to say, early in the fifteenth century, when a new Buddhist civilization, based upon contemplative and poetic insight into nature had arisen, that the inchoate Japanese drama, fostered in the Shinto temples, could take on a moral purpose and a psychologic breadth that should expand it into a vital drama of character. The Shinto god dance, the lyric form of court poetry, the country farces, and a full range of epic incident, in short, all that was best in the earlier Japanese tradition, was gathered into this new form, arranged and purified. (*Translations*, p. 278)

What Fenollosa called "all that was best in the earlier Japanese tradition" was very close to what the *Cantos* would single out as best in the western tradition. Both the Noh and the *Cantos* incorporate courtly lyric poetry, country farce, and epic incident in a new purified form. Both have enough ampleness to include a large range of cultural history. Both are rooted in a primitive vision of man's relation to nature. And both focus on characters in the middle of a spiritual odyssey. ("A play very often represents some one going on a journey. The character walks along the bridge or about the stage, announces where he is and where he is going, and often explains the meaning of his symbolic gestures, or tells what the dance means, or why one is dancing") (*Translations*, p. 222).

The Noh cycle was perhaps most attractive to Pound when he considered its formal arrangement. The Noh play's structure of exposition, development, and resolution could not be separated from its ritual function, and thus the Japanese plays embodied the intersection of Pound's thinking about form and content, music and myth. In their ritual rhythms, it appears, he found a vehicle like the canzone which, through repetitive form, might be "good art as the high mass is good art." It is no wonder that in 1914 when he began to think about a long Vorticist poem he immediately thought of the Noh: "I am often asked whether there can be a long imagiste or vorticist poem. The Japanese, who evolved the hokku, evolved also the Noh plays. In the best 'Noh' the whole play may consist of one image . . . enforced by movement and music. I see nothing against a long vorticist poem."[34]

Pound placed special emphasis on one play—"Takasago"— which traditionally appeared first in the Ban-Gumi, and which served the double function of an overture to the cycle and an invocation to the gods. Indeed, "Takasago" became something of a touchstone for the plays in general. Being an Oriental version of Ovid's myth of Baucis and Philemon, it is a ritual enactment of the harmony that exists in an ideal relationship between man and nature.

The play starts with a priest's announcement that he is breaking a long journey at Takasago. As his speech ends, a saintly old couple appear, chanting the *issei*, or prelude, which establishes a mood of spiritual peace. They sing of the eternal winds of spring and of the waves of the sea and of the ancient pine trees of Takasago. They identify their lives with the simplicity and endurance of the pine tree. When they stop singing, the priest addresses them, and, quoting from the Japanese equivalent of the Confucian Odes, he recounts the myth of the male pine tree at Sumiyoshi and the female pine tree at Takasago, which grow separately but present the semblance of a wedded couple. He compares the trees in the myth to the old couple, and he bids the husband finish the story. The husband agrees, but he and his wife do more than tell the rest. They sing and then dance a ritual piece that serves to relate man with the pine tree and with all of nature. During the ritual, the saintly

---

[34] See above, Chapter Two, p. 23.

couple reveal themselves to be the god and goddess of Sumiyoshi and Takasago. After an intermission, the priest journeys
to Sumiyoshi, and is again greeted by the pine-god, who per-
forms a ritual dance of blessing. The play ends with the god
and a chorus chanting that the land is under divine protection.

When Pound sent the manuscript of *Three Cantos* to Harriet Monroe, he told her that their "theme is roughly the
theme of 'Takasago,' which story I hope to incorporate more
explicitly in a later part of the poem."[35] Reading over *Three
Cantos I*, we discover what Pound meant. Just as the *issei*
of "Takasago" was used at the beginning of the Noh cycle
to initiate the theme of man's harmony with natural energies,
so the action of *Three Cantos I* begins with an evocation of
the "old gods" who inhabit Lake Garda. The movement of
the poem will be a series of journeys, witnessings, and revelations like that of the Noh plays, leading to a reconciliation of
man with the will of nature. Pound wrote that the pine is
"the symbol of the unchanging. It is painted right on the
back of the [Noh] stage, and, as this cannot be shifted, it
remains the same for all plays" (*Translations*, p. 222). By
Canto IV, the *Cantos'* sacred pine was introduced, with the
intention of it being as firmly painted in the readers' memory
as the Japanese pine has been painted on the Noh stage:

> The pines at Takasago
> grow with the pines of Isé!

Harriet Monroe published *Three Cantos* in *Poetry*, and
the poem's readers discovered that Pound had incorporated
other Noh plays in addition to "Takasago." I will consider
which ones in the next section of this chapter, but for a
moment I would like to examine the influence not of individual plays but of one of the "types" of plays that, Pound
wrote, combine to make a Ban-Gumi or Noh cycle. In *'Noh'
or Accomplishment*, he defined four such "types" — battle

---

[35] In the Yale letters, cited by Slatin, p. 186.

pieces, love pieces, spirit pieces, and moral pieces — and he expressed particular interest in one of them. The spirit pieces, he wrote, represent "the results of carelessness" to ritual duties, and present confrontations between men and gods. He added that "the lover of drama and of poetry will find his chief interest in the psychological pieces, or the Plays of Spirits; the plays that are, I think, more Shinto than Buddhist. These plays are full of ghosts, and the ghost psychology is amazing. The parallels with Western spiritist doctrines are very curious" (*Translation*, p. 222).

On one of those plays, "Suma-Genji," Pound commented that "I dare say the play . . . will seem undramatic to some people the first time they read it. The suspense is the suspense of waiting for a supernatural manifestation — which comes. . . . The reader will miss the feel of suspense if he is unable to put himself in sympathy with the priest eager to see 'even in a vision' the beauty lost in the years, 'the shadow of the past in bright form'" (*Translations*, pp. 236-237). Later in *'Noh' or Accomplishment*, Pound wrote that the most "striking thing" about the spirit plays "is their marvellously complete grasp of spiritual being. They deal more with heroes, or even we might say ghosts, than with men clothed in the flesh. Their creators were great psychologists. In no other drama does the supernatural play so great, so intimate a part" (*Translations*, p. 280).

In 1908, Pound had written that he was interested in character only in a "moment of song, self-analysis, or sudden understanding or revelation" (L, p. 4). In 1913-1915, the Noh Spirit plays reinforced this inclination and, with "their marvellously complete grasp of spiritual being," they added to the store of technique Pound had acquired from Ovid, Browning, and Yeats to dramatize such moments. Canto II, with its lyric introduction to Ovid's Acoetes-Dionysus episode, owed a great deal to the Spirit-Noh's techniques of "waiting for a supernatural manifestation — which comes."

But more than anything else, it was the setting of the Spirit-Noh in a complete cycle that affected Pound's developing notion of the *Cantos*. By its juxtapositions of the spirit plays alongside more traditional heroic plays and in front of eternal symbols of spiritual verities, the Ban Gumi (Noh Cycle) provided a continuing spiritual reference, an achieved medium for incorporating diverse secular and spiritual material. The religious context of the cycle insured that the ultimate meaning of any of its dramatic fragments would come out only in relation to the framework of divine reference. The cycle thus afforded Pound a structure that could include the whole of life and that was based upon the perception of limited patterns of recurrence and divine intervention. In 1913's *Patria Mia*, he had written that in the study of history "one wants to find what sorts of things endure . . . recur."[36] In *'Noh' or Accomplishment*, he asserted that those recurrences were rhythms of nature, and he held up the Noh cycle as a model of true imitation: "The Noh holds up a mirror to nature in a manner very different from the Western convention of plot. I mean the Noh performance of the five or six plays in order presents a complete service of life. We do not find, as we find in *Hamlet*, a certain situation or problem set out and analysed. The Noh service presents, or symbolizes, a complete diagram of life and recurrence" (*Translations*, pp. 221-222).

The Noh-cycle was an example of how values could organize an extended but loosely structured literary work. It demonstrated how incidents could be given a sequence derived from a primary value structure and yet not be locked into a Dantesque linear progression. Through his study of the Noh, Pound developed a feeling for sequential development that was based on the ebb and flow of perception of spiritual reality. In the Noh plays, the pine tree that symbolized eternal values was constantly in view, and it provided a running but silent commentary on the awareness or obtusity of the characters. As the cycle advanced, the meaning of the pine became clearer to both the characters and the audience. The

---

[36] *Patria Mia* (Chicago, 1950), p. 68.

Cantos present a mind in contemplation of a Noh-like ritual cycle, where certain mysteries work themselves through into consciousness as spiritual images clarify and resolve. In the events of his epic, Pound transformed the "plot" of the *Odyssey* to accommodate just such a notion of ritual development. The late *Cantos* shift the climax of the *Odyssey* from Odysseus' physical return to a more spiritual nostos. The great Odyssean moment of *Thrones* is the appearance of Leukothea, the maidservant of Athena. Odysseus, from the beginning of his wandering, had been denied the appearance of his divine protectress. For more than 90 Cantos, his spirit had been too darkened by the years of war to perceive her. But as his soul is clarified, images of the divine presence take on a shape and voice. Cantos 95-96 present the end of the journey as a supernatural manifestation in just the way that we might expect from a reading of 'Noh' or *Accomplishment*.

iii: *Three Cantos I and II*

"When any man is able, by a pattern of notes or by an arrangement of planes or colours, to throw us back into the age of truth, everyone who has been cast back into that age of truth for one instant gives honour to the spell which has worked, to the witch-work . . ."[37] (1915).

Pound published what became parts I and II of 'Noh' or *Accomplishment* in May 1915. The composition of *Three Cantos* was begun in September. I hope I have conveyed some feeling for the stages of the poem's genesis from 1912-1915. What has been missing is a clear picture of the substance of *Three Cantos*. An examination of these drafts[38] will establish that although Pound later discarded *Three Cantos* for stylistic reasons, he never really repudiated many of the formal and thematic patterns they began. I intend to concentrate on two facets of *Three Cantos* in particular — their

[37] Ezra Pound, "Affirmations: Arnold Dolmetsch," *The New Age*, XVI, 10 (January 14, 1915), p. 246.

[38] Other readings may be found in Guy Davenport's unpublished Harvard dissertation, pp. 56-106, and *The Analyst*, xxv (April 1969).

elements of primitivism and their use of phrases as motifs to
articulate thematic development.

As we have seen, *Three Cantos I* begins with an exordium
devoted to the poetics of the poem to follow. As the exordium
fades, Pound's narrator describes his personal situation. He
locates himself in the surroundings of Lake Garda, and he
presents himself within a literary tradition and a continuum
of beliefs that stretch back to the primitive roots of antiquity:

> I walk the airy street,
> See the small cobbles flare with the poppy spoil.
> 'Tis your "great day," the Corpus Domini,
> And all my chosen and peninsular village
> Has made one glorious blaze of all its lanes —
> Oh, before I was up — with poppy flowers.
> Mid-June: some old god eats the smoke, 'tis
>   not the saints;
> And up and out to the half-ruined chapel —
> Not the old place at the height of the rocks,
> But that splay, barn-like church the Renaissance
> Had never quite got into trim again.
> As well begin here. Began our Catullus:
> "Home to sweet rest, and to the waves' deep laughter,"
> The laugh they wake amid the border rushes.
> This is our home, the trees are full of laughter,
> And the storms laugh loud, breaking the riven waves
> On "north-most rocks"; and here the sunlight
> Glints on the shaken waters, and the rain
> Comes forth with delicate tread, walking from
>   Isola Garda —
>   *Lo soleils plovil,*
> As Arnaut had it in th' inextricable song.
> The very sun rains and a spatter of fire
> Darts from the "Lydian" ripples; *"locus undae,"* as Catullus,
>   *"Lydiae,"*
> And the place is full of spirits.
> Not *lemures,* not dark and shadowy ghosts,

112

But the ancient living, wood-white,
Smooth as the inner bark, and firm of aspect,
And all agleam with colors — no, not agleam,
But colored like the lake and like the olive
    leaves,
Glaukopos, clothed like the poppies, wearing
    golden greaves,
Light on the air.
Are they Etruscan gods?

The poem's technique is at first that of "Provincia Deserta," where Pound wrote: "I have walked there / thinking
of old days." In "Provincia Deserta," however, he invoked
the image of Provence to deride the present for its emptiness
("That age is gone"), and to damn contemporary artists for
their passivity (*I have thought // of them // living*). *Three
Cantos I* calls up the past to establish vital elements of it
still extant, unnoticed, hidden in traditions whose beginnings
have been forgotten. The passage I have cited is a pastiche
in which Pound creates a traditional context for certain words
and images that become the *motifs* of the poem. The full
implications of the motifs are not provided by the narrator,
even in these early and relatively straightforward Cantos. The
convention of the poem is for the speaker to be in quest of
meanings. He knows he is lost. He knows where to look but
not what he is looking for, and the task of the reader is to
follow not the speaker, but rather the poem's developing
pattern of motifs.

    "Poppy spoil" (fallen red petals) represents the first part
of the exordium's "catch." The petals "flare" on the "small
cobbles" as Pound said in the exordium he was going to dump
his catch "flapping and slipping on the marginal cobbles."
Ostensibly, the poppies are only traditional "decor" of
Pound's "chosen and peninsular village" (Sirmio) during
the feast of Corpus Domini (Browning's "great day" —
Sordello iii, 766). In fact, they are part of the passage's ghostly background. As Frazer, one of the "corn-god encyclo-

paedists" whom Pound had compared to Upward, wrote in *The Golden Bough*, the poppy was in antiquity a "symbol" of the goddess Demeter.[39] The "flaring" of the poppy introduces "flare" as an emblematic verb indicating divine impingement, and presents the first of a series of correspondences that relate Christian observances to pagan roots. Pound follows it up with a reference to Corpus Domini, which (as we find out in *Three Cantos II*) he conflates with St. John's Day, the 24th of June, a day that the Christians took over from the older celebration of Midsummer's day. On this purportedly Christian feast day, a god has "eaten" the sacrificial smoke. Not a Christian saint, but "some old god," perhaps the pagan fertility god about whom Pound had written in 1914's "Coitus":

> The gilded phaloi of the crocuses
> > are thrusting at the spring air.
> Here is there naught of dead gods
> But a procession of festival,
> A procession, O Giulio Romano,
> Fit for your spirit to dwell in.
> Dione, your nights are upon us.
>
> The dew is upon the leaf.
> The night about us is restless.

The speaker walks out of the town to the "half-ruined chapel." Not to the "old place" (maybe the Castello Scaligero or may be the so-called villa of Catullus), but to a still older one, "that splay, barn-like church the Renaissance / Had never quite got into trim again." The barn-like church is

[39] J. G. Frazer, *The Golden Bough: A Study in Magic and Religion.* Twelve Volumes (New York, 1935), VII, p. 43. Note: Hereafter, page references to *The Golden Bough* will be integrated in the text. Whereever possible those references will be to the abridged version that is conveniently available in a one-volume paperback published by Macmillan (New York, 1963). When no volume number is provided, therefore, the reader should assume that the reference is to the paperback.

San Pietro in Mavino, which was constructed upon the ruins of an antique pagan temple.

In this milieu, alive with presences from pre-antiquity, the narrator begins his story. Here is the place where the way was lost, and here he will re-begin the search. Not in Browning's Asolo, but in Sirmio, where Catullus lived and wrote. He calls up Catullus, the civilized poet who still understood the psychological reality of the myths. (Even the brutal ones, as Carmina LXIII will testify.) The citation of "Home to sweet rest, and to the waves' deep laughter" (from Carmina XXXI) calls up the spirits that Catullus had seen, and that Upward had "understood." As the pagan temple still could be perceived beneath San Pietro, so now Catullus' vision of the vital universe alive around Lake Garda is seen to stand behind Arnaut Daniel's *Lo soleils plovil* (the light rains). "Provencal song," Pound wrote, "is never wholly disjunct from pagan rites of May Day" (SR, p. 90). Pound's narrator meditates upon Catullus' poetry, and comes finally to quote from the Latin of Carmina XXXI, "*o Lydiae lacus undae.*"[40] He clearly perceives the phenomena before him, but does not impose traditional names and form on them. Athena is hovering about, as are other gods, but they are given to us here only as "the ancient living, wood-white/Smooth as the inner bark," and later as "folk," "silvery almond-white swimmers."[41] The narrator comes close to naming the gods but never does. Pound follows the convention of Dante in the *Commedia*, who retrospectively describes his experiences as he had seen them and not in the light of what he later discovered. As soon as the narrator's meditation begins to strain

[40] Davenport, p. 72, suggests the ripples are Lydian because Catullus was alluding to Sappho's Lydian coast, and therefore contends that Pound's look back into the past extends beyond Catullus to Sappho.

[41] Pound remembered Frazer's treatment of Attis, the sacrificial subject of Carmina LXIII, whose "mother, Nana, was a virgin, who conceived by putting a ripe almond or a pomegranate in her bosom. Indeed in the Phrygian cosmogony an almond figured as the father of all things, perhaps because its delicate lilac blossom is one of the first heralds of the spring" (p. 403).

after premature conclusions, his concentration breaks and
Catullus gives way to an image of his youthful self:

> Your "palace step"?
> My stone seat was the Dogana's curb,
> And there were not "those girls," there was
> one flare, one face.
> 'Twas all I ever saw, but it was real. . . .
> And I can no more say what shape it was . . .
> But she was young, too young.
> True, it was Venice,
> And at Florian's and under the north arcade
> I have seen other faces, and had my rolls for
> breakfast, for that matter;
> So for what it's worth, I have the background.
> And you had a background

He turns to face this younger self ("My stone seat *was* the
Dogana's curb"), and we recognize the outline of E. P. in
Venice circa 1908). The narrator tells us that for E. P. there
were not "those girls" (*Sordello*, iii, 700), there was "one
face, one flare." We guess by the word "flare" that E. P.
experienced a vision of some sort, but the narrator's falling
rhythms tell us that in 1908 E. P. was too young, still incapable of asserting the shaping power of his "germinal consciousness." ("I can no more say what shape it was . . .").
He reinforces that judgment with the brusqueness of "True,
it was Venice . . . So for what it's worth, I have the background." That is, E. P. at the time affected to understand
Venice, but such understanding can come only through the
experience of a lifetime. Browning called Venice a figure for
life:

> Venice seems a type
> Of life — 'twixt blue and blue extends, a stripe,
> As life, the somewhat, hangs 'twixt nought and nought.
> (*Sordello*, iii, 725-727)

In *Three Cantos*, Venice becomes E. P.'s vanished Troy and Pound's Ithaca to come.

Three Cantos I goes on to take a swipe at Browning's looseness with fact, and discusses at length why the convention of a "progress" (Browning's "elementary masque") is inadequate for a modern poem. *Three Cantos II* is more interesting and important, and I would like to get on with it. However, during the second half of *Three Cantos I*, Pound introduces motifs that are developed not only by *Three Cantos* but by later Cantos as well. Therefore, I have provided a tabular gloss in the appendix to this chapter as a way of noticing these motifs without getting bogged down in many pages of explanation. My gloss begins with line 99, "Whom shall I hang my shimmering garment on."

At the beginning of *Three Cantos II*, the narrator half-regretfully soliloquizes, "Leave Casella." As he leaves the limited beauty of lyric poetry for his epic journey across the waste plain of the *Cantos'* inferno, Pound adjusts the poem's narrative technique. The persona of the narrator, firmly established, recedes from center stage into the inflections of a less prominent speaking voice. Instead of a monologue, he presents his readers with a series of what I have chosen to call "radicals in design" — a series of paratactically arranged but not unrelated vignettes. The narrator "discourses" with images of many joyless ghosts, each fixed in a type of spiritual blindness.

Three Cantos II is important for several reasons. For one, its less prominent narrator anticipates the sophisticated theatre of consciousness of *A Draft of XVI Cantos*. Secondly, its organization of radicals around the theme of "drear waste" recalls the same thematic variations in Canto IV, whose sophisticated texture has disguised its origins. Finally, *Three Cantos II* develops Pound's technique of layering the vital past and the empty present into an extended sequence capable of use in the more compressed Cantos to come. Chapters Four and Five will deal in some detail with the topics of narration and structural revisions. The intricacy of Pound's "ply over ply"[42] of religious consciousness, however, can best be dealt with in the process of explication.

The Canto begins with a lyric prelude that combines dull memories of former spiritual awareness with epiphanies of spiritual loss. Using the techniques of imagism, Pound renders that loss with an allusion to the Mantuan Palace of the Gonzagas, once full of creativity, now "Drear waste, great halls, / Silk tatters . . . in the frame." As for the gods, the "ancient people," they exist only in half-remembered and insufficiently valued remnants. The narrator reaches back and remembers a Provençal song, a vision of a "flare of color," and therefore divine, not "wholly disjunct from the pagan rights of May-Day." But in the drear waste of the present, "all the rest" of the song save one stave has been forgotten. E. P. has lost the copy he had in Paris. The roots of the loss are to be found in the image of Richard at Chalus. Richard went to Chalus in order to claim a golden antique artifact that was found by one of his vassals and kept from him. Richard needed the gold to pursue his endless wars, and did not care about the artifact's treasure of ancient wisdom and mystery. He was as heedless to the true value of the piece as E. P. is to Joios' Alba, or as the old man who closes Canto XXI "beating his mule with an asphodel" is to the flower's Elysian potency. It is in the economic best interest of the modern citizen to devalue the sacred.

Joios and Arnaut are highly sensitive registers, recording the radiations of love as they were recognized in that age when the "rose-leaf" was a metaphysical emblem. (See Pound's remarks on the *Romaunt of the Rose*, SR, p. 85.) The objective correlative to their sensitivity is a "ringing glass," which, like a transducer, converts patterns in one

---

[42] Pound's source for this phrase is once again *Sordello*:

Hildebrand
Of the huge brain-mask welded ply o'er ply
As in a forge

(v, 162-164)

medium of energy into patterns in another. Arnaut converted the vibrations of the psyche into patterns of word and music. (In Canto XVII "the great alley of Memnons" will register the first light of dawn by ringing.) The narrator wishes out loud that Arnold Dolmetsch, the man who rediscovered the unique tonalities of renaissance instruments, might build our age in "witching music." That is, in the "witch-work" that we have heard Pound say is able to "throw us back into the age of truth."

But the wish is not enough. With the quick movement of the mind characteristic of the *Cantos,* Pound projects an image of the sacred springs of affection polluted by their misapplication. The appearance of the lute girl ("out of the night comes troubling lute music") unmistakably invokes the appearance of one of the damned to Dante. Her story tells of the divine music of love cheapened by materialism into a parody of itself:

> "Many a one
> Brought me rich presents; my hair was full of jade,
> And my slashed skirts, drenched in expensive dyes,
> Were dipped in crimson, sprinkled with rare wines.
> I was well taught my arts at Ga-ma-rio,
> And then one year I faded out and married."
> The lute-bowl hid her face.

Reaching out for a meaning for the lute girl's "drear waste," the narrator seeks the guidance of Catullus' shade, standing beside him in Sirmio. In sometimes cryptic transitions, he ponders the way the terrible awareness of the power of love had diminished from Sappho's sacred hymns to Catullus' "cribs." Frazer (pp. 388-389) had recreated the rites of Aphrodite vividly enough for Pound to understand the terror behind the prettiness of Sappho's *Poikilothron*; and Frazer's discussions of how primitives believed in animal embodiments of the gods once more allowed the *Poikilothron's* sparrows to be properly appreciated. Like the lute girl, Catullus, for "society," forgot Aphrodite's wrath. The tamed birds of his Carmina II and IV toy with a sacred image. Catullus' poems, in fact, provide Pound with an immortal "equation" for neglect of one's duties to Aphrodite. Catullus suffers the "way of [profane] love," passing from playful involvement to the divine punishment of Carmina LI ("along my veins / Runs the slow fire") to the jaded disgust of Carmina LVIII:

> That Lesbia, Caelius, our Lesbia, that Lesbia
> Whom Catullus once loved more
> Than his own soul and all his friends,
> Is now the drab of every lousy Roman.

"So" (Pound, quoting *Sordello*) "the murk opens." The morass of history begins to take form. But the murk opens to reveal that the past is full of unexplored veins, and that the truth exists for that mind quick enough to sense connections. The narrator is beginning to understand that "all ages are contemporaneous." Lines 65-73 record his perception of the "ply over ply" complexity of the emotional equations surrounding him. The centaur who comes "spying the land," registering relations, is the poetic faculty: "Poetry is a centaur. The thinking word-arranging, clarifying faculty must move and leap with the energizing, sentient, musical faculties" (LE, p. 52, circa 1913). And so, the narrator continues his research into the way men have dealt with the terrible goddess. Digging into his fisherman's bag of world literature, he dumps out his "catch at Dordoigne," his evidence from Provence. As Catullus had felt "the night . . . thrust down upon me," so now out of the murk appears Viscount St. Antoni, who feels "the night air full of subtle hands." The narrator records *"Si com, si com"* (Provençal for "for as"), and the properly alert reader hears the motif of Venus approaching ("she comes / Apparelled like the Spring"). Venus in the St. Antoni story, however, once again is throttled by life-killing conventions. The Viscountess of Pena affects to love St. Antoni in the chivalric convention of extramarital dalliance. But the report of her husband's death

"upset the whole convention," and showed her desire up
for the inauthentic thing it was:

> St. Antoni in favor, and the lady
> Ready to hold his hands —
> This last report upset the whole convention.
> She rushes off to church, sets up a gross of candles,
> Pays masses for the soul of Viscount Pena

In its next movement, *Three Cantos II* presents its narrator meditating upon another part of the "drear waste." A
second blocked wellspring of psychological growth has deprived the present of significant action. Ire harnessed by religious discipline once nourished virtuous action. Homer and
Chaucer both depicted ennobling action. Modern blindness
to the importance of emotional force, however, has created
action divorced from both the divine and the demonic. The
modern world is a wasteland of action driven by calculated
self-interest. To indicate the disparity between modern and
ancient times, Pound once again places his subjects among
settings that the informed reader will recognize as vestiges
of a more primitive period.

The narrator begins his reverie with the memory of a fair
on the eve of St. John's day. He recalls a masquerade of
battle, and his imagination begins to wander in the glories
of the past. Ostensibly, the place and day of the fair are
realistic details of the narrator's past. In fact, Pound chose
St. John's Eve because it points toward the primitive foundations of modern rituals. The gloss for St. John's Eve comes
from *The Golden Bough*, which tells us "A faint tinge of
Christianity has been given to them [Midsummer Eve (the
twenty-third of June) or Midsummer Day] by naming Midsummer Day after St. John the Baptist, but we cannot doubt
that the celebration dates from a time long before the beginning of our era. The summer solstice, or Midsummer Day,
is the great turning-point in the sun's career. . . . Such a
moment could not but be regarded with anxiety by primitive
man . . . and having still to learn his own powerlessness in

face of the vast cyclic changes of nature, he may have fancied that he could help the sun in his seeming decline . . ." (pp. 720-721).[43] One explanation for the fires characteristic of St. John's day celebrations is that they are "purificatory" (p. 744). That is, they symbolize the purification of sacrifice.

Pound may have used Chambers' *The Medieval Stage* (1903) to gather the pagan background to medieval pageants that were performed on St. John's Day (Vol. I, p. 126). Leaning on the anthropologists, Chambers recounts that in the "shows" and "watches" of Midsummer, "elements borrowed from the pageants of the miracle-plays occasionally form an odd blend with the 'giants' and other figures of the 'folk' tradition" (Vol. II, p. 165). He explains that part of that folk tradition was sword-dancing, where "the dancers were young men who leapt with much agility amongst menacing spear-points and sword-blades" (Vol. I, pp. 190-191). And Chambers conjectures that "the use of swords in the dance . . . was to suggest not a fight, but a mock or symbolical sacrifice" (p. 203). The musing narrator of *Three Cantos II* is unconsciously led by the primitive and sacrificial overtones of the St. John's day folk-fair to a consideration of historical action in a sacred context.

From the St. John's Eve Fair, the narrator's mind jumps to other episodes in which noble warriors confront the "drear waste" of secular society. First the Cid and then the Count of Nieblas[44] reflect light amid the darkness. Afterwards, to reinforce the spiritual context of these "gestes of war," the poem doubles back to a brief reference to the Noh. "Kumasaka's ghost" comes from the play *Kumasaka*, which Pound called "the Homeric presentation of combat" between the spirit of a warrior hero and a young boy. In *Kulchur*, Pound wrote that "The ghost of Kumasaka returns not from a grudge and not to gain anything; but to state clearly that the very

[43] Another gloss is Lope's play, *La Noche de San Juan*, which is full of lovers' confusion and folk conceptions of honor.

[44] From Juan de Mena's *El Libertino de Fortuna*. Pound mentions the story obliquely in SR, p. 34.

young man who had killed him had not done so by a fluke
or slip, but that he had outfenced him." The two-line allusion
in *Three Cantos II* provides an example of the function of
conflict refined to its spiritual essence, which is the production
of brilliant nobility. It is meant as contrast to the contingent
and hamstrung actions of the Cid and Nieblas, and ultimately
to Homer. In Canto 79 Pound wrote:

> Greek rascality against Hagoromo
> Kumasaka vs / vulgarity.

An episode of the Noh here functions like the Noh image of
the eternal pine in order to keep the ideal in the mosaic of
impurity.[45]

The last geste of war considered by the speaker from Lope's
Las Almenas de Toro telescopes unhealthy psychological
states of both anger and love. Pound presents the story of
how King Sancho besieged his sister Elvira's city (Toro)
and became excited by a woman on the battlements, without
realizing it was Elvira (see SR, pp. 191-193). Sancho's anger
is misdirected by his intelligence, and it turns upon his family,
a situation that can only freeze his affections. Though "a star,
/ Lights the king's features" he can respond to the light only
with psyche-destroying incest. He projects his consternation,
cursing Elvira: "*Mal fuego s'enciende!*" (May an ill flame
be kindled in her). Though the flame of passion is the only
real path to light, when misappropriated it can also be the
path to eternal torment. The stories of Kumasaka and Sancho
present a diptych of infernal and purgatorial passions.

The Canto concludes with a historical progress of images
that illustrate a fading perception of god in the flame as
Western culture becomes older and more commercial. First
comes the story of Pedro's unfortunate fiancée, and the way
he let her death freeze his passion. Pedro marries the corpse,
and, his passion dead, himself becomes a living corpse. He

[45] The citations and the general reference of this paragraph are discussed by Walter Baumann, *The Rose in the Steel Dust* (Coral Gables,
1970), pp. 74-77.

belongs with St. Antoni's wife, and Canto VII's grieving Dido. Camoens recognized the horror of the situation and universalized it by comparing it with the myth of Demeter and Proserpine. Proserpine was carried away in the fields of Enna and Demeter caused the earth to wither and waste in grief. However dimly, Camoens was still in touch with the rhythms of the vital universe. His "resonant bombast" was still retelling the Homeric Hymn to Demeter, and was in a sense still worshipping her.

The Canto goes on to depict the disappearance of the worship. "What have we now of her?" refers back to both Proserpine and Ignez. After Camoens, "Houtman, lying in jail for debt at Lisbon, planned the Dutch East India Company. . . . Portugal fell, Holland seized the oriental trade, and soon after Roemer Visscher was holding a salon, with which are connected the names of Rembrandt . . ." (SR, p. 221). The gods are forgotten in the rush of commercial prosperity. Forms are lost and with them the perception of the gods in the forms. As Canto V would put it, "Fades the light from the sea." "The old tale out of fashion," Venus falls into the hands of Raphael, Rubens, and Rembrandt. As Pound wrote elsewhere, "the metamorphosis into carnal tissue becomes frequent and general somewhere about 1527. The people are corpus, corpuscular, but not in the strict sense 'animate,' it is no longer the body of air clothed in the body of fire; it no longer radiates, light no longer moves from the eye, there is a great deal of meat, shock absorbing, perhaps — at any rate absorbent. It has not even Greek marmoreal plastic to restrain it. The dinner scene is more frequently introduced, we have the characters in definite act of absorption; later they will be stuffing for expensive upholsteries."[46]

At the very end of *Three Cantos II*, Pound looks back at the last and dearest figure in his inferno. William Brooke Smith, to whom Pound dedicated *A Lume Spento* and

---

[46] From "Medievalism," which *Literary Essays* dates 1910-1931. Reprinted in LE, p. 153.

whom he there called a "painter, dreamer of dreams," is presented now as an artist in an age of darkness, a figure who could not work his way through the past, but could only "dream" his renaissance. In a willful cry of exultation and defiance, Pound concludes the Canto by calling out, Dante-like, to the friendly ghost: "Take my Sordello!" Take my resurrection, my renaissance.

iv: Ulysses, and My Ulysses?

In an essay called "Homer's Sticks and Stones," Hugh Kenner described the provenance of Joyce's belief in the concreteness of Homer's Odyssey.[47] Relying on J. L. Myres' Homer and His Critics, Kenner reviewed the growth of archaeological evidence that had changed the nature of Homeric criticism. Joyce, he argued, came to understand that a retelling of the Odyssey had to be in terms as concrete in their reference as Homer's own. The archaeologists had superannuated in a stroke the Victorian Homer, whose noble outline rendered details unimportant. Joyce's Homer, Kenner implied, was a *contemporary* Homer "made not of mere sonorous words which neither hurt nor nourish, but of cups and saucers, chairs and tables, sticks and stones." What Kenner chose not to emphasize is that there were *other* contemporary Homers. It is possible that he was misled by the emphases of Myres' book, which was heavily oriented to the Homer of the mid-century, an assuredly archaeological Homer. Myres slid over the fact that a mythological bias toward Homer continued into the century by means of the Cambridge anthropologists, who first brought field-studies to the aid of philology. About Frazer, Jane Harrison, and Tylor, Myres wrote only a cursory paragraph,[48] and Kenner was correspondingly silent.

[47] In *James Joyce Quarterly*, VI, 4 (summer 1969), pp. 285-298.
[48] See pp. 207-208. "While the Aryan hypothesis held the field, in the spacious days of the nineteenth century, it was inevitable that Achilles should in due course be sublimated into a Sun God, and the whole Trojan War into a diagram of the whole course of Nature.

Much of the background for Pound's notion of Homeric primitivism can be reconstructed from two or three of the books that came out of the Cambridge school. Early in her career, Jane Harrison published a book entitled *Myths of the Odyssey in Art and Literature* (London, 1882). This rather modest work attempted to apply the "unread commentary" of ancient art to the stories of the *Odyssey*. In most of the volume, Miss Harrison merely juxtaposed scenes in the *Odyssey* with ancient art-work picturing those scenes. She did, however, occasionally bring to bear studies of an already large literature of comparative ritual. In Chapter IV, "The Myth of the Descent into Hades," she alluded to Tylor's *History of Primitive Cults*, and wrote that Odysseus, "like the hero of many other mythologies, must descend into Hades." "It may," she speculated, "be that these stories took their rise in some nature-myth . . . but surely from very early days, about this simple notion that there must have been woven a complex web of keen sorrow and vague aspiration. . . . How else should the Greeks have their Cimmerian land for Odysseus . . . the Teutons their swamps of Drömling, whither departed souls have access; the Kelts their island on Lough Derg, sacred still as St. Patrick's purgatory; the Aztecs their subterranean temple Michtan . . . South African savages their cavern Marimatle . . . Egyptians their sacred lake . . . Fijians their 'calm and solemn place of cliff and forest, where the souls of the dead embark for the judgment-

---

When, however, comparative mythology began to give place to comparative religion, or rather, perhaps we should say, to comparative ritual, in the hands of the new anthropological school of Mannhardt and Wilcken, Usener and Durkheim, Tylor, Frazer and Jane Harrison, it was only to be expected that among the sources of Homeric episodes and personages, place should be found for the three-spirits, the scapegoats, the sacred marriages, the grisly apparatus of totems and *tabus*, which were conceived as the stock-in-trade of Aegean religion until with the coming of the Olympian theology 'the flood came and destroyed them all; and yet did not destroy them utterly, for there was a grim undertone of chthonic observance under that limpid flood water, which surged up now and again, clouding and defiling it.'"

seat of Udengei, and whither the living come in pilgrimage, thinking to see ghosts and gods?' " (pp. 97-98) As early as 1882, then, Miss Harrison was using the evidence of other primitive societies to explain the archaic mind, and to make sense of the details in Homer.

As her work developed, Miss Harrison enlarged her knowledge of the "keen sorrow" of primitive life and her work became more fully documented. *Prolegomena to the Study of Greek Religion* (1903) pieced together classical authorities and reconstructed the darker side of classical religious ritual and belief. In the first chapter, "Olympian and Chthonic Ritual," she dissociated herself and future scholars from the Victorianism of Ruskin's statement that "there is no dread" in the hearts of the ancient Greeks, only "joy such as they might win . . . from beauty at perfect rest." Donning the hat of an anthropologist, she called "the rest of mankind" to witness, and argued that the Greeks, like every other once archaic people, "needed to learn the lesson that in the Fear of the Lord is the beginning of Wisdom." *Prolegomena* painstakingly described elements of darkness in the ritual calendar of Athens. Most pertinently, it touched on the ritual background of the Nekyia. Odysseus' blood offering to Tiresias, Miss Harrison wrote, is "a clear reminiscence" of the ritual of ghost raising that "went on at many a hero's tomb, for . . . every hero was apt to be credited with mantic powers" (p. 75). The letting of blood was one of numerous ritual acts that had two aspects. It was at once an affirmative communion with the Olympian gods and a fearful purificatory exorcism of the chthonic powers. The Odyssean Nekyia, then, depicted an archaic ritual still meaningful to the Homeric bard. The same ritual experience, we are later told, persisted into Periclean Athens in the cult of Orphism. Chapter xi described how descent and rebirth were part of the initiation to the Orphic mysteries, an initiation necessitated by the Orphic's belief that the soul was plagued by spirits because of its "hereditary taint" (p. 592).

Jane Harrison's major work, *Themis: A Study of the Social*

Origins of Greek Religion (1912), laid the groundwork for connecting the ritual exorcisms of pre-Homeric religion to the work of Frazer. In *Themis*, Miss Harrison argued that Athenian customs had their roots in fertility rites, and that the archaic Greek heroes, whether they began as historical or legendary figures, became important only as they acquired the status of fertility daimons. According to *Themis*, both rite and myth recreate the cycle of those fertility or "eni-autos" daimons "from the cradle to the grave and back again, to life and marriage" (p. 332). The Homeric epics, she wrote, do not mirror that cycle, because they came "late": "Homer marks a stage when collective thinking and magical ritual are, if not dead, at least dying" (p. 335). However, both *Themis* and its companion work, Murray's *The Rise of the Greek Epic*, discussed the possibility that chthonic religious practices persisted in the background of the *Iliad* and the *Odyssey*.

In 1914, James Alexander Ker Thomson overreached Jane Harrison. In a work entitled *Studies in the Odyssey* (read, as his preface tells us, by Frazer, Harrison, and Murray), he attempted to demonstrate that the *Odyssey* was much closer to "traditional" origins than his colleagues had allowed. He argued that Odysseus had begun as a historical figure and then had been transformed into a hero-daimon. Whether Pound (or Upward) actually read the book cannot be ascertained. *Studies in the Odyssey*, though, is worth considering in any case because it provides us with a fully modeled contemporary Homer unrelated to the archaeologists, and because it enables us to ground Pound's Odysseus in a major current of turn-of-the-century criticism.

Thomson's predecessors had argued that the most primitive parts of the *Odyssey* must have been remnants of an earlier poem, and Thomson began his revisionist work by rebutting them. The Nekyia, he wrote, was not part of an earlier poem that had been taken into the Odysseus story. Instead, it was one of the story's earliest and most important elements: "But is the Visit to the Dead an original

128

part of the Odysseus saga? The answer is, yes; THERE IS NO PART OLDER THAN THAT" (p. vii). According to Thomson, the *Odyssey* grew out of an archaic core, and, if we are to understand the heart of the poem, we must understand the poem's original resonances. Therefore, Thomson undertook an extended exploration of the religious background of the Nekyia. He traced Odysseus' visit to Tiresias back to records of pre-Homeric rites at a grave site near Tilphossa in Boeotia. Even before Homer's time, Thomson wrote, Tiresias was regarded as a prophet and had acquired an oracle whose shrine men journeyed to consult. "The core of the Odyssean Nekyia," he reasoned, "is an actual, very ancient Boeotian tradition of a visit to consult Tiresias . . . at the prophet's Boeotian home" (p. 26). The *Odyssey* then must have crystalized around the story of a hero making such a visit, and Thomson suggested that the epic poem partook of the ritual unity of all such stories. It was originally the saga of a fertility god's cycle of life, death, and rebirth. The *Odyssey*, he concluded, was probably a religious poem chanted by a priestly caste of cantors on certain ritual occasions.

Whether or not he ever read Thomson, Pound's instincts led him to ritualize the *Odyssey* in a parallel manner. Like Thomson, he based his perception of the poem on the scene of the Nekyia, and like Thomson he regarded the Nekyia as a pervasively archaic document. In 1935, he wrote that "The Nekuia shouts aloud that it is *older* than the rest, all that island, Cretan, etc., hinter-time, that is *not* Praxiteles, not Athens of Pericles, but Odysseus" (L, p. 274). It is probable that Pound's decision to include the *Odyssey* as one of the *Cantos'* archetypes was influenced by a desire to incorporate a "hinter-time" awareness of the power of natural forces.

Certainly, in *Three Cantos III* (1915), Pound emphasized the primitive nature of the *Odyssey*. It was not sufficient to suggest that the actions of the *Odyssey* had modern equivalents. Pound wanted to emphasize that archetypal recurrences were rooted in primeval truth, and that the recognition of archetypes in their modern avatars would lead to educating modern man to lost perceptions, "to throw us back into the age of truth." Consequently, although he grounded his version of the *Odyssey* in words as particular as Joyce's, they were words of a different order. Here, for example, is Joyce's version of the pouring of the blood in *Ulysses*:

> The Botanic Gardens are just over there. It's the blood stinking in the earth gives new life. Same idea those jews they said killed the christian boy. Every man his price. Well preserved fat corpse gentleman, epicure, invaluable for fruit garden. A bargain. By carcass of William Wilkinson, auditor and accountant, lately deceased, three pounds thirteen and six. With thanks.
>
> I daresay the soil would be quite fat with corpse manure, bones, flesh, nails, charnelhouses. Dreadful. Turning green and pink, decomposing. Rot quick in damp earth. The lean old ones tougher. Then a kind of a tallowy kind of a cheesy. Then begin to get black, treacle oozing out of them. Then dried up. Deathmoths. Of course the cells or whatever they are go on living. Changing about. Live for ever practically. Nothing to feed on feed on themselves. (pp. 108-109)

Consider along side it this passage from *Three Cantos*:

> Here did they rites, Perimedes and Eurylochus,
> And drawing sword from my hip
> I dug the ell-square pitkin, poured we libations
>   unto each the dead,
> First mead and then sweet wine,
> Water mixed with white flour.
> Then prayed I many a prayer to the sickly death's-
>   heads
> As set in Ithaca, sterile bulls of the best,
> For sacrifice, heaping the pyre with goods.
> Sheep, to Tiresias only,

Black, and a bell sheep;
Dark blood flowed in the fosse.
Souls out of Erebus, cadaverous dead
Of brides, of youths, of many passing old,
Virgins tender, souls stained with recent tears,
Many men mauled with bronze lance-heads,
Battle spoil, bearing yet dreary arms:
These many crowded about me,
With shouting, pallor upon me, cried to my men
                for more beasts;
Slaughtered the herds — sheep slain of bronze,
Poured ointment, cried to the gods,
To Pluto the strong, and praised Proserpine
Unsheathed the narrow steel,
I sat to keep off the impetuous, impotent dead
Till I should hear Tiresias.

The *Ulysses* passage adapts Homer to the words and rhythms of Bloom-speech.[49] Joyce, that is, uses the Flaubertian technique of *le mot juste* to characterize the way Bloom reacts to death and renewal. His interest lies in the way the experience of death and renewal feels *today* for *un homme moyen sensuel*. Pound's rendition has an entirely different purpose. He wants his readers to exercise historical imagination, and try to feel what it may have been *then*, in a more "sensitive" age. The "Seafarer" rhythms and the archaism distance the passage, make it unfamiliar and unsettling. The practices of libations, funeral burnings, of crying out loud to the gods, all conjure up the experience of an archaic ritual.

Pound not only used the Nekyia in *Three Cantos III* for certain primitive resonances, he seems to have been aware that they were resonances of a particular kind. According to Harrison's *Prolegomena*, the Nekyia was a ritual type of "ἀποδιοπομπεῖσθαι," an attempt "to effect riddance by magical imprecation or deprecation" (p. 27). It was, in other words,

---

[49] This particular passage, of course, represents only one of the ways Joyce makes use of myth in *Ulysses*.

a purification of spiritual taint, performed to appease pursuant demons. In Pound's poem, the Nekyia occurs in the context of an inferno that is already three Cantos underway. In *Three Cantos*, Odysseus is one in a series of heroes lost in individual dark nights. Pound first presented Odysseus as a capable man who has been careless in his duties to the gods, and, like a figure in one of the Noh spirit-plays, who must suffer the consequences. Those who emphasize the adventurous aspects of Canto I would do well to remember that Pound's understanding of Homer was colored by a reading of Dante's story of "crime and punishment":

> Re punishment of Ulysses, no one seems to note the perfectly useless, trifling, unprovoked sack of the Cicones in the *Odyssey*. Troy was one thing, they were inveigled.
>
> Helen's father was trying to dodge destiny by a clever combination, etc., but for the sack of the Ciconian town there was no excuse handy, it is pure devilment, and Ulysses and Co. deserved all they got thereafter (not that there is any certainty that Dante had this in mind).
>
> It gives a crime and punishment motif to the *Odyssey*, which is frequently overlooked, and is promptly and (?) properly snowed under by the human interest in Odysseus himself, the live man among duds. Dante definitely accents the theft of the Palladium, whereon one could turn out a volume of comment. It binds through from Homer to Virgil to Dante.[50]

Pound's Odysseus is not being punished for a single crime but (as in the Spirit-Noh) is suffering the "results of carelessness" to his duties toward the gods. He represents a state of mind whose disharmony and impiety comes out in his theft of the Palladium, about which "one could turn out a volume of comment." In *Kulchur*, Pound wrote about Odys-

---

[50] LE, pp. 212-213. The interpretation of the *Odyssey* that Pound advances was available in Denton J. Snider's 1895 *Homer's Odyssey: A Commentary*. Snider contends that the plot describes not so much punishment for sin as "spiritual restoration" from the "grand estrangement caused by the Trojan expedition."

seus' "maritime adventure morals" (p. 38), and the restlessness of Odysseus, the sailor at sea, was one of the Dantesque images he never forgot.[51] It is remarkable that none of Pound's critics has thought to remember that the lines that Pound elected to begin his translation are the same ones that begin Odysseus' speech in *Inferno* xxvi: "When I parted from Circe, who held me more than a year . . . I put forth on the open deep with but one ship and with that company which had not deserted me." But, of course, none of those critics had ever suspected that the Odysseus of Canto XLVII, who tells his men "Yet must thou sail after knowledge/Knowing less than the drugged beasts," might be less than an admirable adventurer. Dante, it seems, thought otherwise. His Odysseus, who sailed after knowledge without putting his own will in order, followed the currents of impious learning ("seguir la corrente" in Italian means to go with the stream) off the end of the earth: "O brothers . . . take thought of the seed from which you spring. You were not born to live as brutes, but (*ma per seguir virtute e canoscenza*) follow virtue and knowledge."

Pound was not the first to emphasize the unseemly side of Homer's Odysseus. Denton Snider had used Dante to read the *Odyssey* as a tale of purification,[52] and classical scholars were at the start of the century beginning to understand that Odysseus bore a strange resemblance to his grandfather Autolykos, who had named him "son of wrath" (*Odyssey*, xix, 403). Thomson, for example, wrote that the grandfather was "the reflection or double" of the chthonic Hermes-Dolios, god of thieves. ("The stories speak of him [Autolykos] as above all a thief of cattle, like Hermes in the [Homeric] *Hymn*" [p. 16].) According to Thomson, Hermes was one of the archaic dieties who, when other gods were being trans-

---

[51] To cite one example among a great many: In '*Noh*' or *Accomplishment*, when Pound wanted to give an example of Dante's clarity, he offered this line from *Purgatorio*, viii: "Era già l'ora che volge il disio"—It was now the hour which turns back the longing of Seafarers. (See *Translations*, p. 264.)

[52] See above, note 50.

formed into Olympians, always retained some of his chthonic ambivalence. Thomson argued that Autolykos, the reflection of Hermes, bequeathed Odysseus the character and the reputation of a rogue and a dissembler. In the Homeric "Hymn to Hermes," it is Hermes who kills the cattle of the sun. In the *Odyssey*, Odysseus' relation to Hermes-Dolios is suggested but censored, and Odysseus' men commit the offense. Still, Thomson noticed, Hermes extends a patron-like protection to Odysseus on two occasions: "the first, when he visits Kalypso in her island to announce the will of the gods that Odysseus return home; the second when in that other island of Kirke he appears to Odysseus in the likeness of a young man" (p. 19). Odysseus, therefore, grandson to Autolykos and reflection at second remove of Hermes, is a very special (and mischievous) kind of hero.

Pound, whether or not he was aware of Thomson's views, had obviously thought of the gods as dividing themselves up along Olympian-Chthonic lines, and had used Hermes to represent the darker group. In "Surgit Fama," he wrote:

> The tricksome Hermes is here;
> He moves behind me
> Eager to catch my words,
> Eager to spread them with rumour;
> To set upon them his change
> Crafty and subtle;

And in Canto XVII, he made the dualism of the gods explicit. Describing an approach to Venice with the images of Odysseus' return to Ithaca, he depicted the dual nature of his Odyssean hero "trembling" between Olympia and Chthonos:

> Gods,
> Hermes and Athene,
> As shaft of compass,
> Between them, trembled-

Sixteen Cantos earlier, in the Nekyia, the poem had begun a ritual process that would allow Hermes' chthonic energies to be harnessed.

A Glossary for *Three Cantos I*, ll. 99-193

l.99 "shimmering garment." see Yeats's "coat covered with embroideries/Out of old mythologies" (*A Coat*). Pound means a full panoply of mythic correspondences.

l.100 "featherly mantle, *hagoromo*." Hagoromo was the name of the feathery mantle in the Noh play of the same name. The character who chances upon the mantle trades it back to a spirit in return for learning a magic dance that embodies knowledge of the stages of the moon. (See *Translations*, 308-314.) Pound glosses the play in one place by lines from the *Paradiso*. The character who figuratively wears Pound's hagoromo will endure a ritual dance leading to such knowledge.

l.110 "Zanze" See *Sordello*, III, 879.

l.114 "The lyre should animate but not mislead the pen" Taken from Wordsworth's sonnet, *Plea for the Historian* (*Memorials of a Tour in Italy*, VI). The octet reflects Pound's attitude toward historical veracity in diction that probably made him wince:

> Forbear to deem the Chronicler unwise,
> Ungentle, or untouched by seemly ruth,
> Who, gathering up all that Time's envious tooth
> Has spared of sound and grave realities,
> Firmly rejects those dazzling flatteries,
> Dear as they are to unsuspecting Youth,
> That might have drawn down Clio from the skies
> To vindicate the majesty of truth.

Pound wrote that the *mot juste*, which poets must be encouraged to use, was not the same as Wordsworth's common word, "not by a long way. And it is possible to write in a stilted and bookish dialect without using clichés." (G-B, p. 115.)

l.122 "Puvis." Pierre Puvis de Chavannes, a nineteenth-century French painter of mythological allegories. Too pretty for Pound's taste. The implication is that Puvis did not know the gods well enough to paint their power. Cf. the last paragraph of Yeats's "The Tragic Generation": "I say: 'After Stephane Mallarmé, after Paul Verlaine, after Gustave Moreau, after Puvis de Chavannes, after our own verse, after all our subtle colour and nervous rhythm, after the faint mixed tints of Conder, what more is possible? After us the Savage God.' "

l.128 "Metastasio." Poet to the Viennese Court. An Arcadian. Apparently, Pound respected his treatment of mythology, believing it personally witnessed. He wrote in 1912:

> Time was when the poet lay in a green field with his head against a tree and played his diversion on a ha'penny whistle, and Caesar's predecessors conquered the earth . . . and let him alone . . . looking back upon this naïve state of affairs we call it the age of gold.
>
> Metastasio, and he should know if any one, assures us that this age endures. . . ." (LE, p. 8)

l.131 Pound had already located Metastasio in the Sirmio of his own world, for the very next paragraph glosses "folk upon them/Going their windy ways, moving by Riva": "I would much rather lie on what is left of Catullus' parlour floor and speculate the azure beneath it and the hills off to Salo and Riva with their forgotten gods moving unhindered amongst them, than discuss any processes and theories of art whatsoever." (LE, p. 9.)

ll.136-39 "naif ficinus." Ficino was "naif" because he created a systematic allegory of already allegorized and unfeared gods. In the process he made all religions so aesthetic that even the Christian God ceased to be immediately experienced. Pound wrote earlier in 1915:

> Ficino was seized in his youth by Cosimo dei

Medici and set to work translating a Greek that was
in spirit anything but "classic." That is to say, you
had, ultimately, a "Platonic" academy messing up
Christian and Pagan mysticism, allegory, occultism,
demonology, Trismegistus, Psellus, Porphyry, into a
most eloquent and exciting and exhilarating hotch-
potch, which "did for" the mediæval fear of the
dies irae and for human abasement generally. Ficino
himself writes of Hermes Trismegistus in a New
Testament Latin, and arranges his chronology by
co-dating Hermes' great-grandfather with Moses."
(G-B, p. 112)

Pound had too much respect for "the results of carelessness" to one's divine duties to endorse the hotch-
potch. Ficino here gets treated like Browning, a genuine
personality of considerable learning who never really
put it all together in an authentic way.

l.136   "Hotep-Hotep." Pound wrote about his reaction to
Gaudier's hieratic bust: "Oh, well, *mon pauvre carac-
tère*, the good Gaudier has stiffened it up quite a lot,
and added so much of wisdom, so much of resolution.
I should have . . . the firmness of Hotep-hotep, the
strength of the gods of Egypt." (G-B, p. 50)

Pound may have wanted to contrast Ficino with
the primitive power of art that is vitally connected
with the gods. The rest of the progress describes arts
more ritualistic than the quattrocento's.

ll.141-42   "Exult . . . bronzes." Pound is constructing a history of art based on one Gaudier wrote and Pound
reprinted in G-B, pp. 20-24. After the Egyptian of
Hamite vortex eventually comes the paleolithic Chinese vortex:

The black-haired men who wandered through the
pass of Khotan into the valley of the YELLOW
RIVER lived peacefully tilling their lands, and they
grew prosperous.

Their paleolithic feeling was intensified. As gods

they had themselves in the persons of their human ancestors — and of the spirits of the horse and of the land and the grain.

THE SPHERE SWAYED.

THE VORTEX WAS ABSOLUTE.

The Shang and Chow dynasties produced the convex bronze vases. (G-B, pp. 22-23)

ll.142-43 "Confucius . . . Perfection." Allen Upward ran a series of articles on Confucius in *The New Freewoman* in 1913. Pound is alluding to the passage that became in Canto XIII, "If a man have not order within him/ . . . He can not put order in his dominions."

ll.145-58 "With Egypt . . . China." Cf. Pound's 1915 essay (LE has it incorrectly dated 1914) "The Renaissance": "our opportunity is greater than Leonardo's: we have more aliment, we have not one classic tradition to revivify, we have China and Egypt. . . ." (LE, p. 224)

ll.146-54 "Daub out . . . above the river": Pound is introducing motifs of the vital relation to the gods of two "living" cultures, Egypt and China. Both the Egyptian scarabs and the grey steps of a Japanese shrine are emblems of divine perception. Early in the *Cantos*, such glimpses out of the drear waste appear only as fragments. They are "colors" that Pound is getting down so that he will have access to them later in the poem, when the light becomes clearer.

When Pound rewrote (and condensed) this passage for Canto III, he retained the details of the grey steps and (until 1930) the scarabs, but he deleted any mention of their ritual function, thus obscuring their significance.

l.153 "Kwannon": A female goddess of mercy, whose avatar is a lotus petal. She is taken from the Noh play, "Tamura," as are the other details of ll. 148-59 (see *Translations*, pp. 259-263). In the later Cantos Pound makes her the divine type of the poem's generous women. She stands behind both Cunizza and the Roman bride (from Catullus LXI) who appears in Canto IV, and about whom Pound writes "Saffron sandal *so petals* the narrow foot."

l.165 "he leapt": The "he" is Guido Cavalcanti. See Davenport, p. 82, and the *Decameron*, sixth day, ninth story.

ll.172-78 "I have but smelt. . . ." The reader be warned. The narrator sounds as if he is rejecting all of the preceding fragments of cultures outside his time and place. In fact, he is rejecting only the simple form of a "progress," the "masque" that Sordello had called an early stage of literature. (*Sordello* v, 583-601.) If we gloss the passage by Pound's prose, we find that the answer to the questions "shall I claim . . . confuse . . . ?" is *yes*.

Though the narrator says he has "but smelt this life," Pound in '*Noh*' or *Accomplishment* is quite keen on smelling:

In the eighth century of our era the dilettante of the Japanese Court established the tea cult and the play of "listening to incense."

In the fourteenth century the priests and the court and the players all together produced a drama scarcely less subtle.

For "listening to incense" the company was divided into two parties, and some arbiter burnt many kinds and many blended sorts of perfume, and the game was not merely to know which was which, but to give to each one of them a beautiful and allusive name, to recall by the title some strange event of history or some passage of romance or legend. It was a refinement in barbarous times, comparable to the art of polyphonic rhyme, developed in feudal Provence four centuries later, and now almost wholly forgotten.

The art of allusion, or this love of allusion in art, is at the root of the Noh. These plays, or eclogues, were made only for the few; for the nobles; for those trained to catch the allusion. In the Noh we find an art built upon the god-dance. . . . (*Translations*, pp. 213-214, emphasis mine)

This passage from '*Noh*' *or Accomplishment* also glosses Canto VII's "Against their actions, aromas." Clearly, Pound does not lament the progress in literary practice from heroic narrative to an "art of allusion."

ll.174-75 "And shall I . . . phantastikon": In "Psychology and the Troubadours," Pound identified the "phantastikon" as the mental faculty the Greeks thought reflected the world, and he compared it unfavorably to the "germinal" consciousness, which does not reflect but transmutes. (See SR, p. 92.) Here, the narrator is asking if he dares to distort his phantastikon by the forms of his imagination. The gods behind him are only actual once he gives them form.

ll.179ff. "How many worlds . . ." The reader should be aware of the dialectical movement of the conclusion. The narrator as tentative Vorticist affirms "How many worlds we have!" Then he draws back into hesitation and reliance on the creations of the Renaissance classics, which have become by the twentieth century mere *décor*, sets for ballet, from which we can only "guess" a soul for man, built from "aery" populations. The final affirmation echoes Gaudier's ringing defense of the moderns as the inheritors of primitive elemental *form* and power. The word "flare" reappears, bringing with it the motif of the flaming gods. The tone of alternating affirmation and hesitation is reinforced by "world enough . . . worlds enough," echoing Marvell and perhaps *Prufrock*.

ll.179-83 "Botticelli . . . blossoms": Simonetta was the bride of Juliano dei Medici and the reputed model for the figure of Venus in Botticelli's "Birth of Venus." As far back as this passage, Pound had decided to make Venus the reigning goddess of his poem. The goddesses of the *Cantos* are really one goddess seen in different lights, all related to Venus genetrix. Aufidius is a stream in Italy.

ll.184-86 "Behold . . . *Pericles*": Pound is quoting from *Pericles* I.i.12, where Pericles describes the daughter of Antiochus with an image of Venus: "See where she comes, apparell'd like the spring,/Graces her subjects." (In Botticelli's "Primavera," Venus is also accompanied by the graces, as she is in the Homeric Hymn to which Pound alludes at the end of *Three Cantos III*.) Pound will pick up "she comes," and use it as an oral motif indicating the presence of Venus in *Three Cantos II*.

ll.192-93 "If . . . Casella!": "Writing to paint" is, of course, imagism, a poetic counterpart to the modernism of Picasso. Pound asserts that imagism deserves a place beside writing to music, or traditional lyric poetry. (See G-B, pp. 81-82.) Casella was the musician in *Purgatorio II* who once set Dante's poems to music and who entrances Dante with a performance of one of them. The exclamation "O Casella" means that Pound is comparing his own duty to transcend lyricism to Dante's. In the *Purgatorio*, Dante is rebuked by Cato for loitering with the musician, and reminded that he must climb the mount. Pound's mountain will be the task of leaving his earlier lyrics and proceeding with the *Cantos*, which intend to establish a "hierarchy of values" in imitation of the *Commedia*.

CHAPTER IV

TOWARD A NEW NARRATIVE VOICE

WHEN Pound took over Browning's "meditative,/ Semi-dramatic, semi-epic" method for *Three Cantos*, he also took over Browning's devices for dramatizing a narrator. The speaking voice of *Three Cantos* achieved a definite tone and a not inconsiderable presence through the agency of a running series of colloquial asides, and the poem's "subjectivist" groundwork was accomplished by a *Sordello*-like paratactic organization. The *Cantos* never relinquished their paratactic techniques. But, between *Three Cantos* (1915) and the publication in 1919 of a very different Canto IV, Pound grew disenchanted with Browning's rhetorical mannerisms, and sought more subtle methods to dramatize a different kind of speaking voice.

In this chapter, I wish to examine the particulars of Pound's prolonged search for the techniques by which he could improve *Three Cantos*. The incidents of both *Three Cantos* and Canto IV occur within the theatre of a dramatized intelligence. In the latter, however, we find a consciousness that has lost its resemblance to *Sordello*'s gesticulating showman and has taken on the tincture of a Jamesian emotional register. After composing *Three Cantos*, Pound followed a road of new imitation and experiment that first enabled him to express the urbane sensibility of "Homage to Sextus Propertius." And, as Hugh Kenner has noted, the ironic tonalities of "Propertius" led the way from Pound's early poetry to the suppleness of the revised Cantos.[1]

---

[1] "The devices by which Pound gleefully riddled the affairs of Cynthia with irony are employed in the *Cantos* to frame and distance and epiphanize tag-ends of governmental intrigue and financial malpractice: the clichés of journalism handled with forceps devised for the clichés

It must not be imagined, though, that Pound's road from Browning's showman to the voice of A *Draft of XVI Cantos* was a straight one. Although in hindsight we may see the *Cantos'* impasse as a problem in narrative technique, Pound's attention centered on the associated question of rendering a subject. Convinced that the great accomplishment of modern literature had been the Flaubertian novel, Pound could not advance until, in the words of Forrest Read, he had "come to terms with the prose tradition."[2] For Pound, reconciliation of the claims of narrative poetry with prose realism proved to be no easy matter.

The pattern of Pound's exploration of dramatic voices between 1913 and 1919 repeated the shape of his earliest experiments with lyric personae. Pound's first dramatic lyrics, as several critics have discovered,[3] sort themselves out into two ideal types: those where the primary interest is in the psychological reality of a persona, and those where a persona allows Pound to express his own emotional states. Hugh Witemeyer designated these types as "Browningesque" and "Yeatsian,"[4] and Pound's remarks made it clear that the "Yeatsian" type was the more interesting.[5] In his post-*Imag-*

---

of passion. A close study of the techniques of *Homage to Sextus Propertius* is recommended to anyone who finds undifferentiated muddle in large blobs of the *Cantos*. These devices for organizing verse by shifts of texture and tone are central to Pound's mature poetic practice." (Hugh Kenner, *The Poetry of Ezra Pound* [London, 1951], pp. 162-163.)

[2] Forrest Read, "Pound, Joyce, and Flaubert: The Odysseans," in *New Approaches to Ezra Pound*, ed. by Eva Hesse (Berkeley and Los Angeles, 1969), p. 127. Although my differences with Read will become obvious, his article provides the best statement of Pound's circuitous progress to date.

[3] See N. Christophe de Nagy, *The Poetry of Ezra Pound: The Pre-Imagist Stage* (Bern, 1968), Chapter Five; and Hugh Witemeyer, *The Poetry of Ezra Pound: Forms and Renewal, 1908-1920* (Berkeley and Los Angeles, 1969), Chapter Four.

[4] Witemeyer, pp. 62-63.

[5] Pound wrote in a letter of 1911 that "The Sestina Altaforte is admittedly Bertrans de Born. —You can see translations in 'The Spirit

iste poetry, Pound developed both types under new influences. As a result of reading Remy de Gourmont, he transformed his "subjectivist" masks into expressions of a civilized sensibility. As a result of reading Flaubert, Joyce, and the early James he transformed his Browningesque portraits into "realistic" presentations. The revised Cantos would have been impossible without either development. Without de Gourmont, the poem would have lacked its ground voice and medium of expression. And without Flaubert, it would never have acquired its characteristic methods of compression and evaluation. To get a sense of how his original conception of the *Cantos* grew and changed, we must understand both these developments and their interaction. Chronologically, Pound's interest in realism came first.

From the start, Pound's preoccupation with prose realism was related to the techniques of the Flaubertian narrator. Pound was compelled by *le mot juste*, but his attraction was not due to superficial considerations of "style." He focused on the way Flaubert's use of *le mot juste* allowed him to condense and invisibly evaluate his portraits. He recognized that, by shading the overtones of a character's speech or rendered vision, Flaubert was able to trim down sequences of revelatory action and also place a character's spiritual inadequacy in the perspective of a larger understanding.

We find Pound's complex attitude toward realism present

---

of Romance.'—I mean translations of words. I NEEDED FREER MODE FOR TRANSLATION OF SPIRIT PLUS EXPRESSION OF MYSELF." (Quoted in de Nagy, p. 176.)

Reprinting an essay of two years earlier, he wrote in 1916's *Gaudier-Brzeska* that: "In the 'search for ones-self,' in the search for 'sincere self-expression,' one gropes, one finds some seeming verity. One says 'I am' this, that, or the other, and with the words scarcely uttered one ceases to be that thing. I began this search for the real in a book called *Personae*, casting off, as it were, complete masks of the self in each poem. I continued in long series of translations, which were but more elaborate masks" (p. 85).

in general terms the first time (1913) he wrote about the "prose tradition" of poetry:

> . . . what may be called the "prose tradition" of poetry, and by this I mean that it is a practice of speech common to good prose and to good verse alike. It is to modern verse what the method of Flaubert is to modern prose. . . . It means constatation of fact. It presents. It does not comment. It is irrefutable because it does not present a personal predilection for any particular fraction of truth . . . it does not deal in opinion. It washes its hands of theories. . . .
>
> The presentative method does not attempt to "array the ox with trappings." It does not attempt to give dignity to that which is without dignity, which last is "rhetoric," that is, an attempt to make important the unimportant, to make more important the less important. It is a lie and a distortion.
>
> The presentative method is equity. It is powerless to make the noble seem ignoble. It fights for a sane valuation. It cannot bring fine things into ridicule.[6]

Good poetry must resemble good prose. It must be natural, unadorned, particular. The phrasing is very reminiscent of Pound's imagist imperatives and therefore very easy to mistake for another demand that the poet cleanse his palette of clichés and empty generalities. Yet it would be a mistake to regard Pound's discussion of "the prose tradition" as merely a restatement of the Imagiste manifesto. The operative word here, the word upon which all the others depend, is "fact": "the 'prose tradition' of poetry . . . means constatation of fact." Buried in Pound's abstract treatment of realism is an awareness that the "facts" of realistic prose are not synonymous with the imagist's natural objects. In Pound's later

[6] From "The Approach to Paris V," *The New Age*, XIII, 23 (October 2, 1913), p. 662.

essays, it becomes apparent that the facts "presented" by the prose tradition are states of mind, or rather those idiosyncratic mannerisms of speech or behavior that give away states of mind. The accurate presentation of such states of mind, he argues, immediately communicates psychological reality.

An author's superimposed rhetoric, his attempts to impose authorial judgments on his characters, can only be "a lie and a distortion" of these facts. To try to persuade a reader that the "facts" of a character's restricted vision are unimportant is (Pound uses Dante's phrase) "to array the ox with trappings." The "presentative" or realistic method, because it does not try to paper over the spiritual ugliness of conventional virtue, "fights for a sane valuation." And the "evaluative" or moral emphasis of Pound's "realism" is, though not traditional, very strong. He sees two poles of character — "noble" and "ignoble." The "noble" character acts on the basis of authentic emotions, and is therefore capable (in a Nietzschean sense) of desiring good. ("Without strong tastes one does not love, nor therefore, exist.")[7] The "ignoble" character is cut off by the prisons of socially imposed, clichéd feelings from authentic tastes, from desire, from love, and from real existence. The moral or evaluative charge of the "prose tradition" is to dissociate genuine from clichéd feeling and "fight for a sane evaluation."

Pound's 1914 essay, "The Prose Tradition in Verse," presents additional evidence concerning his view of "realism." Writing on Hueffer's poetry, he reduced his earlier formulations of the "prose tradition" to a critical shorthand, and informed his readers that he found Hueffer "significant and revolutionary because of his insistence upon clarity and precision . . . upon efficient writing — even in verse" (LE, p. 377). This time, however, Pound alluded to a group of writers who, taken collectively, suggest what kind of prose "clarity and precision" he had in mind:

[7] Cited by Patricia Hutchins, *Ezra Pound's Kensington* (London, 1965), p. 11.

146

Stendhal had said, and Flaubert, de Maupassant and Turgenev had proved, that "prose was the higher art" — at least their prose. . . .

Remy de Gourmont . . . says that most men think only husks and shells of the thoughts that have been already lived over by others. . . . (LE, p. 371)

Stendhal, Flaubert, de Maupassant, and Turgenev all attempted to puncture sentimentality by revealing its ugly and debilitating effects. Their narrative techniques, according to Pound, were devoted to presenting and evaluating certain deficiencies in moral perception. Together they compose a class that de Gourmont's remark helps to describe. Their emotionally limited characters are trapped in *cliché* — "husks and shells of the thoughts that have been already lived over by others." Their work acts as a touchstone for that quality of "clarity" in Hueffer's poetry which Pound wished to endorse.

In 1915, Pound's preoccupation with the "prose tradition" led him frequently to mention the subject of realistic literature in his journalism. In an essay in *The New Age* he wrote that "realism" or "words that conform precisely with fact," had been absent from English literature since Sterne, and was desperately needed.[8] Once again he neglected to explain the word "fact," but in one of the columns that followed he provided his readers with their most specific illustration to date. Alluding to Flaubert's *L'Education Sentimentale,* he wrote that America will be lost until she "can understand that a satire . . . [consists] merely in a statement of fact (undistorted fact, known perfectly well to the reader)."[9] The "facts" of *L'Education Sentimentale,* at least, are clear. The novel deals with the disastrous effects of romantic misper-

---

[8] "American Chaos I," *The New Age,* xvii, 19 (September 9, 1915), p. 449.

[9] "American Chaos II," *The New Age,* xvii, 20 (September 16, 1915), p. 471.

ceptions, and its achievement is based on the presentation of clichéd attitudes in a character's mind by the techniques of *le mot juste*. Here again we are forced to draw the conclusion that Pound's interest in the "prose tradition" centers around narrative technique and psycho-moral considerations.

Pound's fullest explanations of the prose tradition came in the pieces he wrote about his contemporary English realists James Joyce and Henry James. In "Meditatio" (1916), Pound compared Joyce to Flaubert and lamented the publishers' resistance to *A Portrait of the Artist as a Young Man*. In order to put Joyce's accomplishment in perspective, he invoked Edmond de Goncourt's preface to *Germinie Lacerteux* (the preface that Pound later said "states the case and the whole case for realism,"[10] and excerpted passages for citation:

> the novel . . . has become, by analysis and psychological inquiry, the history of contemporary ethics-in-action (how shall one render accurately the phrase "l'histoire morale contemporaine"?) . . . .
>
> It would be insulting (*injurieux*) to us, the young and serious school of modern novelists, to forbid us to think, to analyse, to describe all that is permitted to others to put into a volume which has on its cover "Study," or any other grave title. You cannot ask us at this time of day to amuse the young lady in the railroad carriage. (P/J, pp. 71-72)

Pound applied the citation to Joyce, and stressed the "realism" of *Dubliners* and *Portrait*. In them, Pound wrote, Joyce analyzed "*l'histoire morale contemporaine*," the "contemporary ethics-in-action" of modern Dublin. *Dubliners* and *Portrait* exposed the way Dublin had allowed unanalyzed sentimentality to bankrupt its moral discrimination. The argument was continued in Pound's essay, "James Joyce: At Last the Novel Appears" (1917):

[10] In "Joyce" (1918), reprinted in P/J, p. 140.

The Portrait is very different from *L'Education Senti-mentale*, but it would be easier to compare it with that novel of Flaubert's than with anything else. Flaubert pointed out that if France had studied his work they might have been saved a good deal in 1870. If more people had read *The Portrait* and certain stories in Mr. Joyce's *Dubliners* there might have been less recent trouble in Ireland. A clear diagnosis is never without its value. . . .

. . . Mr. Joyce's realism . . . [is] of a piece with . . . the style, the actual writing: hard, clear-cut, with no waste of words, no bundling up of useless phrases, no filling in with pages of slosh.

It is very important that there should be clear unexaggerated, realistic literature. . . . The mind accustomed to it will not be cheated or stampeded by national phrases and public emotionalities. (P/J, pp. 90-91)

Pound described Joyce's realism, then, as the hard, clearcut description of "public emotionalities." The moral insight of Joyce's stories, had it been understood by the people of Ireland, would have prevented the Irish from being stampeded into the 1916 uprising (the "recent trouble in Ireland"). Once again we discover that, although Pound seems to desire fine technique for its own sake, he actually admires it for the way it can serve the purposes of a "sane" morality.

Between January 1916, when Henry James died, and August 1918, when Pound edited the *Little Review* memorial issue for James, Pound read all of James's work.[11] Henry James became a constant subject of his journalism, and, although he would later appreciate other qualities of James's technique, Pound concentrated during this period on James's realism. In *The New Age* for July 1917, he wrote that "the bulk of the work in Henry James's novels is precisely an analysis of, and thence a protest against, all sorts of petty

[11] See Hugh Kenner, *The Pound Era* (Berkeley and Los Angeles, 1971), p. 14.

tyrannies and petty coercions, at close range."[12] Pound saw
James's characters trapped in the artificial constraints of
American and European emotional clichés. And, he wrote,
just as the scholar is constantly engaged in an attack on the
provincialism of time, so "the realist author is engaged in an
attack on the provincialism of place."[13] He saw James as a
heroic figure who devoted his life to analyzing social and romantic clichés. James was the archetypal realist and "Realist
literature is a letting out the big cat. It is giving away the
gigantic or established show, when the show is an hypocrisy;
it is giving away with an ultimate precision. . . . The realist
novelists let out the cats of modernity, many forms of oppres-
sions, personal tyrannies, and group tyrannies."[14]

Pound's notion of realism, then, remained consistent
from 1913 to 1918. For him, Flaubert, Joyce, and James were
among the major authors of his time because of their analysis of the "facts" of "public emotionalities." They taught him
that realism depended on the techniques of an invisible narrator and the device of *le mot juste*, by which a narrator
could unobtrusively portray the extent to which a character's
emotional response was *clichéd* or inauthentic. And Pound,
ever the conscious craftsman, often paid as much attention
to their techniques as to their moral intentions. He wrote that
James's "emotional centre is in being sensitive to the feel of
the place or the tonality of the person" (LE, p. 306), and
that "these atmospheres, nuances, impressions of personal
tone and quality *are his subject*; that in these he gets certain things that almost no one else had done before him"
(LE, p. 324). He was even more specific in an essay on Joyce's
Exiles. Defending Joyce's need to use certain risqué words,
he wrote in 1916: "I admit that Mr. Joyce once mentions a

[12] In "Provincialism the Enemy, II," *The New Age*, xxi, 12 (July
19, 1917), pp. 268-269.

[13] In "Provincialism the Enemy, III," *The New Age*, xxi, 13 (July
26, 1917), pp. 288-289.

[14] In "Studies in Contemporary Mentality, IX," *The New Age*, xxi,
25 (October 18, 1917), pp. 527-528.

garter, but it is done in such a way . . . it is done in the only way . . . it is the only possible means of presenting the exact social tone of at least two of the characters" (P/J, p. 51).

In Pound's pre-1918 "realist" poetry, he managed in a very limited way to apply the techniques of a Flaubertian "presentation" to verse. In the very early "Les Millwin," for instance, he "presented" a few vacant young ladies by means of catching the tone of their dress and speech. The "little Millwins" do not see but "behold" a ballet, and their souls are fashionably "mauve":

> The Little Millwins attend the Russian Ballet.[15]
> The mauve and greenish souls of the little
>   Millwins
> Were seen lying along the upper seats
> Like so many unused boas.
>
> The turbulent and undisciplined host of art
>   students —
> The rigorous deputation from "Slade" —
> Was before them.
>
> With arms exalted, with fore-arms
> Crossed in great futuristic X's, the art students
> Exulted, they beheld the splendours of *Cleopatra*.
>
> And the little Millwins beheld these things;
> With their large and anaemic eyes they looked out
>   upon this configuration.
>
> Let us therefore mention the fact
> For it seems to us worthy of record. (1913)

Despite the small successes of "Les Millwin" and his other realist verse, however, and despite his respect for the "prose tradition," Pound was then unable to turn realism into major poetry. We have already seen how lightly he regarded his

---

[15] For the exact intellectual tone of the Russian Ballet (only haltingly modern), see Pound's review in *Athenaeum*, xciv, 4, 689 (March 12, 1920), pp. 348-349.

realistic "sketches," and how small a part the claims of realism played in *Three Cantos*. It appears (to me at least) that his sense of poetry could never quite brook realism's ugly honesty or its "invisible author" techniques. We have seen that his early dramatic lyrics were invariably slanted toward "expressive" rather than "objective" personae, and that he was attracted to the form of *Sordello* principally because of its dramatic possibilities. In 1913-1918 Pound was willing to admire the modern techniques of Henry James, but for his own poetry he needed a model that would allow more freedom for his bent toward self-expression. When he compared Henry James unfavorably to Remy de Gourmont in 1919, it was obvious who that model was. Pound wrote:

> The mind of Remy de Gourmont was less like the mind of Henry James than any other contemporary mind I can think of. James' drawing of *moeurs contemporaines* was so circumstantial, so concerned with the setting, detail, nuance, social aroma, that his transcripts were 'out of date' almost before his books had gone into a second edition. . . .
> He has left his scene and his characters, unalterable as the little paper flowers permanently visible inside the lumpy glass paperweights. He was a great man of letters, a great artist in portrayal; he was concerned with mental temperatures, circumvolvulous social pressures, the clash of contending conventions, as Hogarth with the cut of contemporary coats. . . .
> In contradiction to, in wholly antipodal distinction from, Henry James, Gourmont was an artist of the nude. He was an intelligence almost more than an artist; when he portrays, he is concerned with hardly more than the permanent human elements. His people are only by accident of any particular era. He is poet, more by possessing a certain quality of mind than by virtue of having written fine poems; you could scarcely contend that he was a novelist.
> He was intensely aware of the differences of emotional timbre; and as a man's message is precisely his *façon de voir*,

his modality of apperception, this particular awareness was
his "message." (LE, pp. 339-40)[16]

James had given Pound a model with which to render the
imprisoned intelligences of other people. The example of
Gourmont allowed him to present the resonant intelligence
of a mind like his own. Such conclusions can be read fairly
easily from this excerpt from the 1919 Gourmont essay. What
the following pages show is that the Gourmontian ideal had
been present as early as 1915. Until mid-1919, Gourmont was
a greater influence on Pound's poetry than the "realistic"
James, and Gourmont's influence continued to grow throughout the writing and revising of the early Cantos.

§§

Pound's ambivalence toward the theatre may begin to
explain his admiration for Remy de Gourmont. To Pound,
important events were the events of the mind, and the theatre was much too crude to re-create them. In his review of
Joyce's *Exiles*, he had contrasted Shaw with Ibsen on this
basis:

> Of course, oh, of course, if, *if* there were an Ibsen stage
> in full blast, Mr. Joyce's play would go on at once.
> But we get only trivialized Ibsen; we get Mr. Shaw, the
> intellectual cheese-mite. That is to say, Ibsen was a true
> agonist, struggling with very real problems. "Life is a com-
> bat with the phantoms of the mind" — he was always in
> combat for himself and for the rest of mankind. . . .
> There is in Shaw nothing to restrain, there is a bit of
> intensity in a farce about Androcles, but it is followed by
> a fabian sermon, and his "comedy" or whatever it is, is
> based solely on the fact that his mind moves a little bit
> faster than that of the average Englishman. You cannot

[16] The essay was originally printed as "De Gourmont: A Distinction
(Followed by Notes)" in *Little Review*, v, 10/11 (Feb-March 1919),
pp. 1-19.

conceive any intelligent person going to Mr. Shaw for advice in any matter that concerned his life vitally. He is not a man at prise with reality. . . .

The trouble with Mr. Joyce's play is precisely that he *is* at prise with reality. It is a "dangerous" play precisely because the author is portraying an intellectual-emotional struggle, because he is dealing with actual thought, actual questioning, not with clichés of thought and emotion. (P/J, pp. 51-52)

Pound was saying that Shaw presents thought as smoothed-over and tarted-up generalization. The real intelligence of Ibsen and Joyce, he argued, was a struggle within the mind, a struggle between "intellectual-emotional" impulses that were not yet clichés. The reality with which they are "at prise" was the reality of a modern mind that can have no certainties. Pound described Ibsen, the "real dramatist," almost as if his play was only the expression of his mind:

in your problem plays you must remember that all the real problems of life are insoluble and the real dramatist will be the man with a mind in search; he will grope for his answer and he will differ from the sincere auditor in that his groping will be the keener, the more far-reaching, the more conscious, or at least the more articulate; whereas, the man who tries to preach at you, the man who stops his play to deliver a sermon, will only be playing about the surface of things or trying to foist off some theory. (P/J, p. 56)

Pound's comments attempt to transform drama into something more congenial, into the dramatization of an individual intelligence. (In fact, his remarks recall his description of the "meditative,/ Semi-dramatic, semi-epic" nature of *Sordello*, and it is interesting to note that, according to Read, the review was written "while he was in the very middle of struggling with the first drafts of *The Cantos*" [P/J, p. 48].)

Pound continued the preoccupations of his *Exiles* review

in an obituary notice he wrote in late 1915 for Remy de Gourmont.[17] In that notice, Shaw was still sticking in his throat: "And I call the reader to witness that he, de Gourmont, differed from Fabians, Webbists, Shavians (all of whom, along with all dealers in abstractions, are ultimately futile). He differed from them in that his thoughts had the property of life" (PD 1, p. 120). The last phrase, "the property of life," recalls Pound's remark that Ibsen was (and Shaw was not) "at prise with reality," and attributes Ibsen's caliber of intelligence to de Gourmont. Other passages in the obituary clarify Pound's sense of that intelligence:

> The tedium and the habit of the great ruck of writers is that they are either incoherent and amorphous, or else they write in conformity to, or in defence of, a set of fixed, rigid notions, instead of disclosing their thought . . . which might, in rare cases, be interesting. . . .
>
> [To quote Gourmont] "A few only, and without gain or joy to themselves, can transform directly the acts of others into their own personal thoughts, the multitude of men thinks only thoughts already emitted, feels but feelings used up, and has but sensations as faded as old gloves. When a new word arrives at its destination, it arrives like a post-card that has gone round the world and on which the handwriting is blurred and obliterated with blots and stains." (PD 1, p. 119)

[17] Stock, in his *Life* (p. 112) says that Pound was "put on" to de Gourmont in February 1912. He mentions the incident in 1913 when de Gourmont telegraphed his encouragement to the Paris meeting of "*les jeunes*" that Pound attended. The first major entry in Stock about de Gourmont is for 1914: "Although they had never met, Pound had been in touch with him by letter. De Gourmont contributed an article on Lautréamont to *The Egoist* in 1914 and in June 1915 he offered to co-operate in Pound's plans for a new magazine to maintain communications between New York, London and Paris."

Pound's obituary tribute was entitled "Remy de Gourmont," and it originally appeared in *The Fortnightly Review*, xcviii (n.s.), 588 (December 1915), pp. 1159-1166.

For Pound, then, Shaw and "the great ruck of writers" could not transform external reality into the contours of "their own personal thoughts." His bias is derived from both Pater and Nietzsche, and he insists that the kind of "thought" that is accepted from society rather than being transformed by the inner contours of an individual's passion is not expression but slavery. (Elsewhere he wrote that "Mr. Shaw goes down into the limbo of those who put their trust in abstractions,"[18] and that "Shaw slips into the kultur error . . . where he speaks of a man being no use until you put an idea inside him. The idea that man should be used 'like a spindle,' instead of existing 'like a tree or a calf' is very insidious.")[19] Pound imagined Gourmont, however, as a man "absorbed in . . . the struggle for the rights of personality" along with "the subtlest thinkers for the last thirty years."[20] In the citation above, Pound praised Gourmont for imposing his personality upon the social world of clichéd ideas.[21] Later in the obituary, he added that Gourmont allows truth to cease being a function of logic and become instead a function of sensibility. "Ideas came to him," Pound wrote, "as a series of fine wines to a delicate palate, and he was never inebriated" (PD 1, p. 115).[22]

The extent to which Gourmont's assertion of the "rights of personality" crystalized Pound's most fundamental tenets can be appreciated only when we recognize where Pound

[18] From "Affirmations, VII; The Non-existence of Ireland," *The New Age*, xvi, 17 (February 25, 1915), pp. 451-453.

[19] From "Provincialism the Enemy, II," *The New Age*, xxi, 12 (July 19, 1917), pp. 268-269.

[20] *Ibid.*

[21] Earlier, Pound had used a similar notion of Gourmont in his theory of the image. According to De Nagy, Pound's theory of *imagisme* adapted Gourmont's "premise that it is the specific task of the artist to render the world as it is 'deformed' by his personality." See De Nagy's *The Critical Decade*, p. 74.

[22] Compare this with Eliot's famous remarks on the quality of metaphysical poetry, written a decade later. Both poets were strongly influenced by de Gourmont.

placed Gourmont in the cultural tradition. Although Pound believed that culture was ultimately a series of creative masterpieces, each made possible by a new technical "donation," he also speculated that each "donation" was preceded by a change of mentality that liberated new areas of treatment. He often cited the rigor of Aquinian disputation, for example, as something that went hand-in-hand with the scientifically precise metaphors of Cavalcanti and Dante. He associated the name of Montaigne with that of Shakespeare because Montaigne's skepticism prepared for Shakespeare's secular humanism. For Pound, each epoch possessed a mind or group of minds that embodied its highest and most advanced thought. These minds represent the "civilisation" of the period, the forces that function "to depreciate material values and build up values of the intelligence."[23] Pound conceded that, as each civilized mind builds upon the subtleties of the last, civilization does, haltingly, advance.[24]

Pound envisioned Gourmont in the direct line of modern culture, a culture that began when Renaissance Italy "proclaimed the individual": "Modern civilisation comes out of . . . renaissance Italy, the first nation which broke away from Aquinian dogmatism and proclaimed the individual; respected the personality. That enlightenment still gleams in the common Italian's 'Cosi son io!' when asked for the cause of his acts."[25] In a nutshell, Pound's view of civilization since the Middle Ages consisted of three advances. The Renaissance freed men from the political tyranny of the church-state; Voltaire freed men from the intellectual tyranny of

[23] From "The Revolt of Intelligence, IX," *The New Age*, xxvi, 19 (March 11, 1920), pp. 301-302.

[24] That is, advances with two steps forward, one step back. Pound wrote that "civilisation does *not* 'advance' with anything resembling solidarity . . . the Middle Ages threw aside Roman civilisation . . . the nineteenth century cast out many of the intellectual freedoms of the eighteenth." See "The Revolt of Intelligence, VI," *The New Age*, xxvi, 11 (January 15, 1920), pp. 176-177.

[25] From "Provincialism the Enemy, III," *The New Age*, xxi, 13 (July 26, 1917), pp. 288-289.

religious authority; and Flaubert and James freed men from the emotional tyranny of socially imposed states of feeling.

Pound attributed whatever advances civilization had made in his own generation to Gourmont. Gourmont had surpassed Voltaire in that he denied the validity not only of religious absolutes but of abstract moral truths of any kind. Pound wrote in 1919 that "He had passed the point where people take abstract statement of dogma for 'enlightenment.' An 'idea' has little value apart from the mind which receives it" (LE, p. 341). Gourmont had also surpassed Henry James's feel for individual tone. "Where James is concerned with the social tone of his subjects, with their entourage, with their *superstes* of dogmatized 'form,' ethic, etc., Gourmont is concerned with their modality and resonance in emotion" (LE, p. 340). In 1919, Pound called Gourmont's oeuvre the best record "of the civilized mind from 1885-1915":

> Gourmont's wisdom is not wholly unlike the wisdom which those ignorant of Latin may, if the gods favour their understanding, derive from Golding's *Metamorphoses*.
>
> Barbarian ethics proceed by general taboos. Gourmont's essays collected into various volumes . . . are perhaps the best introduction to the ideas of our time that any unfortunate, suddenly emerging from Peru, Peoria, Oshkosh, Iceland, Kochin, or other out-of-the-way lost continent could desire. A set of Landor's collected works will go further towards civilizing a man than any university education now on the market. Montaigne condensed Renaissance awareness. Even so small a collection as Lionel Johnson's *Post Liminium* might save a man from utter barbarity. . . .
>
> Needless to say, Gourmont's essays are of uneven value as the necessary subject matter is of uneven value. Taken together, proportionately placed in his work, they are a portrait of the civilized mind. I incline to think them the best portrait available, the best record that is, of the civilized mind from 1885-1915. (LE, p. 344)

Gourmont's special attraction for Pound may be inferred from the last paragraph of the above citation. Pound writes that Gourmont's essays are a "portrait of the civilized mind" even though "they are of uneven value as the necessary subject matter is of uneven value." He was rephrasing his 1915 observation that "it is not any particular phrase, poem, or essay that holds you, so much as a continuing sense of intelligence, of a limpid, active intelligence in the mind of the writer" (PD 1, p. 113). For Pound, Gourmont's ability to unify an arbitrary conglomeration of subject matter by a sense of antecedent intelligence was uniquely attractive. *Three Cantos*, we remember, started out as a "rag-bag" of the modern world, held together by the clumsy persona of a *Sordello*-like narrator. In Gourmont he saw that a "rag-bag" of subject matter need not be unified by the external characterization of a speaker. Gourmont imposed the personality of an intelligence on his various works by the inflections of a single sensibility — what we have seen Pound call a *façon de voir* and an emotional "modality." Moreover, he provided a counter-example to the realist's completely invisible narrator, and once more made it respectable for a work to reflect the personality of its author.

Pound had been fruitlessly experimenting with realistic verse that allowed him no possibility for self-expression, and in 1915 he jumped to endorse Gourmont's essays and his poetry. In his obituary, he paid the Frenchman's prose "sonnets" an extraordinary compliment:

> These "sonnets" are among the few successful endeavors to write poetry *of our own time*. I know there is much superficial modernity, but in these prose sonnets Remy de Gourmont has solved the two thorniest questions. The first difficulty in a modern poem is to give a feeling of the reality of the speaker, the second, given the reality of the speaker, to gain any degree of poignancy in one's utterance.
>
> That is to say, you must begin in a normal, natural tone of voice, and you must, somewhere, express or cause a deep

feeling. I am, let us say, in an omnibus with Miscio Itow. [Itow was a Noh actor, a friend of Pound and Yeats who performed in "At the Hawk's Well."] He has just seen some Japanese armour and says it is like his grandfather's, and then simply running on in his own memory he says: "When I first put on my grandfather's helmet, my grandmother cried . . . because I was so like what my grandfather was at eighteen."

You may say that Itow is himself an exotic, but still, there is material for an hokku, and poetry does touch modern life . . . though it does not much appear in modern verses.

De Gourmont has not been driven even to an exotic speaker. His sonnets begin in the metropolis. The speaker is past middle age. . . . (PD 1, p. 121)

Pound then cited passages from Gourmont's prose "sonnets" and remarked that they overcame their unlikely material (intellectual bric-a-brac) by the feeling of poignancy Gourmont was able to create by a constantly felt dramatic voice. Gourmont's meaning, he commented, was in "the tone, the conversational, ironic, natural tone of the writing, the scientific dryness, even." He concluded that Gourmont "has worn off the trivialities of the day, he has conquered the fret of contemporaneousness by exhausting it in his pages of dry discussion, and we come on the feeling, the poignancy, as directly as we do in the old poet's —

$$\text{Λέγουσιν αἱ γυναῖκες}$$
$$\text{Ανακρέων γέρων εἶ}$$

'Dicunt mihi puellae
Anacreon senex es'

(PD 1, pp. 122-123)

From the beginning of his career, Pound had been a dramatic poet, and had attempted to "give a feeling for the reality of a speaker." However, his early dramatic lyrics had been mainly Yeatsian lyric expressions of a Romantic, pastoral voice. In his comments on Gourmont we see him confronting a kind of lyricism that could express not just Romantic reaction to nature, but a complex and intelligent (and still poignant) response to a vast range of *modern* subjects. Gourmont's "sonnets" treated material as diverse as *Three Cantos*, but in a more immediate and subtle way. They were civilized poems of "the metropolis," and they demonstrated how a "limpid active intelligence" might be dramatized with no Browningesque fireworks but simply a "conversational, ironic, natural tone." Gourmont's sonnets gave life to the otherwise lifeless "fret of contemporaneousness" by raising the meaningless flux of modern reality into a sentient mind. We shall see that his "modern," "metropolitan," "conversational," "ironic," voice would provide Pound with the terms and the prototype to recognize the value of Laforgue's technical ability. Out of Gourmont's solution to "the two thorniest questions" of "poetry of our time" would eventually come the dramatic continuity of the revised *Cantos*.

It is significant that in 1915's obituary, however, Pound wrote only about the general qualities of Gourmont's verse and not about its technique. Although he sensed Gourmont's achievement, he could justify it by no more than the following: "The man was infused through his work. If you 'hold a pistol to my head' and say: 'Produce the masterpiece on which you base these preposterous claims for De Gourmont!' I might not be able to lay out an array of books to equal those of his older friend, Anatole France" (PD 1, p. 113). It is a statement Pound would hardly have made about Flaubert, or Joyce, or Eliot, and it suggests why in 1915 he was unable to absorb the Gourmontian qualities he so admired into the body of his own poetry. We shall see that a long process of assimilation and association was necessary before the *Cantos* became in any meaningful way reflections of Gourmont.

§

In his post-1915 prose, Pound consciously tried to imitate Gourmont by experimenting with a series of civilized and urbane dramatic voices. In 1916, Yeats set Pound on to Landor's *Imaginary Conversations,* and Pound became interested enough to go back to Landor's model, Fontenelle's *Dialogues des Mortes.*[26] In May 1916 (six months after his Gourmont obituary), *The Egoist* began to publish Pound's translations — the *Dialogues of Fontenelle.* In them, Pound used Landor's precise but neutral diction to portray the easy conversation of figures from diverse periods of history.[27] The pattern of most of the dialogues was the same. Exceptional, intelligent individuals were allowed to assert themselves over more "respectable" characters. In one, Anacreon convinced Aristotle that the poet is more disciplined than the philosopher. In another, Stratonice argued the claims of an Ovidian sexual sophistication:[28] "A painter at the court of my husband . . . was discontented with me, and to avenge himself he painted me in the arms of a soldier. He showed the picture and fled. My subjects, zealous for my glory, wished to burn the picture in public, but as I was painted admirably well and with a great deal of beauty . . . I forbade them the burning; had the

[26] For Yeats's suggestion, see Stock's *Life,* pp. 189-190. Landor sometimes uses the same characters as Fontenelle, but in general his figures are more emotional, and less brilliant. Some idea of the difference can be obtained by comparing Fontenelle's "Agnes Sorel-Roxelane" with Landor's "The Maid of Orleans and Agnes Sorel" (*Imaginary Conversations,* Fourth Series, No. 10).

It should not be forgotten that Pound praised Landor in the context of his 1919 essay on de Gourmont, and in these terms: "A set of Landor's collected works will go further toward civilizing a man than any university education now on the market."

[27] For a discussion of the techniques of Landor's urbanity, with some reference to Pound, see the first chapter of Robert Pinsky, *Landor's Poetry* (Chicago, 1968).

[28] Pound's contempt for the restriction of sexual nature by an imposed morality was also voiced by Rabelais in "An Anachronism at Chinon": "As for personal morals: There are certain so-called 'sins' of which no man ever repented. There are certain contraventions of hygiene which always prove inconvenient. None but superstitious and ignorant people can ever confuse these two issues. And as hygiene is always changing . . . intelligent men will keep pace with it."

painter recalled, and pardoned him" (PD 1, p. 54). In a
third, Seneca rebuked Scarron and verbalized the collection's
unifying, Gourmontian theme: "wisdom . . . [is] not a result
of . . . reason, but merely of temperament."

His translations finished, Pound went on to write a series
of prose sketches which were later collected and entitled
"Pavannes."[29] Two of them (*An Anachronism at Chinon*
and *Aux Etuves de Weisbaden*) were dialogues cut from
the same cloth as the *Dialogues of Fontenelle*.[30] In the others,
Pound experimented with sophisticated narrative voices to
control unusual material, and to create a stylistically interesting texture. *Jodindranath's Occupation*, for example, was
ostensibly a description of an admirable but exotic species of
man. Its real subject, however, was the sophisticated mind of
the narrator, rendered by the manners of his voice:

[29] They appeared in the *Little Review*, in the following order: "Jodindranath Mawhwor's Occupation" (May 1917); "An Anachronism at
Chinon" (June 1917); "Aux Etuves de Weisbaden" (July 1917);
"Imaginary Letters" (a series of five pieces, starting in September 1917
and continuing until November 1918); "Our Tetrarchal Precieuse"
(July 1918); "Genesis, or The First Book in the Bible" (November
1918).

[30] However, *Aux Etuves de Weisbaden* touched on two subjects of
interest. Anticipating *Propertius*, it asserted the virtues of Roman
civilization:

> "Maunsieur: Being clean is a pagan virtue, and no part of the light
> from Judaea.
> "Poggio: Say rather a Roman, the Greek philosophers died, for
> the most part, of lice. Only the system of empire, plus a dilettantism
> in luxuries, could have brought mankind to the wash-tub." (PD 1,
> p. 27.)

Echoing Gourmont, it asserted the superiority of personal values over
an imposed ethic or pattern:

> "Poggio: What dignity have we over the beasts, save to be once,
> and to be irreplaceable!
> I myself am a rag-bag, a mass of sights and citations, but I
> will not beat down life for the sake of a model." (p. 30.)

Poggio's image of his "self" ("a rag-bag . . . of sights and citations")
significantly mirrors the words of *Three Cantos I*: "the modern world/
Needs such a rag-bag to stuff all its thoughts in."

Jodindranath rose in the morning and brushed his teeth, after having performed other unavoidable duties as prescribed in the sutra, and he applied to his body a not excessive, as he considered it, amount of unguents and perfumes. He then blackened his eyebrows, drew faint lines under his eyes, put a fair deal of rouge on his lips, and regarded himself in a mirror. Then having chewed a few betel leaves to perfume his breath, and munched another bonne-bouche of perfume, he set about his day's business. He was a creature of habit. That is to say, he bathed, daily. And upon alternate days he anointed his person with oil, and on the third day he lamented that the mossy substance employed by the earliest orthodox hindoos was no longer obtainable. He had never been brought to regard soap with complaisance. . . .

The evening was given over to singing. Toward the end of it Jodindranath, as the head of his house, retaining only one friend in his company, sat waiting in the aforementioned perfumed and well arranged chamber. As the lady with whom he was at that time connected did not arrive on the instant, he considered sending a messenger to reproach her. The atmosphere grew uneasy. His friend Mohon fidgeted slightly.

Then the lady arrived. Mohon, his friend, rose graciously, bidding her welcome, spoke a few pleasant words and retired. Jodindranath remained. And for that day, the twenty fifth of August, 1916, this was his last occupation. In this respect the day resembled all others.

This sort of thing has gone on for thirty five hundred years and there have been no disastrous consequences.

As to Jodindranath's thoughts and acts after Mohon had left him, I can speak with no definite certainty. I know that my friend was deeply religious; that he modeled his life on the Shastras and somewhat on the Sutra. To the Kama Sutra he had given minute attention. He was firmly convinced that one should not take one's pleasure with a woman who was a lunatic, or leprous, or too white, or too black, or who gave forth an unpleasant odor, or who lived an ascetic life, or whose husband was a man given to wrath and possessed of inordinate power. These points were to him a matter of grave religion. (PD 1, pp. 4-6)

Writing about Gourmont, Pound said that "a man's message is precisely his *façon de voir*," and in this citation the "message" is located in how the narrator's tone anticipates, manipulates, and mocks the attitudes of the average reader. Ostensibly, he is describing the daily routine of an exotic. Actually, however, he is playing an intellectual game with' tonalities of the normal and the abnormal. At first he insinuates that the activities of this Indian are perfectly average. Jodindranath, after all, "munches" his breakfast like any good Englishman. These expectations of the pedestrian, though, do not last. Soon he slaps his reader (and Pound is playing to the kind of unthinking reader who likes his stories "straight") with an offensive detail. The breakfast that Jodindranath is munching happens to be perfume. The pattern is repeated when the narrator uses the comfortable cliché, "creatures of habit," and pretends to assume the attitude of a bourgeois reader. But, again, the pretense is short-lived. The phrasing of the line, "That is to say, he bathed, daily," is a comeuppance that creates a distance between narrator and reader with joltingly unexpected formality.

By the end of the penultimate paragraph, the narrator's tone has communicated that these exotics are much saner than modern Englishmen. Jodindranath's evening has been spent in the sixteenth-century English style of decorous singing. His friendship is based on an admirable code of respectful deference. His assignation is merely "the last occupation" of the day, a ceremony, an accepted need. Jodindranath's every activity has been civil and sane on that day: on "the twenty fifth of August, 1916" — a day when the peoples of Europe were busy committing the barbarities of World War I.

Pound's experiments with civilized voices extended beyond his creative prose to his journalism. Readers of *The Egoist* were verbally assaulted not only by Ezra Pound and E. P., but by Ferrex, Henery Hawkins, Bastien von Helmholtz, Herrmann Karl Georg Jesus Maria (!), and Alf Arpur. In the *Little Review* Pound wrote "Imaginary Letters" in the full persona of Walter Villerant, and signed short pieces by the names of John Hall and Thayer Exton. The most significant of the disguises, however, were B. H. Dias and William Atheling, pseudonyms he adopted for his art and music reviews in *The New Age* between November 1917 and January 1921. Dias and Atheling had opinions very similar to Pound's, but the poet took special delight in varying their personalities and maintaining an artistic distance between himself and them. Of William Atheling Pound later wrote:

> "William Atheling" wrote fortnightly in *The New Age* from 1917-20; he was more a secondary personality than a nom de plume, that is to say he had a definite appearance (baldheaded) and a definite script (crabbed and with an old fashioned slant); he sympathized with Arnold Dolmetsch' opinions, even when not wholly in agreement therewith. That is to say he might very well have thought that music ended with Bach. He existed in order that I might study the actual sounds produced by performing musicians.[31]

With B. H. Dias, Pound had the rare pleasure of complaining publicly that his own circumspect review of Wyndham Lewis had not gone far enough. He wrote *in propria persona* to *The New Age* about Dias:

> Sir, — What is the use of Mr. Dias' treading on eggs? Mr. Wyndham Lewis is one of the five or six painters in this country whose work has any significance, or who would take any sort of rank among the French "independents." Neither Mr. Dias nor anyone else is qualified to speak of

[31] See *The Transatlantic Review*, I, 2 (February 1924), p. 109.

Mr. Lewis's work unless they have seen both the Baker collection and the collection of fifty "drawings" (mostly in rich colour) which I sent to New York for the Vorticist Exhibition, at which they were all of them sold, the best of them now in Mr. John Quinn's collection.[32]

§

Gourmont's poetry and Pound's experimental prose prepared for a change in Pound's poetic technique, but did not accomplish it. In the summer of 1917, Pound published *Three Cantos* in *Poetry*, and their narrative texture was not significantly different from 1915's "Provincia Deserta." Late in 1917, however, something happened that changed the career of Pound's poetry. Through a combined study of Gourmont, T. S. Eliot, and Jules Laforgue, he developed a critical insight that enabled him to create the voice of his unprecedented "Homage to Sextus Propertius."

Eliot's *Prufrock and Other Observations* appeared in 1917, and Pound reviewed it in two different periodicals. In the August number of *Poetry*, he began a tribute to Eliot with this epigraph from Remy de Gourmont: "Il n'y a de livres que ceux où un écrivain s'est raconté lui-même en racontant les moeurs de ses contemporaines—leurs rêves, leurs vanités, leurs amours et leurs folies."[33] Under Gour-

[32] *The New Age*, XXIV, 17 (February 27, 1919), p. 283. Pound made the game even rarer by having Dias reply:

"Mr. Pound mistakes both my tone and my attitude; but whatever I might think of Wyndham Lewis' work, I cannot, in fairness to other artists, use these columns for the criticism of any painting save that which has been publicly exhibited. I have, as a matter of fact, seen the Baker collection, but I can include neither that nor the works which Mr. Pound sent to New York in an estimate of Mr. Lewis' work unless I am also to include the unexhibited work of Mr. Lewis' contemporaries. I am, however, quite willing to admit [!] that Mr. Lewis is one of the dozen, or perhaps even the half-dozen English painters, whose work merits international attention."

[33] Pound later translated the remark himself as "There are no books (real books) save those where an author has presented himself in

mont's aegis, Pound then went on to describe Eliot's poetry
as poised between realistic treatment of others (*racontant les
moeurs de ses contemporaines*) and a dramatic treatment of
poetic apperception (*où un écrivain s'est raconté lui-même*).
Pound acknowledged the source (Laforgue) of Eliot's satiric
irony, and complimented the contemporaneity of Eliot's
realistic settings ("he has placed his people in contemporary
settings, which is much more difficult than to render them
with romantic trappings"). But Pound also admired the mind
that expressed itself in the intelligence of the poetry, and he
wrote that "the supreme test of a book is that we should
feel some unusual intelligence working behind the words."

The same characteristic ambivalence between subjective
expression and impassive observation was expounded more
clearly in 1917's other "Prufrock" review.[34] In the June 1917
Egoist, Pound made a strong case for the quality of Eliot's
"realism." Defending his friend from an earlier attack by the
Quarterly Review, he placed Eliot in the tradition of the last
generation of French poets. He compared "Conversation
Galante" to the "marvelous neatness" and "finesse" of Laforgue's *Votre âme est affaire d'occuliste*." He cited "La
Figlia che Piange" and "Prufrock," and emphasized the importance of Eliot's achievement in English poetry: "Mr.
Eliot has made an advance on Browning. He has also made
his dramatis personae contemporary and convincing." Pound
added that Eliot's technical innovation had been to "make a
. . . new refinement, a new method of turning old phrases into
new by their aptness." Pound was saying that, thanks to
Laforgue, Eliot had made a quantum leap in the "presenta-

---

presenting the customs of his contemporaries, their dreams, their vani-
ties, their loves, and their follies." (See "The Revolt of the Intelligence, IV," *The New Age*, xxvi, 9 [January 1, 1920], pp. 139-140.)
At that time he stressed the expressive side of Gourmont's axiom by
adding, "the hallmark of journalism is precisely that the author does
not "present himself."

[34] "Drunken Helots and Mr. Eliot," *The Egoist*, iv, 5 (June 1917),
pp. 72-74.

tive" abilities of English realistic verse. Whereas Pound's
realistic poems, for instance, could only invisibly render a
third person subject, a poem like "Conversation Galante"
was able to render a speaking voice by the realistic device of
consciously used clichés. Pound may have been thinking of
a stanza like this one, in which Eliot's rhythms make his
speaker pause self-consciously over the cliché, "exquisite noc-
turne":

> And I then; "Someone frames upon the keys
> That exquisite nocturne, with which we explain
> The night and moonshine; music which we seize
> To body forth our own vacuity."

Once again, however, Pound's admiration extended beyond
Eliot's realistic achievements. In phrases that recalled earlier
discussions of Gourmont, he remarked upon the "personal
quality" of the mind that pervaded "Prufrock and Other Observations": "He has been an individual in his poems. I have
read the contents of this book over and over, and with a continued joy in the freshness, the humanity, the deep quiet
culture. . . . His practice has been a distinctive cadence, a
personal modus of arrangement, remote origins in Eliza-
bethan English and the modern French masters, neither
origin being sufficiently apparent to effect the personal quality." If Eliot was now England's premier realist poet, Pound
seemed to believe he was also the poet most capable of trans-
figuring the subjects of his poetry by a personal presence.
And, significantly, he put his finger on some of the poetic
techniques by which Eliot made his presence felt: "a distinctive cadence" and a "personal modus of arrangement." (I
take the last to mean a private symbolic autonomy.) Pound's
awareness of these techniques marked him on the way to
becoming a poet who could revise the narrative voice of *Three
Cantos*.

According to Christophe de Nagy, Eliot was the impetus
behind Pound's intensive reading of Laforgue, a reading that

occurred some time between 1914 and 1917.[35] Pound once remarked, "I was a man in a hurry. When I got to London in 1908 I was an extremely unsophisticated individual. Eliot was born with all that, Laforgue and so on. I had to acquire it."[36] In 1917, Pound began to write about the Frenchman with an urgent involvement. He mentioned Laforgue in both "Prufrock" reviews, of course, and later that year he confronted him directly. The result, "Irony, Laforgue, and Some Satire" shows Pound in the grips of a major poetic influence, and also indicates that the tension in his development between Flaubert and Gourmont, realism and self-expression, was veering toward a resolution in Gourmont's favor.

In the "Laforgue" essay, Pound referred to Flaubertian realism by his other name for it—satire[37]—and he was still in part respectful. However, he was also at pains to reiterate that Laforgue had surpassed satire, and in Pound's remarks we can read a transformation of his old "realistic" aspirations. "I think Laforgue implies definitely," he wrote, "that certain things in prose were at an end" (LE, p. 282). Then, repeating his judgment, Pound quoted one of Laforgue's tercets, and differentiated him from Corbière, a Flaubertian poet and the principal model for Pound's earlier realist verse:

Je ne suis pas "ce gaillard-là!" ni Le Superbe!
Mais mon âme, qu'un cri un peu cru exacerbe,
Est au fond distinguée et franche comme une herbe.

This is not the strident and satiric voice of Corbière, calling Hugo "*Garde Nationale épique,*" and Lamartine "*Lacrimatoire des abonnés.*" It is not Tailhade drawing

[35] De Nagy (*The Critical Decade,* p. 101) dates the influence immediately after the 1914 meeting with Eliot. Ramsey's article (see below) dates it from Pound's reading of the *Complaintes* in 1915. Stock's *Life* talks about Pound's "sudden interest in 1917" in Laforgue. The earliest reference to Laforgue in the published *Letters* is in 1916 (p. 92).

[36] Cited by Warren Ramsey in "Pound, Laforgue, and Dramatic Structure," *Comparative Literature* (winter 1951), p. 47.

[37] See above, p. 147.

with rough strokes the people he sees daily in Paris, and bursting with guffaws over the Japanese in their mackintoshes, the West Indian mulatto behind the bar in the Quartier. It is not Georges Fourest burlesquing in a café; . . . Laforgue was a better artist than any of these men save Corbière. He was not in the least of their sort. (LE, p. 282)

Finally, to insure that no reader had missed the point, Pound repeated it a third time: "I do not think one can too carefully discriminate between Laforgue's tone and that of his contemporary French satirists" (LE, p. 283).

When we examine Pound's essay from the beginning, we discover that the standards by which he judged Laforgue's superiority were Gourmont's standards. The essay started almost with a paraphrase of Pound's eulogy for de Gourmont: "As Lewis has written, 'Matter which has not intelligence enough to permeate it grows, as you know, gangrenous and rotten'" (LE, p. 280). When Pound continued, he applied all of the key words he had used to praise Gourmont's poetry to Laforgue: intelligent, modern, civilized, ironic, personal. He called attention to Laforgue's "delicate irony" and denominated it "the citadel of the intelligent" (LE, p. 281). Recalling his description of Gourmont as the center of French civilization and the source of "a personal, living force . . . a personal light" (PD 1, p. 113), he characterized Laforgue as "a Numa Pompilius, a father of light" (LE, p. 283). Finally, and most important, Pound wrote that the significant achievement of Laforgue's technical advances was his ability to make them "a vehicle for *the expression of his own very personal emotions, of his own unperturbed sincerity*" (italics mine) (LE, p. 282). It was apparent that (through the lens of de Gourmont) Pound saw Laforgue's self-ironies to be as much the expression of a civilized voice as the realistic presentation of dramatic clichés.

The "Laforgue" essay acquires even greater significance when we note that Pound here first developed a critical concept to handle Laforguian techniques. He called Laforgue's delicate irony "verbalist," and went on to distinguish "verbalism" as a class of poetry co-equal with "lyricism" and "imagism": "I do not think one can too carefully discriminate between Laforgue's tone and that of his contemporary French satirists. He is the finest wrought; he is most 'verbalist.' Bad verbalism is rhetoric, or the use of *cliché* unconsciously, or a mere playing with phrases. But there is good verbalism, distinct from lyricism or imagism, and in this Laforgue is a master" (LE, p. 283). "Verbalism," of course, is the prototype of "logopoeia," that *How to Read* (1929) called "the dance of the intellect among words."[38] And the phrase "dance of the intellect" perfectly renders the Gourmontian, subjectivist bias with which Pound took up Laforgue and Eliot into his critical terminology. In the "Homage" and the *Cantos*, Pound's "realism" would be as much the demonstration of an antecedent intellect as the rendering of an external object.

We have several times noticed how Pound's critical formulations seemed to precede a poetic breakthrough,[39] and the case of 1917's verbalism was no exception. On the first page of "Irony, Laforgue, and Some Satire," Pound suggested he had begun to speculate about using Laforgue for his own purposes: "The innovator most damned for eccentricity, is often most centrally in the track or orbit of tradition, and his detractors are merely ignorant" (LE, p. 280). Pound's "inno-

[38] Between the two Pound developed his terms for the three types of poetry in the following places: In "A Study in French Poets," done for the *Little Review* (February 1918), he reiterated praise of Laforgue's "good verbalism." In his review of the *Others Anthology* for the *Little Review* (March 1918) he used "Melopoeia" and "logopoeia," but retained "imagism." In the *Little Review* (November 1918) he coined "phanopoeia" for the title of a poem. In 1920, in *The New Age*, XXVII, 25 (October 21, 1920), p. 356, the three terms are used together for the first time.

[39] De Nagy also noticed this propensity, and wrote: "Pound is not the sort of critic who would invent a term like *logopoeia* without wanting to make use of it for his own poetry." See *The Critical Decade*, p. 106.

vator most damned" was a compound figure of himself and
Eliot, and his remarks declared that the "tradition" of Laforgue might soon be perpetuated by new composition. He
was already extending the tradition beyond Laforgue, however. In 1929 he told his readers: "Unless I am right in discovering logopoeia in Propertius . . . we must say that Laforgue invented [it]" (LE, p. 33). In 1917 Pound began the
composition of "Homage to Sextus Propertius."

In his "Study in Creative Translation," J. P. Sullivan
enumerates the local devices that make "Homage to Sextus
Propertius" a type of logopoeia, and I direct the reader interested in such a discussion to his study.[40] I wish now to
consider only the relation of the "Homage" to the dialectic
of realism and self-expression that we have been following.
In "Homage," Pound set about imitating not only Propertius
but also Laforgue and Gourmont. He wanted to make his
speaker "modern," "metropolitan," and "civilized," and so
he chose a Roman poet for his subject. "The latin," he wrote,
"is really 'modern.' We are just getting back to a Roman state
of civilization" (L, p. 179). We are just getting back, that
is, to the "Mediterranean sanity" that, Pound wrote in "Medievalism," was "the conception of the body as perfect in-
strument of the increasing intelligence" (LE, pp. 152, 154).
Consider the beginning of the poem's part iv:

> Tell me the truths which you hear of our
>> constant young lady,
>>> Lygdamus,
> And may the bought yoke of a mistress lie with
>> equitable weight on your shoulders;
> For I am swelled up with inane pleasurabilities
>> and deceived by your reference
> To things which you think I would like to believe.

The various claims Pound made for modern poetry come
to bear on this citation. First of all, it is realistic in the La-

---

[40] See J. P. Sullivan, *Ezra Pound and Sextus Propertius: A Study in
Creative Translation* (Austin, 1964), especially pp. 81-82.

forguian manner, and satirizes what Kenner called "the clichés of passion."[41] Propertius has just been informed of his unexpected return to Cynthia's favor. With reflexes conditioned by popular romance, we expect him to respond with heart-swell, but Pound punctures our expectations with an "aptly" used (i.e., jarringly inappropriate) cliché: "I am swelled up with inane pleasurabilities." Fighting for a "sane valuation" of life and literature, this kind of realism was meant to defuse the respectability both of our reflex and the instrumental cliché.

If "Homage" is realistic, however, it is realistic only in the sense of Gourmont's dictum: "Il n'y a de livres que ceux où un écrivain s'est raconté lui-même en racontant les moeurs de ses contemporaines." For every comment on a piece of emotional folly, "Homage" reflexively suggests the intelligent apperceptiveness of its speaker. Pound had commended Gourmont for his creation of "new modes of sanity," and here he was attempting to render Gourmont's modality, his sophisticated *façon de voir*. The manner of "Propertius" is not the epigrammatic conciseness of Laforgue's "Votre âme est affaire" or Eliot's "Conversation Galante." Rather, it is a discursive, periodic style devoted to rendering the movements of an antecedent consciousness. Pound, in fact, made use of a syntax and linear arrangement that was considerably more irregular than the smoothness of a standard translation, and even more difficult than the original Latin. The syntax implies the unevenness of perception, and suggests that Pound's persona, Propertius, is both aware of the unexpectedness of his response and delighted with his own urbanity. Eliot and Laforgue had also utilized discursive manners for the effect of self-irony, but Pound's Propertius is not Prufrock or Pierrot. He is less susceptible to romantic despair, more willing to distrust feeling, more vital, more skeptical. He is a characteristically Poundian cross between Pierrot and the intelligence of Voltaire.

[41] Hugh Kenner, *The Poetry of Ezra Pound* (London, 1951), p. 163.

Of all Pound's descriptions of modern poetry, the one most appropriate to "Homage to Sextus Propertius" came from his tribute to the prose sonnets of Remy de Gourmont. "The first difficulty in a modern poem," Pound wrote, "is to give a feeling of the reality of the speaker, the second, given the reality of the speaker, to gain any degree of poignancy in one's utterance." If the "Homage" endures the test of time, it will endure because Pound was able to "gain" and control a sustained emotional poignancy. Propertius is a character both deeply in love and aware of love's folly. In the gestures and attitudes of his voice, we hear the drama of caring and not-caring, a drama whose poignancy would be crushed by any techniques save the most "superficial" and delicate. In the citation above, Pound employed subtleties reminiscent of Ben Jonson[42] to suggest an emotional involvement beneath Propertius' apparent irony. (One example may illustrate what I mean. In the fourth line, Propertius uses two words emphasized by a spondee, "bought yoke" rather than simply "yoke." He thus both reminds Lygdamus of his servant status and also indicates his own awareness that there are other yokes that are not bought.)

§

Before Canto IV, "Propertius" was probably the single most important fruit of Pound's search for new modes of dramatic presentation. Yet the voice of Propertius was still a formal "mask," and thus in part dependent on elements of social and psychological characterization. For the narrator of the *Cantos*, however, Pound needed techniques to present not so much a "mask" or "character" as a sensibility — a pervasive but nowhere visible register that could absorb images into the unity of an emotional *façon de voir*. In 1917 he

---

[42] To me, the virtues of Pound's "Homage" appear to be those of Jonson's "On my first sonne," a poem in which Jonson plays off intonations of despair and resignation to achieve an almost unbearable "poignancy of utterance."

suggested his awareness that Eliot had created something comparable through the agency of what Pound called a "distinctive cadence" and a "personal modus of arrangement." That is, Eliot had expressed his own antecedent sensibility in his poetry by absorbing images into the magnetic hold of his personal symbolic arrangement, and by rhythmically imposing his own emotional signature.

In the summer of 1919 Pound finished Canto IV, and his 1919-1920 prose revealed the existence of two final critical formulations that had permitted him to complete his narrative development. In the late novels of Henry James he found a prose style whose involutions and participial constructions permitted the energies of perception to be absorbed into drama. And in Aeschylean drama he discovered classical authority for a syntax even more "obscure" than James's — a syntax designed to connect grammatically disparate but related facets of racial memory.

Pound's assimilation of Henry James seems to have been double-tiered. From 1916 to mid-1919 he concentrated on James's "realism," and emphasized the early part of James's career. In his August 1918 essay in the *Little Review*, he was at best ambivalent about the late novels. He wrote that "perhaps the grip was relaxing," and only grudgingly accepted James's late style:

> At any rate in sunnier circumstances he talked exactly as he wrote, the same elaborate paragraph beautifully attaining its climax; the same sudden incision when a brief statement could dispose of a matter.
>
> Be it said for his style; he is seldom or never involved when a direct bald statement will accurately convey his own meaning, *all of it*. He is not usually, for all his wide leisure, verbose. He may be highly and bewilderingly figurative in his language. . . . (LE, p. 311)

As late as Spring, 1919, Pound still limited this estimate of James's oeuvre to certain "realistic" accomplishments, and wrote: "Where James is concerned with the social tone of his subjects, with their entourage, with their *superstes* of dogmatized 'form,' ethic, etc., Gourmont is concerned with their modality and resonance in emotion" (LE, p. 340). Many years later, however, he paid James the ultimate tribute of attributing to him the creation of a representatively American "form" of consciousness: "I'll tell you a thing that I think *is* an American form, and that is the Jamesian parenthesis. You realize that the person you are talking to hasn't got the different steps, and you go back over them. . . . The struggle that one has when one meets another man who has had a lot of experience to find the point where the two experiences touch, so that he really knows what you are talking about."[43] In his tribute, Pound could only have been talking about the extended "parentheses" of James's final phase. He had changed his opinion radically, and there is some evidence to indicate the date of that change between spring 1919 and spring 1920, that is, during the year in which Canto IV was composed in a dramatically altered narrative style.

In May 1920 Pound published the first of his serialized "Indiscretions," a kind of running, "reticent autobiography" in which the poet (at least according to his 1923 "Postscript") attempted to fill the gap between "the place the Great H. J. leaves off in his 'Middle Years' and the place where the younger writers try to start some sort of faithful record" (PD 2, p. 50).[44] The very first page of his "record" was written in an exaggerated imitation of the late Jamesian style:

> Whereafter two days of anaesthesia, and the speculation as to whether, in the development and attrition of one's faculties, Venice could give one again and once more either the old kick to the senses or any new perception; whether coming to the belief that human beings are

[43] *Writers at Work: The Paris Review Interviews*, ed. Kay Dick (Bungay, Suffolk: Penguin Books, 1972), p. 95.

[44] *Indiscretions* was first published serially in *The New Age* from May 27 to August 12, 1920. The postscript was added when it was published in book form by Bird's Three Mountains Press in 1923.

more interesting than anything possible else—certainly than any possible mood of colours and footlights—like glare-up of reflection turning house-façades into stage card-board; whether in one's anthropo- and gunaikological passion one were wise to leave London itself — with possibly a parenthetical Paris as occasional watchtower and alternating exotic *mica salis*; and whether—*the sentence being the mirror of man's mind, and we having long since passed the stage when "man sees horse" or "farmer sows rice," can in simple ideographic record be said to display anything remotely resembling our subjectivity* . . . (italics mine). (PD 2, p. 3)

Pound's full sentence runs on for over a page, but the section I emphasized gives us its point: "The sentence being the mirror of man's mind . . . [we have] long since past the stage when 'man sees horse' or 'farmer sows rice' can in simple ideographic record be said to display anything remotely resembling our subjectivity."

As Pound for five years had been trying to find means to "display" the "subjectivity" of his speakers, the above remark must be taken as a personal testament. In 1915-1916, he had been taken with the "aesthetic" of Fenollosa's "big essay on verbs, mainly verbs" (L, p. 82), and he had tried to write epigrammatic miniatures to catch the transitive action described by Fenollosa's aesthetic. However, he had also written that Shaw's "abstractions" could not compare to an author who was "at prise with reality" and portrayed "an intellectual-emotional struggle . . . actual thought, actual questioning." Now, Pound recognized that the sentences of a novel like *The Ambassadors* did indeed reflect "the different steps" of *how* a man thought, and not just *what* a man thought. The late Jamesian discursive style, with its endless convolutions and cunning use of gerunds, was a better "mirror" of the "steps" of a mind than Fenollosa's "simple ideographic record." James's endless sentences caught the energies of perceived actions in participles, and held those energies suspended while the mind of his speakers turned them over and over.

Pound began to see that poetry did not need the actual presence of verbs so much as a syntax that could incorporate their action and relate it to other actions. When he finally published the "Chinese Character" essay in the *Little Review* (December 1919), he printed Fenollosa's statement that "We should avoid 'is' and bring in a wealth of neglected English verbs," but he also appended this note: "These precautions should be broadly conceived. It is not so much their letter, as the underlying feeling of objectification and activity that matters."[45] And when he composed Canto IV in a revised narrative style, he avoided verbs and rendered "an underlying feeling" of "activity" by taking over the techniques of James's long participial constructions. The dramatic voice of Canto IV had become a Jamesian emotional register, and "displayed" its "subjectivity" in this manner:

> Actaeon . . .
>   and a valley,
> The valley is thick with leaves, with leaves, the trees,
> The sunlight glitters, glitters a-top,
> Like a fish-scale roof,
>   Like the church roof in Poictiers
> If it were gold.
>   Beneath it, beneath it
> Not a ray, not a slivver, not a spare disc of sunlight
> Flaking the black, soft water;
> Bathing the body of nymphs, of nymphs, and Diana,
> Nymphs, white-gathered about her, and the air, air,
> Shaking, air alight with the goddess,
>   fanning their hair in the dark,

[45] The note is printed at the bottom of p. 69 in *Little Review*, VI, 8 (December 1919). Since the text had been previously submitted for publication, it is hard to tell when the note was written. The footnote was reprinted with the essay in *Instigations* (p. 383) but was removed from subsequent publication. It is not in the Stanley Nott (London, 1936) printing or the City Lights edition (San Francisco, 1950).

Lifting, lifting and waffing:
Ivory dipping in silver,
   Shadow'd, o'ershadow'd
Ivory dipping in silver,
Not a splotch, not a lost shatter of sunlight.

Perhaps the lone disadvantage of using late James as a narrative model for the *Cantos* was that James's personal histories lacked the mythical scope Pound required. However, in 1919, Pound discovered an analogue to James's late syntax that did not suffer from the same drawback. Writing on Browning's translation of *Agamemnon* in *The Egoist*, Pound mused over the difficulties of Browning and Aeschylus. The pertinence of these remarks to the *Cantos* is indisputable, for Pound took the occasion to recall the relation of *Sordello* to the life of his art: ". . . if I have been extremely harsh in dealing with the first passage quoted it is still undisputable that I have read Browning off and on for seventeen years with no small pleasure and admiration, and am one of the few people who know anything about his *Sordello* . . ." (LE, p. 269).

Pound wrote that some of the obscurities of Browning's translation were inexcusable, and he singled out Browning's unthinking retention of Greek syntactical inversions. However, he went on, there were functional obscurities even within the original, and these should not be smoothed over by a too-natural translation. Unconsciously repeating Gourmont, Pound asserted that *these* obscurities result whenever an author forsakes received "ideas" for his own *personal* thought. They "occur when the author is piercing, or trying to pierce into, uncharted regions; when he is trying to express things not yet current, not yet worn into phrase" (LE, pp. 268-69).[46] Pound then explained that Aeschylus'

[46] Compare Pound's 1915 translation of Gourmont: "A very few only, and without gain or joy to themselves, can transform directly the acts of others into their own personal thoughts, the multitude of men thinks only thoughts already emitted, feels but feelings used up, and has but sensations as faded as old gloves" (PD 1, p. 119).

originality can be located in his functionally obscure syntax, a syntax that "pierces into" new mental connections between the past and the present:

> It seems to me that English translators have gone wide in two ways, first in trying to keep every adjective, when obviously many adjectives in the original have only melodic value, secondly they have been deaved with syntax. . . .
> One might almost say that Aeschylus' Greek is agglutinative, that his general drive, especially in choruses, is merely to remind the audience of the events of the Trojan war; that syntax is subordinate, and duly subordinated, left out, that he is not austere, but often even verbose after a fashion (not Euripides' fashion). . . .
> Above suggestions should *not* be followed with intemperance. But certainly more sense and less syntax (good or bad) in translations of Aeschylus might be a relief. (LE, p. 273)

Aeschylus' syntax was "agglutinative." In its tangled complexities, its interwoven clauses, it drew together elements of past and present, history and myth, into a "verbose" mass whose connections "reminded" the Greek audience of all the ramifications of Homer's tale of Troy (that is, of their entire cultural inheritance). To illustrate his point, Pound cited from the *Agamemnon*, and provided H. D.'s translation of the famous chorus which began:

> War-wed, author of strife,
> Fitly Helen, destroyer of ships, of men,
> Destroyer of cities. . . .

It was felicitous that Pound should have mentioned *Sordello* in this essay on *Agamemnon*, an essay that constitutes the last exhibit of his search for an expanded narrative tradition. He thus gave us a token of his five-year progress in miniature. From the "meditative, semi-dramatic, semi-epic" method of his *Sordello*-like *Three Cantos*, Pound had arrived at a technique in which complex, "agglutinative" syntax was able to "mirror" his narrator's sensibility and "pierce into" historical awareness "not yet current, not yet worn into phrase." In 1919 Pound plucked out part of the *Agamemnon*'s choric lament over war-wed Helen, and used it unaltered in Canto VII. He did not disturb the Canto's narration one iota:

Le vieux commode en acajou:
       beer-bottles of various strata,
But *is* she dead as Tyro? In seven years?
Ἑλέναυς, ἕλανδρος, ἑλέπτολις
The sea runs in the beach-groove, shaking the floated pebbles,
Eleanor!

CHAPTER V

STAGES OF REVISION

WITH the aid of unpublished letters in the Paige collection at Yale, it has been possible to construct a chronology of the composition of the *Cantos* between 1915, the year that Pound wrote his father that the first three Cantos were completed, and 1925, when William Bird published the Three Mountains Press edition of *A Draft of XVI. Cantos of Ezra Pound for the Beginning of a Poem of Some Length.*[1] According to that chronology, there were three crucial periods of composition: (1) 1915, when versions of *Three Cantos* were composed and two more Cantos were mapped out; (2) 1919, when the first versions of Cantos IV, V, VI, and VII were written; (3) Spring 1922 to January 1925, when the first three Cantos were re-fashioned and the remaining nine were written. (Pound wrote to his father in August 1923 to report that he had "rewritten the beginning of the poem".)

To understand more about the changes that the Cantos underwent from 1915 to 1925, we must recognize that there were many factors involved in the process of revision, and that the differences between each stage were minor. On the basis of a direct comparison between *Three Cantos I* and the apparently more ideogrammic Canto IV, it might seem that sometime in 1919 Pound suddenly decided to eliminate the Cantos' narrator and make other significant changes in the way the poem was conceived.[2] But such speculation is ill con-

---

[1] See Myles Slatin, "A History of Pound's Cantos I-XVI, 1915-1925," *American Literature*, 35 (May 1963), pp. 183-195.

[2] See John L. Foster, "Pound's Revision of Cantos I-III," *Modern Philology*, 63 (1965-1966), pp. 236-245. Foster attributed Canto IV's new "elastic style" to Pound's discovery of "the ideogrammic structure," and accounted for the post-1919 revision of the first Cantos by claiming that Canto II (originally published as Canto VIII) gave Pound a

ceived. *Three Cantos I* was intended from the beginning only as an exordium. The narrator of *Three Cantos* (see above, Chapter Three) recedes into an unobtrusive voice, and the structure of *Three Cantos II* is genuinely comparable to Canto IV.[3] Although Canto IV does differ stylistically from *Three Cantos II*, it would be incorrect to say that the difference was based on a radically new conception of structure. A careful look at all the revisions reveals that Canto IV was meant to continue the structural principles as well as the thematic motifs of the original *Three Cantos*. We shall see that Canto IV's real innovations have to do with narrative technique and texture.

Three Cantos appeared in the June, July, and August 1917 numbers of *Poetry*. Almost as soon as they appeared in print, Pound began to revise them. We know that he requested and used the advice of T. S. Eliot, whom he was seeing more and more, because he wrote Harriet Monroe, "the printing it [*Three Cantos*] in three parts has given me a chance to emend, and the version for the book [*Lustra*] is, I think, much improved. Eliot is the only person who proffered criticism instead of general objection" (L, p. 115). The revisions included the excision of a long redundant passage,[4] and numerous small improvements. Looking closely, we can isolate certain patterns in the revisions that were beginning to alter the substance of the original: (1) Pound eliminated twenty-

---

"controlling symbol" (the sea as the flux of human experience) with which to re-order what he had written.

[3] Canto IV appears to be structurally different because it is more elliptical and difficult. In fact, the new difficulty exists within the radicals and not in what we would ordinarily call the Canto's structure (the pattern of linkage between the radicals). A comparative structural map of the two Cantos (remember that neither one supplies transitions between images) has been provided for the reader's convenience on pp. 185-186. Both Cantos are organized around a theme that might be characterized "potential splendor and actual waste."

[4] Lines 103-119, "Or shall I do . . . straight simple phrases." The passage only repeated many of the points Pound had already rebuked Browning with in the lines "Tower by tower . . . outside the picture."

Three Cantos II

Prelude: Civilization in Ruins: Gonzaga's Palace
  I. Ubi sunt?
      A. Half Forgotten Artificer: Joios
      B. The Coming Civilization: Dolmetsch
  II. Frustration-Misdirected Will: Love
      A. General: The Lute Girl
      B. Literary: Catullus
              Sappho
  III. Reflective Interlude: Dordogne
  IV. A Tenuous Beam of Light: (In the gloom the gold . . .): Love
      A. St. Antoni
  V. In the gloom the gold: War
      A. Myo Cid
      B. The Count de las Nieblas
      C. *Kumasaka*
      D. Sancho
  VI. Renewed Frustration
      A. Literary: Ignez
      B. Mythic: The Rape of Proserpine
      C. Historic: The Renaissance declines into the mercantile age
  VII. Defiant optimism amid present waste
      A. Pound and the Indiana painter.

Canto IV

Prelude: Civilization in Ruins: Troy
  I. Ubi sunt?
      A. Ancient Artificer: Cadmus
      B. Divine Creation
  II. Frustration-Misdirected Will: Love
      A. Vidal
      B. Intensified:
          1. Historic: Sir Raymond of Castel-Rousillon
          2. Mythic: Tereus, Actaeon

185

III. Interlude: Dim perception of the Gods: "Ply over ply"
IV. In the gloom the gold: Love
    A. Provence
    B. The ritual of Catullus 51
 V. The void the Gods have left
    A. The significance of the wind
    B. Danae
VI. Reprise: Glimpses of the Gods among the ruins
    A. The smoke of Troy
    B. Images of Kuannon
VII. Frustration and obtuseness
    A. Historic: Pierre Henri Jacques
    B. Historic: Polhonac
    C. Historic: Raymond
    D. Mythic: Tereus
    E. Religious: Venus reduced to an opaquely perceived Mary
VIII. Affirmation of Potentiality: Mary, quickened in the mind, reflects Venus.

one personal pronouns from *Three Cantos I*. He seemed to discriminate carefully between the formal exordium of the poem and the beginning of the action. Apparently he decided that although there was a continued need to maintain the narrator's presence in the action, the exordium ought to be impersonal. Impersonalizing *Three Cantos I* altered its dialectical form and its tone. (2) In *Three Cantos II* and *III* Pound retained all of the major radicals but shortened many of them. By so doing, he increased the importance of pattern vis-à-vis incident. (3) The radicals and the transitions between radicals became more elliptical throughout. Consequently, in many cases one needs the original *Poetry* text to make sense of what appeared in *Lustra*.

I would guess that much of Eliot's criticism concerned the first group of revisions. Pound was always rather ambivalent about the presence of personality in his work. On one hand, he believed that personal satisfaction and personal vision were the foundation stones of art. On the other hand, he believed that it was the job of the artist to transmute personal meanings into objective form that could evoke an emotion from any observer.[5] As we have seen, one of the attractions of the form of *Sordello* was that it was a mask of the self in which images were always used to define consciousness. Eliot, however, during this period was evolving his own theory of impersonality, best known to us from 1919's *Tradition and the Individual Talent*.[6] He would have thought *Three Cantos*, Pound's "reticent autobiography," too personal and too rhetorical. He probably recoiled from *Sordello's* contrived dramatic unity, and argued that Pound's poem be founded in a deeper (and less obvious) emotional unity. In short, he would have argued for the "impersonalization" of the *Cantos*.

Pound accepted Eliot's "criticism" because he himself was becoming aware of a fundamental disjunction in *Three Cantos I*. Because of his ambivalence about the presence of an individualized voice, his narrator's vacillation about poetic principles had been at odds with the certitude of the same narrator's eye-witnessings: "The place is full of spirits." "Gods float in the azure air." Pound reduced his narrator's

[5] For Pound's most lucid expression of this ambivalence, see G-B, pp. 84-86.

[6] Even before *Tradition and the Individual Talent* Eliot had expressed his dislike of an author's including himself in his poetry. In Eliot's review of Yeats's *The Cutting of an Agate* (in *The Athenaeum* for July 4, 1919), he disapproved especially of a statement of Yeats's that resembled Pound's standard definition of myth: "The end of art is the ecstasy awakened by the presence before an ever-changing mind of what is permanent in the world, or by the arousing of that mind itself into the very delicate and fastidious mood habitual with it when it is seeking those permanent and recurring things." Eliot's reaction was, "Why introduce the mind? why not say—the recognition of the permanent in the changing, and the recognition of the protean identity of the permanent with the changing?" He went on to call Yeats "extreme in egoism" and "a little crude." Eliot's paraphrase of Yeats's statement is very much the kind of thing Pound did to *Three Cantos* between *Poetry* and *Lustra*.

vacillation, and changed *Three Canto I*'s tone from tentative to assertive. Consider the following passages from *Poetry* and their *Lustra* revisions:

(1) *Poetry*:

(A) Is't worth the evasion, what were the use
    Of setting figures up and breathing life upon them,
    Were't not *our* life, your life, my life extended?
    I walk Verona. (I am here in England.)
    I see Can Grande. (Can see whom you will.)
        You had one whole man?
    And I have many fragments, less worth? Less worth?
    Ah, had you quite my age, quite such a beastly
        and cantankerous age?
    You had some basis, had some set belief.
    Am I let preach? Has it a place in music?

(B) And we will say: What's left for me to do?
    Whom shall I conjure up; who's my Sordello,
    My pre-Daun Chaucer, pre-Boccacio,
        As you have done pre-Dante?
    Whom shall I hang my shimmering garment on;
    Who wear my featherly mantle, *hagoromo*;
    Whom set to dazzle the serious future ages?
    Not Arnaut, not De Born, not Uc St. Circ who has
        writ out the stories.

(2) *Lustra*:

(A) Worth the evasion, the setting figures up
    And breathing life upon them.
    Has it a place in music? And your: "Appear
    Verona"?

(B)   and what's left?
    Pre-Daun-Chaucer, Pre-Boccacio? Not Arnaut,
    Not Uc St. Circ.

Poetry's Canto I was written to depict modern uncertainty, and portrays its narrator deferentially questioning his master. *Lustra*'s narrator, with chopped phrases and a rising voice, displays the curt impatience of a man sure of his ground. (The phrase "Has it a place in music?" was originally prefaced by an apology. The narrator appeared to be departing reluctantly from his master's practice. In *Lustra*, with the apology deleted, the same phrase sounds truculent.) By reducing vacillation, the *Lustra* version gave greater authority to the poem's chief witness. It also made the increased number of elliptical constructions seem less out of place. (One does not expect an impatient voice to spell out every detail.)

The poem became more elliptical as Pound compressed it. His critical touch was usually sharp, but his lapses were responsible for some of *Lustra's* increased obscurity. When Pound refashioned whole radicals, the results were impressive. He altered Canto II's version of Catullus 51, and the new version was denser and more powerful in the proportion it was cut:

> God's peer, yea and the very gods are under him
> Facing thee, near thee; and my tongue is heavy,
> And along my veins the fire; and the night is
> Thrust down upon me.

Pound pared the passage down to the most effective details appropriate to his theme. The speaker's blasphemy (he calls his lover's new paramour god's peer) is now followed immediately by an evocation of the consequences. Pound chiseled away at the externals of Catullus to get at the elements of universal experience. His revised Canto II's St. Antoni section is on the same principle. The *Poetry* version told the St. Antoni story twice—once in Pound's redaction and once using phrases from St. Circ. *Lustra's* version was only half as long, and incorporated the St. Circ citations without fanfare into the telling. *Lustra's* Canto II, with "St. Antoni" and "Catullus" the size of its other radicals, became more obviously a fashioned whole. That is, no section was long enough to distract attention from the whole to its parts.

We can see the unfortunate side of Pound's compressions in those lines in which he condensed the narration's argument. To cite just one case among many, when he revised 1-B (above) to 2-B, Pound left the response to "what's left?" unconnected to anything in the revised version. "Not Arnaut" had answered "Whom shall I conjure up?" a question that does not appear in *Lustra*. Having written it out once, Pound assumed that his readers would understand subsequent abbreviation. We can see the same obtuseness at work in the 1923 revisions (see below, pp. 254-55), where Pound left in allusions after he had excised the Cantos that contained their referents. He frequently did the same thing in his prose. Recall, for example, the series of articles on the "prose tradition in verse." Each discussion became more and more gnomic as Pound replaced his first well-reasoned statements with shorthand.

§

The next stage in the revision of *Three Cantos* was the now difficult-to-obtain version published in *The Future* for February, March, and April of 1918.[7] Pound billed the *Future Cantos* as excerpts, but the manner in which he "excerpted" them so resembles the manner in which he later "revised" the same Cantos that it seems likely the deletions were made as much for his satisfaction as for the demands of space. The *Future Cantos* were the first to acquire the modernistic, demanding brevity that was later to become characteristic of the poem. Pound took advantage of the journal's limited circulation to experiment with minimalizing transitions and excising discursiveness. For instance, *The Future*'s version of *Three Cantos I* eliminated the Canto's beginning and conclusion. Pound threw out *all* of the dramatized vacillation that had seemed so important in 1915-1917. He left only the essentials: the two long appearances of the gods and the image of E. P. stranded in Venice. The reader of "Passages from the opening address in a Long Poem" was left in as

[7] I have reproduced these Cantos in Appendix A.

much darkness about the relevance of *Sordello* as the reader of *A Draft of XVI Cantos*.

"Images from the Second Canto of a Long Poem" left out *Three Cantos II*'s "gestes of war" and its concluding address, reprinting the rest of the poem through the St. Antoni story. *Three Cantos II* had treated "drear waste" vis-à-vis the epic themes of love and war. "Images" limited itself to wasted love. Its four remaining radicals — "Joios," "The Lute Girl," "Catullus," "St. Antoni" — are exposed and forced individually to bear more of the Canto's burden of meaning.[8] "Images" also has an altered movement. *Three Cantos II* was symmetrical. It began with the somberness of Gonzaga's palace in tatters and ended with the death-grip of Ignez and the triumph of bourgeois Holland. The St. Antoni story was the one radical in it that hinted at the possibility of a seed of growth in the "drear waste." (St. Antoni was able to survive the dead convention of the marriage and accept Elis of Montfort's invitations because his troubadour sensibility was too vital to stop growing.) "Images" ended with "St. Antoni's" ambivalence and avoided a tonic resolution. By choosing not to end "Images" with a strong resolution like the Ignez story,[9] Pound was committing himself to a unit less com-

---

[8] That is not to say that the "excerpt" is more effective or successful. True, the "Lute Girl" and "Catullus" stand up remarkably well. In their revised form they glow with such poignant integrity that one thinks of some of the shorter passages of the *Commedia*. Thematically, the Lute Girl is analogous to Francesca, but her brief speech reflects lessons learned from Dante's La Pia, who speaks only seven lines in *Purgatorio* v. Both Pound and Eliot schooled themselves in the possibilities of Dante's capsule treatment of La Pia, and both of them alluded in their master-works to her "Siena mi fè; disfecemi Maremma" —Pound in *Mauberley* and Eliot in *The Waste Land*.

The other radicals do not hold up as well as "The Lute Girl." "St. Antoni," in particular, needs more development to give it substance. "Images" is less than clear, for example, about why the Lady of Pena "dismisses" her husband.

[9] We know that Pound at some stage recognized the Ignez episode as such a resolution because he saved it for a key place in Canto XXX,

plete-in-itself than *Three Cantos II*. He had already begun
to save resolutions for later use, and to emphasize material,
like the troubadour stories,[10] that could point in two directions. "Images" thus represented a significant step in the
Cantos' thickening (and difficulty).

"An Interpolation taken from Third Canto of a Long
Poem" consisted of only a three-line introduction and
Pound's translation of the Nekyia.[11] Aside from the intro-
duction and a few minor revisions,[12] "An Interpolation" had

---

the set piece that concludes *XXX Cantos* and the poem's inferno.
(There is an allusion to "Ignez da Castro murdered" in the present
Canto III, but that reference is a very late edition. It was not included in *A Draft of XVI Cantos*, and seems to have been deliberately
added in *XXX Cantos* to prepare for Canto XXX.)

[10] St. Antoni's story ends with the emptiness of his lady's marriage,
but it is hinted that the troubadour will find satisfaction beyond it. Similar ambivalences are exploited in the troubadour stories in Cantos V and
VI. Canto V shows medieval marriage customs forcing Pierre de Maen-
sac to recreate the Trojan War in order to fulfill his love. Only the
strength of his heart allows him to overcome the times and his own
aggression and keep his Helen. Canto VI, in its original version (Canto
VI as it was published in the *Dial* [August 1921], in *Poems 1918-21*,
and in *A Draft of XVI Cantos*, is not the same Canto as the present
Canto VI. The original ended with "who sheds such light in the air."
That is, it did not include the lines about Sordello, Cairels and Theseus)
ended, like "Images," with the sad and yet promising story of a troubadour lover: Bernart de Ventatour tells us about his affair with the
Lady Ventatour. Like St. Antoni, he was forced by the circumjacent
stupidity of the time to abandon his love, but he lived on to love again
and exercise the compassion created by his clarified affection.

[11] The introduction was:

I've strained my ear for *-ensa*, *-ombra*, and *-ensa*,
And cracked my wit on delicate canzoni.
                    Here's but rough meaning:
And then went down. . . .

[12] "An Interpolation" retained Odysseus' three attempts to seize
Anticlea, Pound's catalogue of women, a gloss for Divus ("plucked
from a Paris stall"), and a judgment on the value of the Cretan's
language ("florid mellow phrase"). All of these details were excised
in Canto I. The catalogue of women may well have been judged ex-
pendable in the summer of 1923 (when Slatin believes the order to

already taken on the form of revised Canto I. The critics will have to deal with the earliness of that transformation. A double significance has always been placed on the 1923 revision, which singled out the Nekyia and placed it at the very beginning of the *Cantos*. It has been said that Pound's repositioning announced his intention to allow the poem's personages to supersede his narrator, to stand as objective representatives of a journey that would have no more general type.

It has also been said that the repositioning declared Pound's intention to make Odysseus the premiere persona and to use the *Odyssey* as a scaffold for his poem. The fact that Pound highlighted Odysseus in early 1918 calls those contentions into question. Pound apparently did decide to give his personae more importance vis-à-vis the narrator, but at an early and fluid stage of revision, and certainly without the intention of displacing the one by the others. The date of the revision argues that Pound began to "objectify" his poem without the benefit of *The Waste Land* or much of *Ulysses*,[13] and that his "objectivity" is not to be equated with theirs. The contention that Pound's revision indicated a post-*Ulysses* decision to use the *Odyssey* as a scaffold may have to be scrapped.

Odysseus was important from the start, and "An Interpolation" argues that Pound began to revalue the *Odyssey* even before he knew the structure of *Ulysses*.[14] Pound had from the beginning seen Odysseus as one analogue of his drifting protagonist. Shifting the Nekyia to a more prominent place did not indicate an architectural decision so much as a change in his judgment about the comparative effectiveness of his characters. "An Interpolation" indicates that Pound in 1918 understood that the image of Odysseus would carry more weight than he first supposed, and that the Nekyia was more powerful alone. In 1923 when he shifted the Nekyia

---

have been changed) because Tyro was one of the women treated by Canto II (originally Canto VIII).

[13] See below, pp. 194-97.   [14] See below, pp. 194-95.

to Canto I, he merely re-affirmed that judgment. He was not oblivious to Joyce, but his major conceptual decisions were made before *Ulysses*. The economy of the *Future Cantos*, however, argues that Pound was in early 1918 already reacting to Joyce's technique.

In most cases it would be naive to inquire what happened to an author between time A and time B to cause him to change his mind about a version of his work. The answer nine times out of ten will only be that he reread it in a different mood. Such a rereading is a private, inaccessible event. It may indeed be naive to ask why Pound so radically revised *Three Cantos* only three months after their once-polished appearance in *Lustra*. There is, however, an event concurrent with the revision that is so striking that one must say the two either form a causal sequence or an amazing coincidence. Between October 1917 and January 1918 Pound received the opening chapters of *Ulysses*.

§

Pound had been vaguely aware of Joyce's project as early as August 1916. At that time he wrote Joyce to ask whether a prospective publisher for *Portrait* might be able to inspect "the Sequel" within a reasonable time (P/J, p. 78). He knew not only that Stephen would be involved but that the *Odyssey* would be a major pattern, for he wrote in the same letter "How much of *Ulysses* is done?" (p. 79). There are several references to the Odyssean character of Joyce's work in progress in the letters during the year following,[15] but Pound gave no indication that he was aware of the radical donation Joyce was preparing. Joyce wrote in April 1917 that the only thing that he might be able to offer for immediate publication "would be the Hamlet chapter, or part of it" (p. 105), but we have no way of knowing whether descriptions of the chapter had been given.[16] The only thing we may guess with any

[15] See P/J, pp. 85, 93, 104.

[16] The pair never met until June 1920 at Sirmione (P/J, pp. 177-178). Any knowledge Pound had must have been by letters that are not now available.

certainty is that Pound had some idea of the bulk of the novel. He wrote in April 1917 that he hoped the format of the *Little Review* would be "big enough to hold *Ulysses*" (p. 111). There is no question of his having anything like full understanding of Joyce's intentions. Pound was quite bowled over by "Telemachus" and again by "Calypso," and as late as November 1918, at which time the *Little Review* had published chapters of the novel through "Aeolus," he was still able to write: "Has 'Ulysses' 24 Odyssean books? I don't want to ask silly questions, and I hope it continues forever, but people are continually asking ME about it and about. Fortunately my ignorance of Bloom's future is complete." (p. 146)

We know only two details of Pound's first reaction to "Telemachus,"[17] but the details are telling. Pound filtered his reading through judgment founded on comparable masterworks, and made two revealing juxtapositions: In the letter to Joyce (dated December 19, 1917) that confirmed his reception of the manuscript, he wrote: "In one or two places your actual writing suggests De Gourmont to me. I say this neither as praise nor the reverse" (P/J, p. 128). In the note that accompanied the chapter to Margaret Anderson, he wrote: "It is certainly worth running a magazine if one can get stuff like this to put in it. Compression, intensity. It looks to me rather better than Flaubert" (P/J, p. 130).

Chapter Four discussed the extent and diversity of Pound's debt to Gourmont. A reading of Gourmont had started him searching for new poetic techniques with which to convey "a feeling for the reality of the speaker" of a poem. At first, he attempted to portray the speaker of *Three Cantos* by the

---

[17] Read (P/J, pp. 128-129) claims that Pound's December 19, 1917 letter was in response to "the first chapters" of *Ulysses* and that he sent on "the first two episodes" to Margaret Anderson. However, Pound speaks in the letter only about "Telemachus" (he announces his intention to subdivide the seventeen pages into three parts), and Anderson (in the *Little Review Anthology*, p. 175) claims that she received the "first three instalments," indicating that she too at first only got "Telemachus." How much Pound saw in December is important vis-à-vis the relation of *The Future* excerpts to *Ulysses*.

device of dramatizing internal conflict. In *Three Cantos I* he rendered the complexity of his narrator by presenting the narrator's "doubts" in dialogue form. After he read Eliot and then Laforgue,[18] however, Pound realized that he could satisfy Gourmont's imperative by depicting sensibility with the nuances of a speaking voice. It is not surprising that he saw Gourmont in the suppleness of Stephen's internal monologue. Joyce's skill at rendering sensibility, though, did not affect the way Pound altered *Lustra's Canto I.* The revisions that produced the *Future* excerpts were concerned with arrangement rather than voice. There is, I believe, enough indication in the nature of Pound's comparison of Joyce with Flaubert to explain the excerpted *Cantos.*

Before and after December 1917 Pound related Joyce to Flaubert primarily in terms of "realism,"[19] but his gut reaction to "Telemachus" was to emphasize its "compression, intensity." Once again Joyce's writing seemed to be valuable because of its emulation of Flaubert's "prose tradition," which was "constatation of fact. It presents. It does not comment."[20] Telemachus' "constatation," its refusal to explain, was so uncompromising that Pound was shocked into uncharacteristic brevity. He did not amplify his description until his next letter to Joyce (in March, after "Calypso" had arrived), where he made a first gesture at explaining what would be one staple of his permanent attitude toward *Ulysses.* He wrote that the novel achieved its compression by the

[18] See Chapter Four. Pound's essays "T. S. Eliot" and "Irony, Laforgue, and Some Satire," both of which bear on his view of Gourmont, were published in August and November of 1917.

[19] In "Meditatio" (March 1916), "At Last the Novel Appears" (February 1917), and in "Joyce" (May 1918), Pound centered his advocacy of Joyce around the Goncourts' preface to *Germinie Lacerteux,* which Pound said "states the case and the whole case for realism" (P/J, p. 140).

[20] See above, Chapter Four, pp. 144-46. The citation is from the *Approach to Paris* (1913) articles. Many years later, Pound wrote to René Taupin that he valued Flaubert for "mot juste, présentation ou constatation" (L, p. 218). See also De Nagy, who devotes an entire chapter to Flaubert in *The Critical Decade.*

technique of juxtaposed *contrast*: "The contrast between Bloom's interior poetry and his outward surroundings is excellent" (P/J, p. 131).

A month later, in a *Future* article entitled "Joyce," Pound polished this aperçu for inclusion in his critical armory. This time, he underlined the relation between constatation and compression by calling attention to Joyce's "swift" comparison: "On almost every page of Joyce you will find just such swift alternation of subjective beauty and external shabbiness, squalor, and sordidness. It is the bass and treble of his method" (P/J, p. 135). Swift comparison, intense compression, uncompromising constatation were the things that most impressed Pound. If we assume that we can read the amplifications of a few months later back into December (usually a valid approach with Pound, for he almost invariably worked by making strong immediate impressions and then reworking them), it is not unreasonable to conclude that "Telemachus" made him feel uncomfortable with the diffuseness of the *Lustra Cantos*. The swift alternations of "Telemachus" compressed it by permitting simple juxtapositions to define their own comparisons. When Pound applied Joyce's method to *Lustra*'s *Canto I*, it emerged in *The Future* as a swift alternation of the shabbiness of Pound's external circumstance with the splendor of his imagination. Suddenly, long explanatory passages no longer seemed necessary and were cut. *The Future* excerpts were a first stab at increasing the level of "compression" of the Cantos to come.

§

Pound's revisions from *Poetry* to *Lustra* to *The Future* have suggested that the new objectivity and the so-called ideogrammic structure of Canto IV can in fact be accounted for by the slow adjustments Pound was making as *Three Cantos* developed. Perhaps I should summarize that development while I fill in a few facts that will continue the history of the *Cantos* from early 1918 to autumn 1919.

In 1915, heavily under the influence of *Sordello*, Pound

created for Canto I a highly visible narrator because he believed that epic truth must be founded in an individual perspective, and because he was convinced that the best way to portray that perspective was to present the internal dialogue of a divided mind. During 1917, Gourmont, Eliot, and Laforgue convinced him that a sensibility could be implied without resorting to dialogue. When the first polished version of *Three Cantos* was published in *Poetry*, Pound was struck by the what now seemed inordinate attention the narrator called upon himself. He changed the poem for *Lustra*, but not radically enough—much of Cantos I and III still retained the discursiveness that originally functioned to render the illusion of a mind-in-question. "Telemachus" made Pound uncomfortably aware of what now was only stuffing, and he improvised three dramatically compressed "excerpts." Still, the excerpts were too rough to replace the original Cantos. Pound was uncertain. He allowed the *Lustra* versions to be reprinted without change in *Quia Pauper Amavi* (October 1919), but he did not publish Canto IV which (he had written his father)[21] was already composed. He continued to work on Canto IV during 1917-1919, at the same time that he was working on *Propertius* and annotating Eliot's new poetry. He finally published Canto IV in October 1919 with a level of compression closer to Joyce, a more expressively supple syntax, and some of the allusive devices of Eliot. However, Pound did not then intend Canto IV to supersede *Three Cantos*.

There is no question that 1919's Canto IV was written under the assumption that *Three Cantos* would be there to refer to. Canto IV begins where *Three Cantos III* had left off (with the effects of Aphrodite at Troy)[22] and a number of lines allude to the beginning of the poem: "The silver mirrors catch the bright stones and flare" refers back to the god-flare and "burnished mirror" of Canto I. "Choros nym-

[21] See Slatin, p. 185.

[22] For a discussion of Troy's place in the *Cantos* (tragedy brought on by blindness), see Chapter Six.

pharum, goat-foot with pale foot alternate" refers back to
Canto II's "There came a centaur, spying the land, / And
there were nymphs beside him." "In the sea foam" catches
the description of Aphrodite which ended Canto III ("light
on the foam, breathed on by zephyrs"). Further on in Canto
IV, "Thus the light rains, thus pours, *e lo soleils plovil*"
depends upon the *"Lo soleils plovil"* passage in Canto I for
clarification. Canto II's "ply over ply" reappears as a tag,
indicating that Pound is counting on an already established
meaning. "Brook film bearing white petals" alludes to the
Noh passage in Canto I, making the sudden appearance of
the pines of Takasago not at all puzzling. "The scarlet
flower is cast on the blanch white stone" parallels Canto II's
"The rose leaf casts her dew on the ringing glass." ("Scarlet
. . . stone" is another 'transducer' metaphor describing the
transfer of form from one medium to another.) "The Peach-
trees . . . no whiter" restates Canto I's lines describing the
same stream, the same rafters, the same gray stone posts.
"Spanish poppies," in the next line, look back to Canto I's
poppies, manifestations of the gods which made the "small
cobbles flare." The final conflation of the Virgin with Venus
is prepared for by wound trellises, which allude to Viscount
St. Antoni's song of Venus.

And yet, although Canto IV was tied thematically to *Three
Cantos*, and although it made no real structural departures,
it did originate the style of the Cantos that followed. *Three
Cantos II* and Canto IV, despite their structural similarities,
are written in two completely different manners. Compare
the opening of both Cantos:

(1) *Three Cantos II*:
  Leave Casella.
 Send out your thought upon the Mantuan palace —
 Drear waste, great halls,
 Silk tatters still in the frame, Gonzaga's splendor
 Alight with phantoms! What have we of them,
 Or much or little?

> Where do we come upon the ancient people?
> "All that I know is that a certain star" —
> All that I know of one, Joios, Tolosan,
> Is that in middle May, going along
> A scarce discerned path, turning aside,
> In level poplar lands, he found a flower, and wept.
> "Y a la primera flor," he wrote,
> "Qu'ieu trobei, tornei em plor."

(2) Canto IV:

> Palace in smoky light,
> Troy but a heap of smouldering boundary stones,
> ANAXIFORMINGES! Aurunculeia!
> Hear me. Cadmus of Golden Prows;
> The silver mirrors catch the bright stones and flare.

Three Cantos II describes. Canto IV presents. If (1) were rewritten in the structural idiom of (2), it would look something like this:

(3)   Palace in phantom splendour,
> Mantua, great halls, silk tatters still in the frame,
> All that I know. Joios.
> Y *a la primera flor*
> Qu'ieu trobei, tornei em plor.

My pastiche (3) should suggest that, under the surface, *Three Cantos II* and Canto IV are very much alike. *Three Cantos II* and Canto IV both treat the theme of "drear waste," but in Canto IV Pound, imitating Joyce, has learned to leave out rhetorical questions. In (1) the question "Where do we come upon the ancient people?" is an implicit response to the emptiness of the palace. Joios, Arnaut, Dolmetsch are Canto II's answer to that question. In Canto IV, the urgency of "ANAXIFORMINGES! . . ." implies such a question, "*ubi sunt?*" The following lines provide an answer by presenting the ancient people (the gods). Compare the similar demands of the opening of the "Proteus" chapter of *Ulysses,* which Pound would have known eighteen months previously:

INELUCTABLE MODALITY OF THE VISIBLE:
AT LEAST THAT IF NO more, thought through my
eyes. Signatures of all things I am here to read, seaspawn
and seawrack, the nearing tide, that rusty boot. Snotgreen,
bluesilver, rust: coloured signs. Limits of the diaphane.
But he adds: in bodies. Then he was aware of them bodies
before of them coloured. How? By knocking his sconce
against them, sure. Go easy. Bald he was and a millionaire,
maestro di color che sanno. Limit of the diaphane in.
Why in? Diaphane, adiaphane. If you can put your five
fingers through it, it is a gate, if not a door. Shut your
eyes and see.

Our great advantage with the Joyce passage is that we
know that behind it is Stephen, thinking. At the time Canto
IV was written, however, Pound might have reasonably assumed that his readers would be aware that the lines had a
speaker (the narrator depicted by Canto I). There are some
ambiguities, it is true. We do not know, for one, the exact
provenance of line three. It may be the speaker quoting, or
the speaker pretending to take on the identity of whoever
originally said these strange words. Or it may be that the
words are rising before him, startling him as well as us. Similarly, we do not know in line four whether the speaker is
addressing Cadmus or pretending for a moment to be Cadmus. (If the latter is true, then ending line four with a semi-
colon rather than a period makes sense.[23] If the speaker had
willed himself into Cadmus' mind, he might see the wonders
of the choros nympharum.)

On the other hand, what did the first readers make out of
Proteus? "Ineluctable . . ." is in English rather than trans-
literated Greek, of course, but would it have been more recognizable as a significant, serious citation? The identification
of "he" as Aristotle is never explicitly made. (Those readers
who recognized the Italian would remember Dante's tribute

[23] The *New Directions* text slides over the punctuation with an exclamation mark.

to Aristotle in Inferno IV.) The question *behind* the paragraph (roughly: "how" are the forms of things) controls both paragraph one and the entire chapter, but it is never made explicit.

By the time he wrote Canto IV, "Proteus" had also reinforced Pound's perception that Joyce's narrative intonations resembled Gourmont's and James's. Joyce, too, desired to render subjectivity by dramatic nuance rather than by a retrospective chronicle of thoughts. If the reader will recall Chapter Four, in which I presented the Jamesian-Gourmontian context of *Propertius*, he will remember that paragraph of *Indiscretions* in which Pound wrote: "we having long since passed the stage when 'man sees horse' or 'farmer sows rice,' can in simple ideographic record be said to display anything remotely resembling our subjectivity." Since Canto IV intends precisely to display the complex subjectivity of a mind, the background behind the *Indiscretions* passage is particularly relevant here. At the risk of being redundant, I wish to recapitulate some of that development. It should, I believe, help to explain why the syntax of Canto IV is so different from that of *Three Cantos II*. Pound's gradual understanding of James involved a growing comprehension that the rendering of psychic movement is bound to variations in syntax. Ways of speaking imply ways of thinking.

The changes in Pound's intentions and techniques from *Three Cantos* to Canto IV can be demonstrated by the following three citations—one from *Three Cantos*, a second from *Cathay*,[24] and a third from Canto IV:

(A)   And the clouds bow above the lake, and there are
            folk upon them
      Going their windy ways, moving by Riva,
      By the western shore, far as Lonato,
      And the water is full of silvery almond-white swimmers.
                              — *Three Cantos I* (1915-1917)

[24] Actually from the expanded *Cathay* presented in *Lustra*.

(B) The clouds have gathered, and gathered,
        and the rain falls and falls,
     The eight ply of the heavens
        are all folded into one darkness,
     And the wide, flat road stretches out.
     I stop in my room toward the East, quiet, quiet,
     I pat my new cask of wine.
     My friends are estranged, or far distant,
     I bow my head and stand still.
                    — To-Em-Mei's "The Unmoving Cloud"
                         (first published June 1916)

(C)   Beneath it, beneath it
     Not a ray, not a slivver, not a spare disk of sunlight
     Flaking the black, soft water;
     Bathing the body of nymphs, of nymphs, and Diana,
     Nymphs, white-gathered about her, and the air, air,
     Shaking, air alight with the goddess,
                         fanning their hair in the dark,
     Lifting, lifting and waffing:
     Ivory dipping in silver,
                    Shadow'd, o'ershadow'd
     Ivory dipping in silver,
     Not a splotch, not a lost shatter of sunlight.
                    — Canto IV
                    (published October 1919)

Three Cantos and Canto IV are controlled by different
poetics. The lines from Three Cantos I describe externals
and depend on the suggestive qualities of substantives and
rhythms to suggest symbolist resonance. Canto IV functions
in a different manner. It intends, in the manner of James,
to render working consciousness. Canto IV records a "seeing"
of the events of Three Cantos I in the instant those events
are being registered by an emotional reflector. The rhythms
and repetitions of Canto IV do not describe or suggest the
reality of objects. Canto IV's "art" structures a mental event

203

by rendering the sequence and impact of perception upon consciousness. *Three Cantos I* told us that there were folk upon the lake. Canto IV renders the experience of confronting a goddess.

Cathay marked a turning point on the road from the early to the later Cantos. The poems of *Cathay* experiment with the way alterations in simple sentences can register the mood of a speaker, and the way images objectify a speaker's feelings. "The Unmoving Cloud" uses simple transitive sentences, but artfully underlines the emotional reality behind them. Repetitions, graphically indicated pauses, and long vowels emphasize oppressive, extended awareness of "The Unmoving Cloud's" images of loneliness.[25] The poem, in fact, demonstrates how effective simple sentences can be. And yet its syntax was not adequate for Canto IV, which was intended to present myth just coming into experience. The style of *Cathay* is understatement. It is a style of small poignancies and sane understandings. It is not a style suited for the shimmering reverences that Canto IV demanded.

By 1919 Pound was beginning to revise his first understanding of Fenollosa's *Chinese Written Character* to accommodate these demands. We have already seen that he wrote in 1920 that Fenollosa's syntax was inadequate to render complex subjectivity. Chapter Four demonstrated that in the *Little Review* text of *The Chinese Written Character* Pound modified Fenollosa's prescriptions by extending approval of literary constructions to gerund constructions. In the same year Pound was praising Aeschylus for his "agglutinative" syntax, which permitted the playwright to indicate the particulars of complex remembrances. A new appreciation of James was behind his comments on both Fenollosa and Aeschylus. James's parentheses (as Pound later wrote) reveal the layers of a man's mind. The long involuted periods of James's late style are able to contain the complex reference of Aeschylus' Greek while they absorb the "activity" of count-

[25] See Kenner's discussion in *The Pound Era*, pp. 207-216.

less verbs. In other words, James's style can render both the complexity and vitality of consciousness. Canto IV was the first of the Cantos to exploit the possibilities of James's syntax. By then Pound had also discovered that Jamesian constructions lent themselves to trochaic rhythms and an elegiac mood. In a real sense, then, Canto IV defined the narrative and metrical pattern of the later Cantos.

We must be careful, however, not to overemphasize Canto IV as *the* turning point in the evolution of the *Cantos*. For one thing, although Canto IV incorporated some of the narrative experiments of *Propertius*, it did not assimilate *Propertius'* tonal range. Canto IV's voice is more flexible than the terse, no-nonsense idiom of *Three Cantos II*, but Pound was unwilling in 1919 to utilize Laforguian ironies. It was not, as we shall see in a few moments, until 1922 that he made any major change in the poem's decorum. Canto IV wished only to recreate the amazed and wondrous voice of Dante — the hushed witness of awesome events and significant loss.

Canto IV is transitional in yet another way. Although a typical reviewer of *Three Cantos* wrote that a "reader feels he has passed no mild literary examination if he can instantly catch every literary allusion," there are no allusions in *Three Cantos* so nude and significant as Canto IV's "ANAXIFORMINGES! Aurunculeia!" Canto IV continued to "communicate" through the musical development of motif typical of *Three Cantos*, but it also began to rely on allusion. I attribute the beginnings of what would become a pillar of the Cantos' style to Pound's association in 1917-1919 with T. S. Eliot, a subject that now must be considered in earnest.

§

Eliot, and not Pound, was the first to publicly endorse the literary value of *Ulysses'* allusiveness. Pound's early remarks are directed either at *Ulysses'* "compression" or its "realism." Only a few months after he received "Telemachus," however, Eliot saw something more. In a mid-1918 review of

Pound's poetry, he pointed out the differences between *Ulysses* and *Three Cantos*:

> James Joyce, another very learned literary artist, uses allusions suddenly and with great speed, part of the effect being the extent of the vista opened to the imagination by the very lightest touch. Pound's recent unfinished epic, three cantos of which appear in the American edition of "Lustra," proceeds by a very different method than that of Joyce in "Ulysses." In appearance, it is a rag-bag of Mr. Pound's reading. . . . And yet the thing has, after one has read it once or twice, a positive coherence; it is an objective and reticent autobiography.[26]

A few months later, Eliot put his observations to practical use. Whereas his earlier poems had made use of local allusions (one thinks of *Prufrock*'s references to John the Baptist or Lazarus) the poems of 1918 began to use allusions systematically to contrast the values of different cultural periods. "Sweeney Among the Nightingales," for instance, began and ended with allusions to Aeschylus' *Agamemnon*. The allusions permitted Eliot to present Sweeney to the imagination against the "vista" of the violence of another era. Joyce's allusiveness allowed him to control contemporary and exotic material, and Eliot was convinced that the increased range of his new poems signaled a growing improvement. He later wrote his brother, "Some of the new poems, the Sweeney one's, especially "Among the Nightingales" and "Burbank," are intensely serious, and I think these two are among the best that I have ever done."[27] Joyce's donation changed what would have otherwise been rather trivial experiments in Laforguian verbal preciosity and Gautiesque rhyming into powerful poems whose ambiguous juxtaposition of era upon

[26] From "A Note on Ezra Pound," *To-Day*, IV, 19 (September 1918), pp. 6-7.

[27] Eliot's letter is quoted in *The Waste Land: A Facsimile and Transcript of the Original Drafts Including the Annotations of Ezra Pound*, ed. Valerie Eliot (New York, 1971), p. xviii.

era compel the imagination. It is hard to imagine Pound, who was committed to innovation, not taking Eliot's critical comparison between *Three Cantos* and *Ulysses* as something of a rebuke, and "Sweeney Among the Nightingales" as something of a challenge. Pound had already attempted to present the ply over ply of history, and he would have been impressed by the effects and economy that Joyce and Eliot achieved. The allusions in Cantos IV through VII were the fruit of his impressions. In fact, the whole provenance of those Cantos exists in the relationship, sometimes master-student and sometimes the reverse, between Pound and Eliot in the years 1917-1919.

In April 1917, Eliot, who had been despondent about his recent unproductiveness, wrote a few poems in French and asked Pound to look them over.[28] Pound corrected Eliot's French, and discussion about the poems led to that now famous conversation in which Pound and Eliot plotted a change in the course of modern poetry through the agency of Gautier and the Bay State Hymn Book.[29] In May, Pound persuaded Harriet Shaw Weaver to allow Eliot to replace the mobilized Richard Aldington as assistant editor of *The Egoist*. Eliot returned the favor by writing, sometime before September 1917, *Ezra Pound: His Metric and Poetry*. Both Pound and Eliot used their journalism to push the other's hobby-horses. As Herbert Schneidau noticed:

> The two kept their heads together: Eliot expands a Pound attack on the amateur spirit in letters, Pound then quotes Eliot; Eliot conducts a symposium in the *Egoist* on Henry James, to which Pound is a major contributor, and eight months later Pound conducts one in the *Little Review* to which Eliot is a major contributor; Pound exposes

[28] See Donald Gallup, *T. S. Eliot & Ezra Pound: Collaborators in Letters* (New Haven, 1970), p. 10; and P/J, p. 112. The latter fixes the date of Eliot's French poems.

[29] See Pound's obituary of Harold Monro in *The Criterion*, XI, 45 (July 1932), p. 590.

in print an infamous section of the U.S. Penal Code relating to importation of "obscene" literature, and within the month Eliot prints it too.[30]

Eliot even wrote a parody in the manner of Bouvard et Pécuchet about their collaboration: *Eeldrop and Appleplex*, which was published in the *Little Review* (September 1917), and makes gentle fun of two litterateurs temperamentally like Pound and Eliot.

By late 1917 Eliot began to write again in English, and despite bouts of depression was able to continue writing poetry until late 1919. The resulting poems, which were eventually to be collected in *Poems, 1920*, were submitted to Pound for his opinion and suggestions. Evidence remains of this collaboration whereby we may reconstruct some of it. Pound's annotations of poems, including "Sweeney Among the Nightingales" as well as "Whispers of Immortality," "Mr. Eliot's Sunday Morning Service," "Sweeney Erect," "Burbank," and (the last to be written) "Gerontion," were preserved on the original typescripts and are now available in the Berg Collection of the New York Public Library.

These manuscripts argue that Pound was intimately aware of Eliot's developing use of allusions. He at first quietly admired Eliot's new device while he was energetically and rigorously hammering Eliot's technique into Gautier-like hardness. The manuscripts Eliot submitted to Pound, with the exception of "Whispers of Immortality," were meant to be near-finished poems. In case after case, Eliot had taken pains to find the right phrase and rhyme, but had neglected the syntactical skeleton of his poems. Pound, relying on the expertise of *Cathay*, changed weak verbs to strong ones, inserted verbs where Eliot had merely improvised syntax, changed "X-of-Y" possessives to their tighter "Y's X" form, and eliminated extraneous words. Under Pound's eye, the poems changed from the flawed work of a gifted beginner to

[30] See Herbert Schneidau, "Vorticism and the Career of Ezra Pound," *Modern Philology*, 65, 3 (February 1968), p. 224.

poetry where no word was extraneous. Given their intended cacophony, the poems needed lucid syntax to hold them together. Pound provided it, and admonished Eliot to train himself in syntactic simplicity. In the one case where Eliot needed real help, "Whispers of Immortality," Pound inked out several of the original stanzas and recommended that new ones be built around several strong lines. He recognized the hard beauty especially of "Who found no substitute for sense," and insisted that Eliot retain the line when subsequent drafts tried to do without it.

The summer of 1919 was the high point of their collaboration. Pound whisked Eliot off for a rest in August 1919 to Périgord, where Eliot visited the cave paintings and Pound the ruins at Montsegur.[31] While they were there Pound received the manuscript for "Sirens,"[32] and *Ulysses* probably was very much a subject of conversation, as it had been for eighteen months before that. (Eliot had recently written about "Scylla and Charybdis," "I have lived on it ever since I read it.")[33] Circumstantial evidence — their mid-year journalism and poetry — suggests that the discussion of *Ulysses* centered around the subjects of history and tradition.

Eliot was preoccupied with the subject of tradition throughout 1919[34] and had made it the focus for "Gerontion," which was written sometime during the summer of that year.[35]

[31] See Stock's *Life*, p. 224; Kenner's *Pound Era*, p. 30; and Gallup, p. 14.

[32] See Stock's *Life*, pp. 224-225.

[33] See R. A. Day's "Joyce's Waste Land and Eliot's Unknown God" in *Literary Monographs*, Vol. 4, ed. Eric Rothstein (Madison, 1971), p. 180.

[34] The first part of *Tradition and the Individual Talent* was published in *The Egoist* in September 1919. A. Walton Litz speculates on how Eliot fit *Ulysses* into his idea of tradition in "Pound and Eliot on Ulysses: The Critical Tradition," *James Joyce Quarterly*, x, 1 (Fall 1972), p. 15.

[35] Eliot sent "Gerontion" to John Quinn on September 29, 1919, to be added to the Knopf edition of his poems. See B. L. Reid, *John Quinn and His Friends* (New York: Oxford University Press, 1968), p. 405.

The "Nestor" chapter of *Ulysses* stands behind "Gerontion." Eliot proofread "Nestor" for the January-February number of *The Egoist*, and remembered Stephen's cry, "History . . . is a nightmare from which I am trying to awake" (*Ulysses*, p. 34). "Nestor" introduces one movement in the novel: Starting from Stephen's anguished perception of the realistic chaos around him, *Ulysses* slowly and indirectly orders the present by the past. One way of describing *Ulysses* is to chart the reader's historical awareness of Dublin life as it progresses from identification with Stephen's myopia to an understanding achieved by layer upon layer of implied literary and historical parallels. By the end of the novel Stephen has been placed in a tradition. "Gerontion," like *Ulysses*, depicts the alienation of its speaker from the meaning of history. Eliot adapted Joyce by making Gerontion's history Christian teleological history and by figuring alienation in the image of a husband estranged from his wife. Without the order of Christian time, history becomes for Gerontion a marriage without contact—an empty and fruitless shell. "Gerontion" acknowledged its debt to Joyce by alluding to "Nestor": "Vacant shuttles/ Weave the wind" comes from the Book of Job but is quoted in "Nestor" — "For them too history was a tale like any other too often heard . . . Weave, weaver of the wind" (*Ulysses*, p. 25).

Pound read and annotated "Gerontion" before September. His advice, which Eliot never followed, is indicative of the type of revision Canto IV had undergone. He bracketed two kinds of words for excision: (1) weak modifiers, and (2) verbs he took to be extraneous either because they were inactive ("is" or "was") or because they were 'unnecessary' repetitions — that is, verbs that Eliot repeated from an earlier line to clarify connections. In every case, the words would not ordinarily be considered extraneous. They were connectives that, if omitted, would have given the lines the appearance of fragmentation. Had Eliot followed Pound's suggestions, "Gerontion" would be less comprehensible than it now is. It would also be more saliently "Poundian," for the suggestions followed principles on which Pound had been revising his own Cantos ever since *Poetry*. The main principle was: never use a word to make the poem easier to read; add words only to particularize sense. The *Lustra Cantos* and Canto IV tend more and more toward appositive constructions, because Pound was becoming convinced that connectives were superfluous forms of indicating mental relationship. The verbs "to be" and "to have" were considered connectives. Had Eliot revised "Gerontion" it would have resembled Cantos IV and V much more than it now does.

In the fall of 1919 Pound was well aware of Eliot's attitudes toward "Nestor" and history. Pound had read "Gerontion," had discussed *Ulysses* with Eliot in France, and had discovered the way Eliot's preoccupation colored his view of the early *Cantos*. In the review of *Quia Pauper Amavi* that Eliot wrote for the *Athenaeum* (October 24, 1919), Eliot wrote about the *Cantos* that "their present importance is . . . as showing what the consummation of Mr. Pound's work could be: a final fusion of all his masks, a final concentration of the entire past upon the present." And, "As the present is no more than the present existence, the present significance, of the entire past, Mr. Pound proceeds by acquiring the entire past." Most of Pound's writing during that fall can be understood as a response to Eliot's theme.

In two articles for *The New Age* for August 1919, Pound lectured on the subject of history with Stephen's *cri de coeur* as his text. "Pastiche . . . The Regional," installments VII and VIII[36] anticipate the themes of Cantos V and VI. Like Eliot, Pound recognized Stephen's position as an example of contemporary misapprehension. "History is not," he wrote, "a dream from which I am trying to awake." Rather, "our apperception" of "a past century" is "correspondingly poorer"

---

[36] The exact references for the two installments are *The New Age*, xxv, 17 (August 21, 1919), p. 284; and *The New Age*, xxv, 18 (August 28, 1919), p. 300. In the above discussion I treat the two as one piece and cite from both.

than our perception of the present because we simplify and
falsify the past until it becomes a lie. Pound related contemporary misunderstandings about history to similarly mistaken etymologies: "an unfamiliar word always tends to be
confounded with and replaced by the familiar. Asparagus
becomes in rural speech 'sparrow grass.' " In order truly to
understand history, the imagination must counteract these
forces of simplification and reconstruct complexity: "Any
historical concept and any sociological deduction from history must assemble a great number of such violently contrasted facts, if it is to be valid. It must not be a simple
paradox, or a simple opposition of two terms." Pound went
on to decry the dogmatic destruction of unpleasant historical
artifacts (reminders), and gave a humble example of one
of his own observations:

> The violence of the Church ultimately profited the
> centralisation of the French monarchy [i.e., the destruction
> of the diverse past aids the forces of conformity and cen-
> tralization].
>
> Richelieu destroyed Beaucaire. Montmorency was taken
> at the altar. Montségur outlasted the treachery against the
> surrendered Albigeois, and was destroyed, I have been
> told, by order of Louis XIV.
>
> If this statement is accurate, the gratitude for the gilded
> chaise-percé should be diminished, seeing that a Can-
> tabrian sun-temple with a Roman superstructure is worth
> a great deal of gilt furniture.

Later on he gave other examples of the complex dynamics
of history:

> Wanting a fair view of a past era, I have sat down with
> a French text-book of history printed in 1862 for the use
> of Catholic schools: "Intrigues Galantes de la Cour de
> France," anonymously printed in Holland in 1694; and
> Zeller and Luchaire's brief reprint of documents contem-

porary with Philippe-Auguste and Louis VIII. Their styles differ, the ex-cathedra statements are inharmonic, but I have found no contradictory statement of facts. The relations between Philippe, Coeur-de-Lion, and the King of Sicily, and their entourages at the start of the crusade in 1191 are as bad as anything in a Henry James novel; the eliminations of the "meagre" historical record have left nothing any simpler than the relations between our friends X., N., and G. Eleanor deserves as much attention as Ninon. But side by side with human and intimate detail one has the constant burning of allegory.

Pound concluded that "Snippets of this kind build up our concept of wrong, of right, of history." At the end of the first article, he made a revealing generalization about the relationship between historiography and civilization: "Liberties as easily acquired have been as easily lost — always for a bribe or a fanaticism." That is, the destruction of historical fact for reasons of cupidity or ideology always destroys liberty. He went on to say that "precedent begins with fratricide" — begins where a prince destroys his brother and covers the evidence for the good of the state.

"The Regional" essays are contemporaneous[37] with Cantos V and VI, for which they provide an admirable gloss. Canto V concerns itself with the difficulty of historical interpretation of two events (fratricides) presented in "snippets" and "contrasted facts." The question that puzzles the questing narrator and his historian guide Varchi is whether the murder of Alessandro by Lorenzaccio is *pia o empia*, righteous or cupidinous. "The Regional" essays put that question in context,[38] and help to explain some of the *Cantos'* secondary

[37] Pound wrote to his father on November 22, 1919, that Cantos V, VI, and VII were finished. See Slatin, p. 188.

[38] A large part of the background to Pound's agonizing over history is, of course, the events of 1919: the postwar disillusion, the economic disaster, Pound's own economic difficulties, the catastrophe of the treaty, the imminence of more senseless violence. Canto V should be properly

detail. According to "The Regional," fratricides in ruling families are luminous details of that kind of inexcusable violence that lends itself to rationalization and leads to falsifying the facts of the past. Although Canto V alludes to Dante, Lorenzaccio is placed in the poem's hell for different reasons than he would have been placed in the *Inferno*. Not for the murder itself,[39] but because Lorenzaccio's act covered up becomes a precedent for lying about history for reasons of state. Canto V lionizes Varchi because he was one "wanting the facts." Lines 100-115 describe Varchi's opposites: The writers Barabello, Mozarello, Francastor, and Cotta, and the General D'Alviano sold out history to authority. They covered or obscured or ignored facts about the death of Giovanni Borgia. They are kindred spirits to Navighero, who burned one of Martial's manuscripts every year and thus destroyed evidence of an alien sensibility by which a later civilization might have liberated itself. Barabello et al. inhabit the same circle of hell ("*Al poco giorno ed al gran cerchio d'ombra*" — at little day and at the great circle of shadow) as Lorenzaccio. They, no less than he, permitted facts to be distorted.

"The Regional's" discussion of Eleanor, Richard, Philippe-Auguste, and the King of Sicily glosses Canto VI, which originally[40] included them all. As does the present Canto VI, the first version recounted the history of Henry II, Louis, and Eleanor. The 1919 version, however, also treated the

---

considered alongside Yeats's "Nineteen Hundred and Nineteen," written in the same year.

[39] For Pound's dislike of abstract condemnation of an action outside its context, see the *Little Review*'s (1919) De Gourmont piece, where Pound wrote: "The relation of two individuals is so complex that no third person can pass judgment upon it. Civilization is individual. The truth is the individual. The light of the Renaissance shines in Varchi when he declines to pass judgment on Lorenzaccio" (LE, p. 355).

[40] The present Canto VI is a considerably altered version of the original, which was first printed in *The Dial* (August 1921), and reprinted in *Poems 1918-21* and in *A Draft of XVI Cantos*. The XVI Cantos version is reproduced in Appendix B.

uneasy alliance of Richard and Philippe-Auguste during the crusade of 1190. It told the story of how King Tancred of Sicily played Richard and Philippe off against each other for his own benefit. Tancred finally informed Richard of Philippe's plotting, and Richard took advantage of the situation to obtain a financially satisfying treaty. Canto VI emphasized that Richard's treaty, as one would expect of an agreement based on belligerence, cupidity, and deceit, was not adhered to for very long.[41] In contrast, the Canto told of another treaty, which might have lasted forever had not respectable Christians intervened:

> And Zion still
> Bleating away to Eastward, the lost lamb,
> Damned city (was only Frederic knew
> The true worth, and patched with Malek Kamel
> The sane and sensible peace to bait the world
> And set all camps disgruntled with all leaders.
> "Damn'd atheists!" alike Mohamet growls,
> And Christ grutches more sullen for Sicilian sense
> Than does Mahound on Malek.)

Frederick II (1194-1250), Holy Roman Emperor, king of Sicily and Jerusalem, a learned ruler over an intellectual court, secured by treaty in 1229 the possession of Jerusalem. He was later roundly condemned by the church for abetting heresy (dealing with the Saracens). He gave the lie to the violence rationalized by generations of Churchmen and Christian monarchs. His presence in Canto VI helps to judge Louis, Henry, Philippe and the rest. Canto VI's emphasis on property settlements in the treaties and on the church's ideologically induced blindness to the value of Saracen culture compel the judgment that Pope and Monarch (as Pound had complained in *The New Age*), destroyed the liberties of civilization "always for a bribe or a fanaticism." They were

[41] Treaties and crusades against the barbarians were topical subjects in 1919.

all save Frederick self-deceivers, and they inhabit a circle of hell that Canto VI momentarily glimpses: "The serpent [Geryon] coils in the crowd."

"Gerontion" and Cantos V and VI were different responses to "Nestor." Based apparently on conversations the two poets had after reading Joyce, they make two different uses of *Ulysses'* treatment of history. Eliot understood the novel's accumulating analogies, and interpreted *Ulysses* as he had interpreted the *Cantos* — as the progressive imposition of knowledge of the past upon an awareness of contemporary chaos. "Gerontion" indicates Eliot's identification with Stephen's anguish, and his understanding of Joyce's analogical technique. Pound, on the other hand, had as little sympathy for Stephen as he did for any other bad student. He was more interested in the techniques by which *Ulysses* "scientifically" constructed history — the way it provided snippets of the concrete moment and only gradually made history out of contradictions. The new direction of Cantos V and VI concerns the manner in which discrete moments build accurate history as well as genuine art.

Once we have recognized that there were differences between "Gerontion" (Summer 1919) and Cantos V and VI (November 1919), we must come to terms with their resemblance, and with the possibility of influence. Consider, if you will, the character of Gerontion. For Eliot, he was one more member of a series that includes Prufrock and the speaker of "Mr. Apollinax." Gerontion loses his will, is unable to affect the future, and can only nervously speculate about what is going to happen to him. (The original manuscript contained an epigraph alluding to Fra Alberigo in *Inferno* xxxiii, whose soul was snatched from his body even before death, and who waits for his physical death with what we may call a sense of alienation.) Gerontion expends considerable effort at prognostication, even though he realizes he has not the acuteness to pierce the future. Ironically, Eliot quotes from Matthew ("We would see a sign") with the implication that the sign has come and gone and Geron-

tion has not the will to act upon it. He is a figure equivalent
to Canto V's Alessandro whose fate was:

> dreamed out beforehand
> In Perugia, caught in the star-maze by Del Carmine,
> Cast on a natal paper, set with an exegesis, told,
> All told to Alessandro, told thrice over,
> Who held his death for a doom.
> In abuleia.

Alessandro is the central figure of Cantos V-VII, which
were published as a unit in *The Dial* in August 1921. These
Cantos confront the questing narrator with the temptation
to accept passively the evil conditions of the world. Cantos
V-VII present history as a riddle: these are the puzzling facts;
you must choose whether to accept their traditional explanations, and be damned; or deduce your own explanation,
which might lead you out of the inferno or might get you
inexorably lost. On one hand is Alessandro, who accepted
"his death for a doom"; on the other hand, Varchi, who
spent "no mean labour" wrestling with the facts, and Frederic, and "the live man" who "*shakes* the dry pods,/ *Probes*
for old wills and friendships,"[42] and Lorenzaccio.

---

[42] For Pound the energy needed to maintain civilization comes out
of the individual's insistence on making up his own mind about the
truth, based on his own experience. It is the same energy, and the same
informing activity with which the individual shapes his language. Consider one more citation from "Pastiche: The Regional . . . VIII," and
notice how certain Pound is of the continuity of apparently dissimilar
paragraphs.

"Ideas suffer . . . battering into the mould of current cliché. Not
only 'in the hands of' (read: under the typewriter keys of) deliberate
cheats, liars, persons of ill-will, persons careless of the subject which
they treat with the sole hope of personal aggrandizement (read: cash,
the glitter of 'getting an article into'), but also in the mouths of people
of good-will, people hurried, people tired, in fact of all people who
have not just that superabundance of energy which is needed to acquire
style or a sense of style in others, ideas suffer this steady attrition.

"I am not trying to give birth to Nietzsche's "Ring of Recurrence"
nor to Machiavelli's circle (poverty-labour-strength-riches-idleness-corrup-

217

As the prelude that links Canto V back to Canto IV fades, we are presented with two images of eternity — the celestial Nile and Iamblichus' light. In the manner of Dante and of the early Cantos, they remain unexplained. What first crystallizes is the narrator in situation. He images the "ciocco"[43] of *Paradiso* xviii, 100. In that Canto, which transpires in Jupiter, the circle of just rulers, lambent angels spell out to Dante the phrase "Diligite Iusticiam Qui Iudicatis Terram" — love justice, ye that judge the earth. Dante begins to see sparks arising from the all-important final M (Monarchia, out of which order comes), and gasps to see the sparks form the eagle of Jupiter:

> Then, as when burning logs [*ciocchi*] are struck rise innumerable sparks, from which the foolish are accustomed to make auguries, so more than a thousand lights appeared to rise again from there and to mount, some much, some little, as the Sun that kindles them appointed; and when each had settled in its place I saw the head and neck of an eagle represented in that pricked-out fire.

Dante's *ciocchi* simile presents an ambivalent view of auguries. Reading the meaning of such sparks on earth would be only "foolish," but in Paradise the sparks tell truth. So, in Canto V, the speaking voice, remembering the *ciocchi*, approaches images of light with some skepticism. Fire or fire? We overhear him pondering as we overheard Gerontion questioning his own power:

> Air, fire, the pale soft light.
> Topaz I manage, and three sorts of blue;
>   but on the barb of time.

---

tion-discord-war-devastation-poverty-etc.); both these concepts have been perfectly well born already, and there is no use my trying to carry them through any further and supererogatory parturition."

[43] In *The New Age*, xvi, 15 (February 11, 1915), p. 415, Pound called Dante's "brand struck on the hearth" an exact image "to present some visionary apparition in his Paradise."

The fire? always, and the vision always,
Ear dull, perhaps, with the vision, flitting
And fading at will.

The narrator's shaken confidence is there in the tone of the passage. Like the speaker of "Gerontion" or *Villanelle: The Psychological Hour*, he comes to a moment of definition with an awareness that he has already failed one test of courage. As the body of the Canto unfolds, it lingers for a few lines on Lorenzaccio and a few lines on Alessandro, whose "abuleia," absence of will, is given special emphasis. Canto V ends with the speaking voice going back to Varchi, still vacillating, still unwilling to condemn Lorenzaccio: "Se pia . . . O empia, ma risoluto."

Auguries urgently demanding judgment and action continued in the *Dial*'s version of Canto VI, which began:

"The tale of thy deeds, Odysseus!" and Tolosan
Ground rents, sold by Guillaume, ninth duke of
    Aquitaine;
Till Louis is wed with Eleanor; the wheel . . .
("Conrad, the wheel turns and in the end turns ill")
And Acre and boy's love . . . for her uncle was
Commandant at Acre, she was pleased with him;
And Louis, French King, was jealous of days unshared
This pair had had together in years gone;
And he drives on for Zion, as "God wills"
To find, in six weeks time, the Queen's scarf is
Twisted atop the casque of Saladin.

"The wheel" in lines three and four comes from Bertran de Born's "Ara sai de pretz quals l'a plus gran." De Born's poem celebrates the courage of Conrad de Montferrat, who defended Tyre against Saladin even when the other western monarchs Richard and Philippe "tarried." The pertinent stanza is this one:

Lord Conrad, the wheel goes turning in this world, but
it has its end in evil, for I know few who are not always

studying how they may deceive friends and strangers, but he who loses does not rejoice, Wherefore let those of whom I say they do thus know well that God records what they have said and done.[44]

Reference to de Born's poem indicates how to evaluate the various characters of the Canto — Eleanor, Harry, Richard, and Philippe — and sustains Canto V's aura of providence dimly perceived. Each time Canto VI changes scene, Pound realludes to the poem, using it like a refrain, a nagging insistence. Harry et al. have tarried in their duty because of quarrels over wealth. Now they appear as in an infernal vision to the narrator, as Mr. Silvero, Hakagawa, Madame de Tournquist, and Fräulein von Kulp appeared to Gerontion.

Canto VII completes Pound's triptych of failed will. It begins with those prototypical old men, the elders of Troy, confronting Eleanor-Helen. The old men are analogues of Louis and Harry, who ignored Eleanor's love in their thirst for her dowry, and thus misappropriated an avatar of Venus. The Trojan elders are in fact less hardened against perception of the goddess, and recognize the divine terror once the damage is done. However, they can no more act upon that recognition than can Gerontion. As the Trojans fade, images of other myopic men, ancient and modern, succeed one another until we arrive at "the old men's voices" of modern times. The rest of the Canto is a "ghostly visit" through the wasteland of modern desiccation, with acknowledgments not only to "Gerontion" but to Remy de Gourmont[45] and to Henry James:[46]

[44] Translation from Barbara Smythe, *Trobador Poets* (London, 1911), p. 87. The original can be found in Antoine Thomas, *Poésies Complètes de Bertran de Born* (Toulouse, 1888), pp. 84-86.

[45] In 1914 Pound had written that "Remy de Gourmont . . . says that most men think only husks and shells of the thoughts that have been already lived over by others" (LE, p. 371).

[46] Pound's ghostly visit through London and Paris was very likely patterned on Henry James's fiction as it was interpreted by A. R. Orage in an August 1918 *Little Review* article, "Henry James and the

Thin husks I had known as men,
Dry casques of departed locusts
                    speaking a shell of speech . . .
Propped between chairs and table . . .
Words like the locust-shells, moved by no inner being;
            A dryness calling for death;

.   .   .   .

But Eros drowned, drowned, heavy — half dead with tears
                    For dead Sicheus.

    Life to make mock of motion:
For the husks, before me, move,
        The words rattle: shells given out by shells.

Like "Pastiche . . . The Regional," Canto VII connects dead
words with dead civilization. Like "Gerontion" (and *Mauberley*) its central metaphor for enervation is "Eros drowned."
Unlike "Gerontion," however, Canto VII ends on a note
of determination:

                    Lorenzaccio
Being more live than they, more full of flames and voices.
Ma se morisse!
        Credesse caduto da sè, ma se morisse.
And the tall indifference moves,
        a more living shell,
Drift in the air of fate, dry phantom, but intact.
O Alessandro, chief and thrice warned, watcher,
        Eternal watcher of things,
Of things, of men, of passions.
        Eyes floating in dry, dark air,
E biondo, with glass-grey iris, with an even side-fall of hair
The stiff, still features.

Ghostly." Orage saw James's achievement as revealing the subconscious
strata of ordinary behavior, which Orage chose to call "ghostly." According to Orage, James's "mission . . . was to act as a kind of Charon
to ferry the understanding over the dark passage of the Styx and to
show us that we are such stuff as ghosts are made of."

After an overview of modern paralysis, the speaking voice suddenly returns to the problem of Alessandro and Lorenzaccio, as if he had been given new evidence with which to judge them. He confronts them drifting in the air of fate, and calls them more living than the modern ghosts in front of him. Recoiling from modern times, the Canto's voice consigns Alessandro to hell for refusing to act. The judgment is pronounced by conflating Alessandro with E Biondo, Obizzo D'Este, who lies eternally paralyzed in the lake of *Inferno* XII. For the moment the speaking voice is willing to endorse the willfulness of Lorenzaccio, who, though dead is "more full of flames and voices" than the living shells of modern London. We know, of course, that such an endorsement cannot endure. The *Cantos'* demonstrated loathing for violence cannot allow Lorenzaccio's values to prevail. The progress of the poem, however, takes the form of an education. The speaker is now willing to throw in with Odysseus, Lorenzaccio, and Malatesta as Dante was at first willing to admire Odysseus, Capaneus, and Farinata. When the light becomes stronger and the speaker's understanding increases, these characters will be put in perspective. Until then, it is still better to be a Lorenzaccio than a Gerontion. As Eliot said, about Baudelaire: "So far as we do evil or good, we are human; and it is better, in a paradoxical way, to do evil than to do nothing: at least we exist. . . . The worst that can be said of most of our malefactors, from statesmen to thieves, is that they are not men enough to be damned. Baudelaire was man enough for damnation" (*Selected Essays*, p. 380). Lorenzaccio, and Malatesta to come, were men enough for damnation.

What probably has prevented readers from noticing the resemblance between "Gerontion" and Cantos V, VI, and VII is the way Pound transformed all of the spiritual underpinning beneath Eliot's shriveled-man motif. One can compare "Gerontion" and, even more tellingly, *The Hollow Men* to Canto VII and see that hollowness means one thing to Eliot and quite another to Pound. There *are* eyes in *The Hollow Men* which exist in death's *other* kingdom, and they have found their home in a kingdom not of eternal activity, but of spiritual peace. Eliot's wasteland has a specifically religious significance. It is inhabited by Christian souls who have not found peace "in His will" and have been exiled to wander endlessly in an ill-lit world. Eliot feels a real empathy for his characters because they present an image of himself.

Pound, however, does not recognize any action as evil because he does not believe in a Christian soul. We notice in Pound's hollow men that it is not their moral freedom that is rotten, but their aesthetic sensitivity. That is, their "selves," after years of conforming to the judgments of others, are so atrophied that they are unable to *feel* what is good for them or to know what is beautiful. Pound has no sympathy for them, and feels no horror. He regrets that they have fallen by the wayside and so cannot make his world more interesting. In some ways he wants more than anything else a world of equals with whom he can joyfully knock heads — a world of stout-hearted men. The only evil he understands is a deprivation of good, and he defines good as perception of the beautiful. This passage from Canto VII is Pound's "death's other kingdom":

> Eleanor!
>   The scarlet curtain throws a less scarlet shadow;
> Lamplight at Bouvilla, e quel remir,
>   And all that day
> Nicea moved before me
> And the cold grey air troubled her not
> For all her naked beauty, bit not the tropic skin,
> And the long slender feet lit on the curb's marge
> And her moving height went before me,
>   We alone having being.

For a moment, the narrator, wrapt in a meditation upon the dead woman, achieves a radiant state of understanding in which he and the woman become part of the ultimate being of perfect form. The *Cantos* revolve around spots of aesthetic radiance, as the *Four Quartets* revolve around points of revelation. Perhaps Eliot's reaction to what Pound did to the motifs of "Gerontion" prepared the ground for his savage attack on the Hell Cantos in *After Strange Gods*. It is an interesting possibility, but one I must forgo, because there remains too much of the two poets' technical collaboration yet to examine.

§

On December 13, 1919, Pound wrote to his father, "done cantos 5, 6, 7, each more incomprehensible than the one preceding it."[47] There are few who would argue with that statement. To a contemporary observer, the work in progress of Pound, Joyce, and Eliot as it emerged from 1919 to 1922 must have seemed part of a contest whose prize was to be awarded for the work of the greatest impenetrability. Joyce once and for all, by a work of indisputable genius, had shattered the literary taboo that prescribed that patient exposition make literature accessible on first reading. The two poets celebrated their new freedom at first gingerly, and then with greater and greater facility and not a little headiness. In a contemporary review, we can see Pound's usual craftsman's reserve melting into enthusiasm:

> It is not necessary, either in the young or in the mature artist, that all the geometry of a painting be tossed up into the consciousness and analysed by the painter before he puts brush to canvas. *The genius can pay in nugget and in lump gold: it is not necessary that he bring up his knowledge into the mint of consciousness, stamp it into either the coin of conscientiously analysed form-detail knowledge or into the paper money of words, before he transmit it.* A bit of luck for the young man, and the sudden coagulation of bits of knowledge collected here and there during years, need not for the elder artist be re-sorted and arranged into coin.[48]

[47] In an unpublished letter cited by Slatin, p. 188.
[48] *The New Age*, XXVI, 4 (November 27, 1919), pp. 60-61.

It is in the context of this heady progress that we must consider the techniques of Cantos V-VII. They had come after much of *Ulysses* and after Eliot had used the allusive compression of *Ulysses* to break poetic ground in "Sweeney Among the Nightingales." Cantos V, VI, and VII pressed on with the new techniques. In Canto VII Pound anticipated Eliot by applying what we now call modernistic techniques to the themes, motifs, and images of "Gerontion," and prepared the way for *The Waste Land*. We know that Eliot had *The Waste Land* "in mind . . . as early as 9 November 1919,"[49] and it seems likely that the two poets compared notes during that summer and fall about how the innovations of *Ulysses* could be minted into the coin of a long poem. It is not necessary to assume that Eliot was influenced by Canto VII. The pair probably worked out their new techniques in conversation before either began using them. One wonders, however, about Eliot during 1920-1922, those years of severe depression and self-doubt. Had Pound delayed using the new elliptical style, would Eliot have had the courage to adhere to the demands of modernism through the protracted effort of writing a long poem?

There are two factors involved in the achievements of 1919-1922. One consists of the technical innovations Pound and Eliot developed concurrently. The other is the way they each assimilated that development to their very different personalities. Let us consider the most important of the new techniques first: (1) a systematic use of allusive fragments, which the poets knew from *Ulysses* could emphasize the immediacy and disorder of existence at the same time as they were opening historical vistas "to the imagination by the very lightest touch"; (2) an adaptation of Jamesian narration[50]

[49] Gallup, p. 15.

[50] For Eliot's contemporary attention to James as a founder of modern art, see A. W. Litz's discussion in *Eliot in His Time: Essays on the Occasion of the Fiftieth Anniversary of The Waste Land* (Princeton, 1973), pp. 17-22. I have already demonstrated the thrust of Pound's contemporary renewed interest in James.

to Gourmont's principles. That is, a rendering of sensibility by a dramatic presentation of mental events.

The dissimilarities between *The Waste Land* and Canto VII testify to how philosophical differences may alter not only material but technique. To begin with fragmentation: although Pound and Eliot used it extensively, they adapted it to familiar patterns based on very different temperaments. From the first publication of *Three Cantos*, Pound had worked within a musical structure in which motifs were introduced casually and developed as the work progressed. He had always understood the concept of structure in the Coleridgean sense: a way in which unconnected material was fused by the force of the shaping imagination. One thinks of the image of the rose in the steel dust, which fascinated Pound throughout his life, or of his advocacy of Vorticism over representational art. Unexplained fragments had no terror for him. Discontinuity was a normal and real part of perception. In 1919 he responded positively to the way *Ulysses* retained the contradictions and fragmentation of history and daily life. He also praised the way *Ulysses* went beyond perception to impose art and harmony upon its material. Pound believed that post-Impressionist art was constructivist, integrative. It did not imitate reality but shaped reality's chaos into order. Given Pound's aesthetics, the use of fragments in Canto VII is entirely predictable. The most exposed and puzzling fragments come at the beginning of the Canto. They follow each other in quick succession, forming a "palette" of (choose your analogy) colors or motifs or themes on which Pound can build.

Fragments in the body of the Canto also follow established patterns. They serve as tags to crystallize a mood the way concluding images had epitomized many of Pound's earlier poems. Consider the sequence:

> Square even shoulders and the satin skin,
> Gone cheeks of the dancing woman,
>   Still the old dead dry talk, gassed out —

It is ten years gone, makes stiff about her a glass,
A petrefaction of air.

. . . .

    Only the husk of talk.
O voi che siete in piccioletta barca,
Dido choked up with sobs, for her Sicheus
Lies heavy in my arms, dead weight
    Drowning, with tears, new Eros.

The first six lines painstakingly build up the image of a
woman for ten years separated from her vital center ("gone
the cheeks of the dancing woman") by her acceptance of the
false postures and "dry talk" around her. The speaker pictori-
alizes her metamorphosis. He tells us that the talk "makes
. . . a glass" of stiffness between her and life, "a petrefaction
of air." The seventh line is a taunt at the reader (the full
passage from the *Paradiso* goes: "O ye who in a little bark,
eager to listen, have followed behind my ship . . . do not put
forth on the deep, for, perhaps, losing me, you would be left
bewildered. The waters I take were never sailed before.")
"O voi che siete . . ." dares the reader to consider the subject
important. In the final three lines, the speaker epitomizes the
woman as Dido in his (Aeneas') arms. Type becomes archetype as the narrator recognizes that the woman, like Dido,
has disavowed the fountain of her affections. She has ceased
to be (that is, to become), and has frozen into "dead weight."
Pound had experimented with like metamorphoses before.
Recall "Pagani's November 8":

Suddenly discovering in the eyes of the
    very beautiful
    Normande cocotte
The eyes of the very learned British museum assistant.

In *The Waste Land*, Eliot used discontinuity in a way
very much his own. The pattern of his poems had always
been disintegrative rather than integrative. His most important earlier poems, *Prufrock* and "Gerontion," began in a

discursive mode with the personality of the speakers tenuously whole, and disintegrated until the speakers were in pieces and the verse was in fragments. Eliot repeated this pattern at two different stages of composition of *The Waste Land*: "The Fire Sermon," probably the first full movement of the poem to be written,[51] ends with the speaking voice's disintegration into fragments of Wagner, St. Augustine, and the Buddha. *The Waste Land* proper ends with a cluster of fragments "shored against" the ruin of the poem's center of consciousness. Discontinuity had connotations of anxiety for Eliot. He responded with sympathetic horror to Stephen Dedalus' "History is a nightmare from which I am trying to awake." We can see the same reaction in a review of Henry Adams' *Education*,[52] where he recoiled from Adams' lifelong becoming, Adams' refusal to finally *be* this, that, or the other: "Conscience told him that one must be a learner all one's life . . . a great many things interested him; but he could believe in nothing . . . Wherever this man stepped, the ground did not simply give way, it flew into particles."

Eliot's instinctive revulsion from discontinuity animates those fragments which serve in the body of *The Waste Land* to deflate easy affirmation. "Burbank" and "Sweeney Erect" had used sudden reversals, accentuated by unexpected rhymes to underline historical incongruities.[53] *The Waste Land* refined those earlier antiphonal effects by endowing unexpected fragments with chilling power. The rising ecstasy of the

[51] See Grover Smith, "The Making of *The Waste Land*," *Mosaic*, VI, 1, pp. 127-141; and Hugh Kenner's article, "The Urban Apocalypse" in Litz, *Eliot in His Time*, pp. 23-49. ["*The Waste Land*: Paris, 1922," Helen Gardner's article in the Litz collection, is of another opinion (pp. 67-94).]

[52] "A Skeptical Patrician," in *The Athenaeum* (May 23, 1919). The review is a companion piece to "Gerontion," which was written at approximately the same time.

[53]   (The lengthened shadow of a man
           Is history, said Emerson
        Who had not seen the silhouette
         Of Sweeney straddled in the sun.)

Hyacinth girl passage is punctured by a reversal, *"Oed' und leer das Meer."* Later in the poem, the popular, gay but specious rhythm of "O the moon shone bright on Mrs. Porter . . ." is suddenly deflated by the icy formality of *"O ces voix d'enfants."* Eliot added the first fragment fairly late in the composition.[54] The sureness of his touch indicates growing ability to control and use the poem's "modernism." The emotional charge of these fragments distinguishes *The Waste Land* from Canto VII, which had reflected Pound's belief that fragmentation and contradiction are a normal part of reality at all times, present or past. Eliot clearly felt that fragmentation was a symptom of modern diseased consciousness.

A second difference between Canto VII and *The Waste Land* involves the way they use Jamesian techniques. *The Waste Land*'s "reflector" is primarily an *emotional* register. We can sense the emotional reactions of a consciousness in the verse even when no speaker is apparent. We feel that there is a narrator, a center of consciousness, because a constant emotional timbre unifies many individual voices. Canto VII has a more obvious narrator, but we tend to disregard him even when he thrusts himself ("lies heavy in *my* arms") in our view. Pound's "reflector" registers images, and often the images are so vivid that they make us forget there is a consciousness behind them.

Moreover, Eliot's emotional and religious temperament narrowed the emotional distance between *The Waste Land*'s narrator and characters. Eliot saw his own damnation in the damnation of others. The narrator of *The Waste Land* has "foresuffered all." He recognizes his spiritual identity with all of the characters. Although more sensitive, he is no less tainted than those he observes. One of Eliot's early drafts describes him well: "A man, contorted by some mental blight / Yet of abnormal powers." Canto VII's narrator, on the other hand, is an elect figure more distanced from his char-

---

[54] See the *Facsimile*, p. 7.

acters than any of James's reflectors. He is lost in an inferno, but remains as emotionally distant from the old men as Dante was from the damned — a "live man" among the dead.

§

According to Slatin, after December 1919, "Unexpectedly . . . the poem stopped; no further reference to the composition of the Cantos seems to have been made until 1922" (p. 188). Pound turned from the *Cantos* to Douglas' economics and to the narrative exercise involved in writing *Hugh Selwyn Mauberley* and *Indiscretions*.[55] By January he was living in Paris, where a new exposure[56] to the cinema reinforced his

[55] Both were completed during the first half of 1920.

[56] *Mauberley*, of course, slurred Georgian art by calling it "A prose kinema." The sneer was typical of Pound's previous remarks about the cinema. In *The New Age*, xxiii, 22 (September 26, 1918), Pound wrote that "cinema is not Art. . . . Art is a stasis. A painter or sculptor tries to make something which can stay still without becoming a bore . . . which will stand being looked at *for a long time*. Art is good in just so far as it will stand a long and lively inspection. . . . Photography is poor art because it has to put in everything, or nearly everything. . . . It cannot pick out the permanently interesting parts of a prospect. It is only by selection and emphasis that any work of art becomes sufficiently interesting to bear long scrutiny. . . . [A cinema frame] is designed to bear but the scrutiny of an instant. . . . One could forgive the cinema for existing if one believed it would kill contemporary theatricals, but this hope no longer survives. . . . It emphasises and glorifies the cheap side of modern theatre. . . . The cinema is the phonograph of appearance" (p. 352).
The Cocteau remarks seem to indicate an aboutface about cinematic possibilities, but probably only signify that Pound was beginning to have a few second thoughts. All his old prejudices are back in an article in *The Dial* (lxxiv, 3, pp. 273-280) for March 1923. It was not until 1928 that he seems to have found a film that would make him a permanent convert. In *The Exile* (Number 4) for autumn of that year, he wrote that the film "Die Simphonie der Grosse Stadt Berlin" was "in the movement, and . . . should flatten out the opposition (to Joyce, to me, to Rodker's Adolphe) with steam-rolling ease and commodity. . . . It would be simple snobism not to accept the cinema, on such terms, as being, on parity with the printed page, L'histoire morale contemporaine, with the national and sociological differences clearly marked."

conviction that fragmentation was the necessary mode of modern art. In a well-known review of Cocteau's *Poésies 1917-1920*, Pound compared modern consciousness to apperceptions of village life: "The life of a village is narrative; you have not been there three weeks before you know that in the revolution et cetera, and when M le Comte et cetera, and so forth. In a city the visual impressions succeed each other, overlap, overcross, they are 'cinematographic,' but they are not a simple linear sequence. They are often a flood of nouns without verbal relations."[57]

The passage is an unequivocal statement that storytelling and syntax must reflect changing modes of consciousness. When Pound arrived in Paris and discovered the frenetic experimentation of the French, his lagging tolerance for experiment was revived. He wrote in the same review that "after twelve years residence I at last and tardily begin to feel the full weight and extent of the British insensitivity to, and irritation with, mental agility in any and every form. . . . The young aesthetic . . . is, in this year of grace 1920, partial to a beauty very rapid in kind." Despite his pretense of commending a new quality in the work of *les jeunes*, however, it is apparent that Pound was judging them according to standards he had himself formulated two years before. In 1919-1920, he had noticed that the complex syntax of Henry James and Aeschylus was able to "mirror" the processes of consciousness. Cocteau's poetry, he now wrote, managed to do the same in a more "rapid" way.

But although Pound wrote admiringly, he seemed to harbor reservations about Cocteau's use of "cinematographic" syntax. It is true, he felt uncomfortable in the role of a tradition-

[57] *The Dial*, LXX, 1 (January 1921), p. 110. The passage may be usefully compared to Eliot's remark in the *Dial* (October 1921) that "Whether Stravinsky's music be permanent or ephemeral I do not know; but it did seem to transform the rhythm of the steppes into the scream of the motor horn, the rattle of machinery, the grind of wheels, the beating of iron and steel, the roar of the underground railway, and the other barbaric cries of modern life; and to transform these despairing noises into music."

bound elder, and wrote that his own fastidiousness was possibly "against the age." But he continued to insist that Cocteau and his contemporaries so far had only toyed with innovations that had previously been used by masters. "I, 'we' wanted and still want a poetry," he wrote, "where the reader must not only read every word, but must read his English as carefully as if it were a Greek that he could not rapidly be sure of comprehending." In contrast, Pound declared that Cocteau's kind of literature was "sometimes incomprehensible [even] if one does read every word and try to parse it in sequence." Finally, Pound called Cocteau's mode "ideographic," and his usage was far from complimentary: "if Cocteau and his semblables wish to reduce this sort of thing to a species of ideographic representation, it is not for us to demand a Virgilian eclogue. They are the 'lyric' (as the word is loosely used) voice of the age — possibly its Demussets. . . ." That is, Cocteau was "ideographic," not in Pound's later, approving sense of that word, but in the pejorative sense of his 1920 statement that we have "long since passed the stage when 'man sees horse' or 'farmer sows rice,' can in simple ideographic record be said to display anything remotely resembling our subjectivity."

The period from summer 1920 to autumn 1921 must have been an ebb tide of Pound's career. All of his old projects had achieved publication, and the sources of both his inspiration and money began to recede. London money dried up in the fall of 1920. In early 1921 John Quinn considerably reduced his interest and patronage. London, which had never been financially supportive, now seemed less welcoming than ever. Eliot had not written anything since "Gerontion," and Joyce, upset over Pound's doubts about "Sirens," sent him no chapters to read between "Oxen of the Sun" in May 1920 and "Circe" in April 1921. Pound had made a few forays into Paris and decided to make his new home there, but he felt out of place. We can see his self-consciousness in the Cocteau review. As with Gaudier-Brzeska in 1913, Pound affected the persona of a man of middle age among the young. He always seemed susceptible to intimidation by new fashions, and his stay in Paris, at a time when many of his old moorings were off, made him question his own technical conservatism. In April 1921, when Joyce handed him "Circe" in Paris, Pound read it with altered vision. As Forrest Read has written, "All of Pound's enthusiasm flooded back. He wrote of "Circe": "Joyce next chapter great stuff"; "Joyce 'Circe' chapter here in transcript. Magnificent, a new Inferno in full sail"; "Joyce's new chapter is enormous — megaloscrumptious-mastodonic."[58]

In London, Eliot, oppressed by demons of his own, had the same reaction to "Circe." He wrote Joyce in response to the manuscript. "I think they [three late chapters of *Ulysses*] are superb — especially the Descent into Hell ["Circe"], which is stupendous. . . . I have nothing but admiration, in fact, I wish, for my own sake, that I had not read it."[59] For the sake of Eliot's admirers, however, it was a stroke of fortune that he did. Ever since the summer of 1919, Eliot had been planning a long poem.[60] He made no serious progress, however, until just the time when he received Joyce's new manuscript. He wrote John Quinn about a month before answering Joyce that "the latter part of Ulysses . . . is truly magnificent," and, in the same letter, that his long poem was now "partly on paper."[61] One fragment of *The Waste Land* which seems likely to have been on paper was "Tom's place," the original opening, which began with a trip to a whorehouse very much like the one in "Circe." Whatever technical debt Eliot may have had in mind that made him half wish that he had not read "Circe," it is apparent that the reading unlocked his energy.

We must now confront Pound's reception of *The Waste Land*. The impact of his annotations on Eliot's poem has been recently and thoroughly considered by several fine crit-

58 P/J, p. 189.
59 May 21, 1921. Cited by Day, p. 183.
60 See Gallup, p. 15.
61 The letter is cited by Day, p. 184.

ics.[62] After noticing their work, I wish to consider the relationship of Pound's labor to the *Cantos*. As precisely as can be established, Eliot took a bundle of fragments to Margate in September 1921 and came back to London with a sequence which included "The Fire Sermon."[63] He spent a week in London with Vivien, and left with her for Paris, en route to a sanitarium in Lausanne. When he got to Paris, he seems to have situated Vivien, left a carbon of the Margate sequence with Pound, and headed off for Switzerland. Pound marked the carbon, most probably before Eliot returned. I shall begin my discussion with these comments.

Some of Pound's judgments reveal nothing because they make obvious decisions. The opening parody of *The Rape of the Lock* was, as Helen Gardner has put it, "beyond help."[64] Conversely, the lines beginning "A rat crept softly . . ." were quite the best thing Eliot had done.[65] The first interesting decision was Pound's deletion of the passage "London, the swarming life you kill and breed." Helen Gardner would have had the lines improved and retained, for to her they represent "a potentially impressive vision of London as a city of automata."[66] Pound did not agree. In fact, when Eliot included the passage in the Lausanne manuscript, Pound put a rude *B ll S* in the margin. He thought the pentameter execrable, but his objection went beyond the rhythm. These "London" lines, unlike the two passages preceding them, do not either indicate or imply a speaker or a situation. They are a disembodied general statement, out of place with the dramatic mode of the rest of the poem. Pound

[62] See the Smith, Litz, Kenner, and Gardner articles on *The Waste Land* cited above.

[63] See Smith's and Kenner's articles on *The Waste Land*.

[64] Gardner, p. 80.

[65] They were fine examples of Eliot the city poet and follower of Baudelaire. The rhythm was admirable, and the concluding verse ran the tonal spectrum from classical eloquence to modern cacophony to macabre reversal.

[66] *Op.cit.*, p. 82.

originally set "vocative" beside them to half ask, half scold Eliot about his lack of dramatic feeling. Very early in his knowledge of the suite, Pound was sure enough of Eliot's intentions to slash out some potentially effective images. He was sure because the two poets had agreed to follow James and Gourmont. Both Pound and Eliot believed that the presentation of sensibility was the major task of the modern poet. The task required continuing attention to the nuances of point of view. Those lines which Pound deleted were not dramatic, although the similar lines above, beginning "Unreal city," were. Pound at first also marked the "Unreal city" sequence "vocative?" but he soon realized that it really did imply a speaker. In fact, he later excised "I have seen and see" from the passage because he felt that introducing the speaker was unnecessarily explicit.

The episode of the typist drew extensive comments. Eliot's quatrains had many of the same problems as his 1917-1919 poems, and Pound set to work with the same bag of surgical instruments. (At one point he gently reminded Eliot of their work on "Grishkin.") Out went inappropriate detail, weak verbs, inversions, extraneous adjectives. Pound once again made the stanzas stress a series of simple actions. Consider the passage which first ran:

> He, the young man carbuncular, will stare
> Boldly about, in "London's one cafe",
> And he will tell her, with a casual air,
> Grandly, "I have been with Nevinson today".
>
> Perhaps a cheap house agent's clerk, who flits
> Daily, from flat to flat, with one bold stare;
> One of the low on whom assurance sits
> As a silk hat on a Bradford millionaire.

Pound recognized that "will stare" and "will tell her" and "who flits" are non-specifying verbs, hypothetical actions that have no particular time or place. The passage was revised so that its emphasis fell on a realizable action, the arrival of the young man:

> He, the young man carbuncular, arrives,
> A small house agent's clerk, with one bold stare,
> One of the low on whom assurance sits
> As a silk hat on a Bradford millionaire.

As Helen Gardner noticed, part of Pound's labor was directed toward destroying "the regularity of the quatrains, which after the revision only establish themselves at the climax of the passage, the rhymes at the beginning being irregular" (p. 83). We may attribute this concern for rhythmic diversity within a series of quatrains to *Mauberley*, which had been written between *Burbank* and *The Waste Land* and where Pound had learned to vary the regularity of the middle stanzas so that regularity in the last quatrains would have special impact.[67]

Perhaps the most distinctively "Poundian" annotations were the ones that dealt with narrative certitude. Pound once wrote that "Art deals with certitude."[68] He meant more or less the same thing when he wrote elsewhere that "Poetry is the statement of overwhelming emotional values . . . and aims at giving a feeling precisely evaluated."[69] Certitude grows out of personal witness. Realism is always individual, and the realistic author sticks to the way he sees things even when the public objects. There is no room for maybes or perhapses in the presentation or in the evaluation. Eliot tried in the typist episode of *The Waste Land* to convey the personal quality of truth by depriving events of external verifiability. Tiresias' epiphany would be "true" about any assignation. Eliot tried to suggest the interchangeability of the

[67] See John Espey, *Ezra Pound's Mauberley: A Study in Composition* (Berkeley and Los Angeles, 1955), p. 45.

[68] See "Affirmations . . . Vorticism" in *The New Age*, XVI, 11 (January 14, 1915), pp. 277-278.

[69] See "Breviora" in *The Little Review*, V, 6 (October 1918), pp. 23-24.

participants in the episode by generalizing: "will stare," "will tell her." Pound at first corrected such verbs as bad writing, but became disturbed when Eliot refused to let Tiresias observe a concrete event. The first time he annotated "The Fire Sermon" he questioned a "perhaps," crossed out "We may have seen," got visibly angry at a second "perhaps," and exploded at the line "Across her brain one half-formed though *may* pass": "make up yr. mind," he told Eliot, "you Tiresias if you know know damn well or else you don't." He was telling Eliot that the episode's "maybes" did more to undercut Tiresias' authority as witness than they did to generalize Tiresias' conclusions. Eliot might have tightened *The Waste Land* so that it better portrayed Johnsonian universality. Instead, Pound altered it so that it presented the obdurate truth of Canto II: "I have seen what I have seen."

When Eliot returned from Lausanne, Pound applied the same tools to the revision of the full manuscript as he had to "The Fire Sermon." His small critical suggestions, which made the poem more precise (and sometimes more obscure), have been extensively discussed by the critics,[70] and do not reveal enough about Pound to warrant consideration here. I wish rather to consider the formal assumptions behind some of Pound's remarks, and what those assumptions suggest about the *Cantos*.

From the beginning, *The Waste Land*'s significant form was Eliot's and not Pound's. Although Pound deserves some credit for perceiving and clarifying the framework of Eliot's suite,[71] and although Canto VII may have provided a precedent for *The Waste Land*, "the famous . . . discontinuity was there from the start."[72] Pound's efforts did not, as critics have always believed, create the poem's discontinuity, and yet they did make it harder to follow. Perhaps one should say they made it more unfamiliar. The *Facsimile* volume shows that

[70] See especially Kenner, "The Urban Apocalypse."
[71] See A. W. Litz, "*The Waste Land*: Fifty Years After," *Journal of Modern Literature*, ii, 4 (November 1972), pp. 455-471.
[72] Gardner, p. 77.

Pound cut out most of "Death by Water" and strongly disapproved of bits of dialogue that he labeled "photographic."
It is possible, as A. Walton Litz has suggested,[73] that Eliot
also removed the "Tom's place" episode at Pound's suggestion. Eliot's deletion of "photographic" details has been
recognized by the critics as a shift in the modality of the
poem away from the drama and realism toward what Grover
Smith has called "the interior monologue . . . in the service
of a narrative of the psyche."[74] Had Eliot left in and improved the segments Pound disapproved of, there would
have been more "facts" from which to make thematic generalizations.[75] As we have seen, however, Pound believed
that the "truth" of facts belongs to the way in which a
sensibility absorbs them and not to any inherent property
of their own. In his eyes, it was not necessary to develop a
full dramatic situation to render sensibility because combinations of images and rhythms could by themselves more ac-
curately present psychic states. He praised those sections of
The Waste Land where Eliot let images objectify a speaker,
and dispraised those sections ("Tom's place" and "Sailing off
Massachusetts") where Eliot gave the speaker a background
and a social voice. In consequence, the poem's literary, historical, and mythical coordinates overwhelmed the few social coordinates Eliot originally provided. I suspect that
Pound regarded even the allusions as evidence about the
speaker's sensibility rather than as "objective" thematic mark-
ers.

As a result of Pound's suggestions, the speakers of *The
Waste Land* lost that degree of tangibility we usually require
to "size up" characters. The literary public has never become as sensitive to nuance as Pound desired. The public
has had to have something to grab on to, some element of the
Jamesian "superstes"[76] of things that Pound believed super-

[73] See "Fifty Years After," p. 461.

[74] *Op.cit.*, p. 135.

[75] The situation of the New England sailors in "Death by Water,"
for example, would have given the drifting condition of the speaker
a social reality.

[76] See LE, p. 340.

238

fluous. And so they have allegorized. *The Waste Land*, like the Cantos, seems obscure because it says less than it appears to say. Much of the cultural bric-a-brac of both poems is intended to be "characterization" and not allegory. *The Waste Land* would have been more satisfying had Pound allowed Eliot to expand the poem's music-hall qualities. Instead, again to quote A. Walton Litz, "Pound changed *The Waste Land* . . . to a condensed and elliptical poetic statement which, for all its dramatic elements, revolves around a series of images or symboliste 'moments.' "[77]

In 1922 *The Waste Land* affected Pound as the year before "Circe" had affected Eliot. After two fruitless years, Pound again began to work on *The Cantos*. Canto VIII, which he had never mentioned in his letters,[78] was published in *The Dial* in May 1922. By mid-July, he had written that he had "blocked in five more Cantos," and a month later that he had "rough draft of 9, 10, 11, 12, 13. IX may be swelled out into two."[79] By the time it was published in *Criterion* (July 1923), Canto IX, the Malatesta Canto, had swelled into four (Cantos VIII-XI). As early as May 1923 Pound was arranging for the Three Mountains Press edition of *A Draft of XVI Cantos*, and in July he wrote to his father that he had "finished Canto XVI, that is fifth after the Malatesta, having rewritten beginning of poem and condensed three cantos into two."[80] Eighteen months after he had seen *The Waste Land*, Pound had more than doubled the size of his poem and revised the beginning Cantos into a sequence that suited his post-*Ulysses*, post-*Waste Land* notion of compression.

Despite the effect of *The Waste Land* on Pound's productivity, we should avoid drawing any neat conclusions. It would not have been like Pound to imitate *The Waste Land*.[81] He had too often expressed the opinion that a

---

[77] "Fifty Years After," p. 461.
[78] Slatin, p. 189.   [79] *Ibid*.
[80] *Ibid*.
[81] A major exception is the apparent relationship between "Sailing off Massachusetts" and what is now Canto II. Pound had already rendered (in *Three Cantos III*) *Inferno* xxvi. He would not authorize *The*

genuine masterpiece cannot be copied without dilution, and besides, he would have been sensitive about being called Eliot's follower. Moreover, *The Waste Land's* subject matter was not very appealing. Beyond the shriveled-man motif, which Cantos V-VII had already appropriated from "Gerontion," *The Waste Land* did not offer a great deal that was adaptable to the *Cantos'* then "historiographic" concerns. What left the most lasting impression on Pound was not Eliot's subject, but the way *The Waste Land* handled seemingly incompatible material — that is to say, *The Waste Land's* decorum.

§

The voice of Cantos I-VII never varied from the reverent tone of ritual chant. The narrator spoke as if charged by a terrifying spirit to report precisely and solemnly what he saw.

Waste Land's retention of a version less accomplished than his own. As Kenner remarked, Eliot's lines have "trouble with idiom, trouble with rhythm, trouble with tone, and we note mechanical efforts to link . . . [them] with the rest of the poem by recalling Dante's Ulysses and working in bits of diction from Tennyson's" ("The Urban Apocalypse," p. 41). After he recommended that "Sailing off Massachusetts" be deleted, however, Pound realized that Eliot had addressed a different facet of Dante's Ulysses than *Three Cantos III*.

Three Cantos III was concerned with Dante's portrayal of the godlike mind of Ulysses as it suffered the mortification of chthonic ritual. "Sailing off Massachusetts" portrayed the minds of Ulysses' sailors as they were confronted and overwhelmed by trancendental force. Eliot's approach interested Pound enough to translate for the main section of Canto II an analogous scene from Ovid. In Canto II Acoetes observes a group of common sailors as they wreck themselves against the power of a god they had never seen.

Pound, however, could not imitate material without transforming it. Whereas Eliot had depicted the psychological state of the sailors, and had denied the reader an explanation of their experience, Pound treated the same action from the standpoint of an evaluating observer. Acoetes' epiphany underlines the spiritual meaning of the sailor's fate. Pound's narratives, like medieval romances, usually concern themselves with moral definition rather than psychological exploration.

In Canto VII, for example, he treated a potentially comic group of pedants with inordinate gravity:

> Another day, between walls of a sham Mycenian,
> "Toc" sphinxes, sham-Memphis columns,
> And beneath the jazz a cortex . . .
> Dry professiorial talk . . .
>   now stilling the ill beat music.

Dante would not have been so solemn. The reader is apt to ask himself whether the man who wrote Canto VII in imitation of Dante was the same Ezra Pound who had gleefully underlined the "grim humour" of *Inferno* xix-xxiii, and who had written, "We lose a great deal if we leave our sense of irony behind us when we enter the dolorous parts of Dante's *Hell.* For sheer dreariness one reads Henry James, not the *Inferno*" (SR, pp. 135-136). Something seems to have kept Pound from applying that perception to his own inferno, for even after writing *Propertius* he regarded ironic wit as inappropriate to *The Cantos.* In May 1922, however, we find the speaker of Canto VIII (what is now Canto II) finally breaking out of his humorlessness:

> The ship landed in Scios,
>   men wanting spring-water,
> And by the rock-pool a young boy leggy with vine-must,
>   "To Naxos? Yes, we'll take you to Naxos,
> Cum' along, lad." "Not that way!"
> "Aye, that way is Naxos."
>   And I said: "It's a straight ship."
> And an ex-convict out of Italy
>   knocked me into the fore-stays,
> (He was wanted for manslaughter in Tuscany)
>   And the whole twenty against me,
> Mad for a little slave money.
>   And they took her out of Scios
> And off her course . . .
>   And the boy came to, again, with the racket,
> And looked out over the bows

Canto VIII's use of irony proceeded to open the way to the civilized urbanity of the Malatesta group and to the sarcasm of the "Hell" Cantos. Behind the composition of Canto VIII lies a change in the poem's decorum — a change that can be associated with the way *The Waste Land* focused *Ulysses* and Dante's *De Vulgari Eloquentia* so that they could be of practical use.

We have seen that in 1918 Pound made several important remarks about the way *Ulysses* alternated beauty and shabbiness. Pound in that year had called Joyce's systematic variation "the bass and treble of his method." In the same year, Pound expressed a renewed interest in that section of Dante's *De Vulgari Eloquentia* that prescribed a decorum of mixed "shaggy and harsh" diction as the proper texture for poetry.[82] (Book II of the *De Vulgari* is a *locus classicus* for the argument that style and diction should vary with subject. High language is said to befit a noble subject and vulgar language a low subject.) It was no coincidence that Pound wrote about Dante so soon after his article on *Ulysses*. Joyce appealed to Pound in 1918 because, like Flaubert, he did not ennoble low subjects. He followed Dante's advice that "we should not describe an ox with trappings or a swine with a belt as adorned, nay rather we laugh at them as disfigured."[83] Joyce's "swift alternation" of the beautiful and ugly called attention to the superiority of the beautiful in a very compressed manner, just as Dante had prefigured: "As to the statement that superior things mixed with inferior effect an improvement in the latter, we say that it is true if the blending is complete, for instance when we mix gold and silver together; but if it is not, the inferior things appear worse, for instance when beautiful women are mixed with ugly ones."[84]

---

[82] See *The New Age*, XXIV, 8 (December 26, 1918), pp. 122-124.

[83] *A Translation of the Latin Works of Dante Alighieri* (J. M. Dent and Sons, Temple Classics edition: London, 1904), p. 67.

[84] *Ibid.*, p. 68.

Pound apparently was not able in 1918 to connect his admiration for the *De Vulgari* and *Ulysses* to his own epic. The *Cantos* continued to be written under the aegis of a single-toned decorum. As he worked with Eliot, however, on Gautier-like dissonances, his tolerance for harsh effects increased. In *Propertius* he employed "logopoeia" to achieve an urbane and elegant surface. In *Mauberley* 1920, he made use of a decorum that permitted not only wit but consciously unpleasant rhythmic effects:

> Invitation, mere invitation to perceptivity
> Gradually led him to the isolation
> Which these presents place
> Under a more tolerant, perhaps, examination.

The "hell" of the fourth and fifth sections of the first part of *Mauberley*, however, were tame exercises for a student of Dante. It took the appearance of *The Waste Land* to make Pound appreciate how *The Cantos* could adapt Joyce's range of material to poetry. Eliot's pub scene (whose "photographic" realism Pound had at first rejected), and his music-hall repertoire of dramatic voices became recognizable at some point in 1922 as derivations from *Ulysses*. Pound began to see how *The Waste Land* also alternated modern squalor with imaginative splendor. After *The Waste Land*, when Pound considered *Ulysses*, he did so with much greater personal involvement.

The composition of *The Waste Land* coincided with the completion of *Ulysses* and with a new round of Pound's praise of the novel in the journals. Pound puffed *Ulysses* most notably in *The Dial*'s "Paris Letter" (June 1922). His review, which began "All men should 'Unite to give praise to Ulysses,'" was a paean to Joyce's ability to vary his style to suit his subject. Pound paused emphatically on the "varigation of dialects" in *Ulysses* that allow Joyce "to present his matter, his tones of mind, very rapidly." Through such deftness, Joyce "does add definitely to the international store of literary [note: not novelistic] technique." In the same article Pound connected Joyce to Dante by calling *Ulysses* the first epic "since 1321" to psychologically resurrect the furies.

A month after *The Dial* article was published, Pound wrote a letter to Felix Schelling which explained that the Hell Cantos attempted a Dantesque accommodation of style to material:

> Next point: This being buoyed by wit. No. *Punch* and the rest of them have too long gone on treating the foetor of England as if it were something to be joked about. There is an evil without dignity and without tragedy, and it is dishonest art to treat it as if it were funny. It is perhaps difficult to treat it at all; the Brit. empire is rotting because no one in England tries to treat it. Juvenal isn't witty. Joyce's isn't harsh enough. (L, p. 180)

Ulysses led Pound once more to take the *Commedia* literally.

Pound was thinking of the *De Vulgari* as well as the *Inferno*, for he wrote about "dishonest art" in just the intonation that the *De Vulgari* had reprimanded works that treated disgusting subjects in an inappropriately noble style. Pound cited the *De Vulgari* later in the same letter to justify the irregular meters of *Mauberley*: "The metre in *Mauberley* is Gautier and Bion's 'Adonis'; or at least those are the two grafts I was trying to flavour it with. Syncopation from the Greek; and a general distaste for the slushiness and swishiness of the post-Swinburnian British line. (Cf. Dante's remarks in the D.V.E.)" (L, p. 181).

Once Pound grasped that *Ulysses* and *The Waste Land* could be used as models for applying the *De Vulgari* to his own work, he was able rapidly to improvise stratagems for material that a short time before had seemed intractable. With new assurance, he mapped out an entire sequence of Cantos. Five days after the Schelling letter, he wrote to Kate Buss that he had "blocked in five more Cantos," meaning the Malatesta, Baldy, Kung, and Hell Cantos.[85] His writ-

---

[85] Cited by Slatin, p. 189.

ing proceeded at a brisk pace, and Pound continued to keep Dante in mind. In an article entitled "On Criticism in General," published in *Criterion* (January 1923), Pound made a formal statement of his new decorum and called it his own *De Vulgari Eloquio*. Forrest Read has perceptively concluded that, by comparing his own essay on criticism to Dante's, Pound was making "On Criticism in General" the "authoritative basis for *The Cantos*."[86]

"On Criticism in General" adumbrates the results of a dozen years of Pound's literary variety of qualitative analysis. The essay's list of significant works is not dramatically different from her lists of ten years earlier.[87] However, "On Criticism

---

[86] Read, *The Odysseans*, p. 129. I believe, however, that Read arrived at his conclusion the wrong way around. Read asserted that the essay could be related to the *Cantos* in part because *On Criticism* finally placed *Ulysses* in a usable epic tradition. As I have argued above, I believe that the direct influence of *Ulysses* on Pound had occurred long before, and that the reorientation of the *Cantos* that was formalized by *On Criticism* occurred because in 1922 *The Waste Land* showed Pound that Joyce's decorum could be adapted to poetry. Although Read recognized the importance of Pound's remarking on Joyce's "tones of mind" for the *Cantos*, he did not connect his recognition to *On Criticism in General*.

The second part of Read's argument that *On Criticism* provided a new theoretical base for the *Cantos* centers around Pound's inclusion of "Fenollosa on the Chinese Ideograph" in the essay's list of the prose tradition. According to Read, Pound thus suggested that "the next work is still to come" in a direct line from Fenollosa. However, it seems to me that Pound referred to the ideograph in *On Criticism* exactly as he had in his Cocteau review—with a kind of groping appreciation that had not yet solidified into appropriation. That at this late date—two years after the burst of energy and redefinition that completed *XVI Cantos*—Pound was still tentative about the ideogram indicates that it had little to do with the first set of Cantos. In the light of evidence I have presented in Chapters One and Four, it seems unlikely that the ideogram per se had much effect on the poem until some time later.

[87] See, for example, "Renaissance I: The Palette" in LE, pp. 214-218. *On Criticism* added to those earlier lists a summary of the prose tradition (collected from other articles that Pound had written during what De Nagy calls his "critical decade"). *On Criticism* also finalized a decade-long history of speculation about the categories of poets (e.g., "in-

in General" took some care to specify the distinctive qualities of each masterwork. There is an enthusiasm behind *On Criticism*'s endorsement of Homer's "actual cadence of voices" or Propertius's "sophistication . . . of the urbs of civilization" that soon makes us realize Pound's grand compilation had a personal relevance. Pound assembled the finest examples of various styles for just those reasons which compelled Dante to write the *De Vulgari*. He wished to define a set of standards for his epic poem. "On Criticism" provides a rhetoric of finely dissociated styles to set alongside the prescriptions of classical decorum. The essay in essence defines the fitness of certain styles to certain subjects. Just as the *De Vulgari* had prescribed the appropriateness of the mode of illustrious language to treat a virtuous knight, and provided examples (II.ii), so *On Criticism*, carrying stylistic analysis beyond high, middle, and low language, prescribes the mode of Propertius to treat a citizen of the metropolis. "On Criticism" defines a "palette" of styles for the *Cantos* ample enough to provide the "tints" necessary for treating, among others, Malatesta, Lloyd George, and Confucius.

§

The final stages of the evolution of *A Draft of XVI Cantos* can now be quickly compassed. After Pound had blocked in Canto XVI, he went back to his notes for "Malatesta" and expanded what was originally intended to be one Canto to four. Were the first version of Canto VI easily accessible, Cantos VIII-XI would not need a great deal of comment. Pound began to treat the world of Malatesta in just the way he had treated the world around Eleanor of Aquitaine. In 1915 he had written that "one seems able to find modern civilisation in its simple elements in the Renaissance."[88] At

---

ventors" and "masters") and poetry (melopoeia, phanopoeia, logopoeia).

[88] *The New Age*, XVI, 15 (February 11, 1915), p. 409.

that time he was interested primarily in the preconditions for art, but by 1919 he had begun to think about the social and economic problems of the twentieth century that were also present in their simple elements during the quattrocento. While researching Canto VI, Pound had read a history of Pope Leo X. From that date (1919) onward, two elements of the Renaissance began to bother him as never before. In 1915 he had a cavalier attitude toward Dante's fears concerning the breakup of the empire:

"That sense, that reawakening to the sense of capital, resulted not in a single great vortex, such as Dante had dreamed of in his propaganda for a great central court, a peace tribunal, and in all his ghibelline speculations; but it did result in the numerous vortices of the Italian cities, striving against each other not only in commerce but in the arts as well" (LE, p. 220).

By 1919 Pound's sense of history was beginning to include a growing abhorrence for violent conflict, and he began to share Dante's belief in the benefits of an empire. He wrote in 1919 that "Universal peace will never be maintained unless it be by a conspiracy of intelligent men."[89] After the war, he saw less to admire in strife among *condottieri*, no matter how cultured. Similarly, although he continued to press for a leisured class that might refine civilization, Douglas was making him see the seeds of capitalist greed in the Renaissance's obsession with luxury. In March 1920 he wrote that Leo X's greed, although his court was as civilized and enlightened as any in Europe, "probably cost the world two hundred years of intellectual progress."[90] Out of Pound's ambivalence toward the Renaissance grew the Malatesta Cantos. Canto VI had depicted greed, duplicity, and internecine struggle in twelfth-century France. The Malatesta Cantos extend the same analysis into the Renaissance, where, as the cultural benefits of competition among armed lords grew, so did the waste.

[89] *The New Age*, xxvi, 3 (November 20, 1919), p. 48.
[90] *The New Age*, xxvi, 19 (March 11, 1920), pp. 301-302.

On a first reading of Cantos VIII-XI one is tempted to attribute the forces of barbarism to the society that surrounds Malatesta, but a closer look indicates that Malatesta contains the evil forces of his age within him. He is the epitome of the Renaissance *condottiere* — no more, no less. Although he possessed qualities of "intelligent constructivity," he was also prone to the *condottiere*'s two misdirections of will — violence and luxury. We learn in what is now Canto VIII that Sigismundo was "a bit too Polumetis," a bit too enthusiastic a "Poliorcetes," a taker of cities. In other words he suffered from "the maritime adventure morals"[91] that permitted Odysseus to sack the Cicones. We also learn, although more subtly, that Sigismundo and his family were participants in the Renaissance progress of luxury.

To stitch the Malatesta Cantos together, Pound used the same device as he had Cantos V-VII. As the fortunes of Malatesta decline, significations of augury come to the surface as they had come to Alessandro. When the eagle lights on the tent pole at the end of Canto X, one may think back to the *"ciocco"* scene in Canto V that alluded to the angels in Paradise forming an Eagle. There is no one in Malatesta's Italy to read true auguries, and the truth, although apparent to the visionary (and the reader), is lost to the blindness of the age. The Latin augury is repeated at the beginning of Canto XI, but the characters pay it no heed.

The difference between Pound's treatment of the Aquitaine circle in Canto VI and his treatment of Sigismundo in Cantos VIII-XI is the new freedom of his enlarged decorum. Whereas the first seven Cantos had been spoken by the narrator in accordance with strict rules of epic gravitas, what is now Canto VIII begins with the "tone of mind" of an urbane character speaking in his own voice. Malatesta is probably Pound's finest persona after Propertius. Cantos VIII-XI achieve effects more subtle than Canto II's colloquialism. They create the full-fledged characterization we find in lines like these:

[91] *Kulchur*, p. 38.

So far as I am concerned, it wd.
Give me the greatest possible pleasure,
At any rate nothing wd. give me more pleasure
    or be more acceptable to me,
And I shd. like to be party to it, as was promised me,
    either as participant or adherent.

As in *Propertius*, Pound here succeeds in portraying attitudes merely by the movements and mannerisms of a dramatic voice. We understand the full range of Malatesta's authority and accomplishment as we hear him shifting from the diplomatic formality of "greatest possible pleasure" to the businesslike precision of "or be more acceptable to me" to the *condottiere*-like persuasiveness of "as was promised me." All such effects would have been too colloquial for inclusion before Pound enlarged the decorum of *The Cantos*. Now, not only could Pound expand his repertoire of characterizations, he was able to utilize types of material that had formerly seemed too prosaic. The letters and historical documents scattered through the Malatesta group are throwbacks to the Cubist inclusivity that Pound experimented with in his monograph *Gaudier-Brzeska* but had rejected as indecorous for the *Cantos*.

Cantos XII-XVI delineate the boundaries of the newly expanded rhetoric of the *Cantos*. The first half of Canto XII presents the exploits of Baldy Bacon in a style of low comedy and crack-brain cataloguing reminiscent of *Bouvard et Pécuchet*. Baldy is a low-life alter ego of Odysseus and Malatesta, a more vulgar brother of Leopold Bloom:

His office in Nassau St., distributing jobs to the printers,
Commercial stationery,
    and later, insurance,
Employers' liability,
    odd sorts of insurance,
Fire on brothels, etc., commission,
Rising from 15 dollars a week,
    Pollon d'anthropon iden

Canto XII's comic treatment of Baldy anticipates innumerable episodes throughout the *Cantos* where a colloquial tone signals the ludicrousness of the contemporary equivalent of a once serious figure. The last segment of Canto XII presents a similar treatment of other parodic characters:

> Jim X . . .
>> in a bankers' meeting,
>> bored with their hard luck stories,
> Bored with their bloomin' primness
>> and the little white rims
> They wore around inside the edge of their vests
> To make 'em look as if they had on two waistcoats,
> Told 'em the tale of the Honest Sailor.

Quinn's banking friends are tailor's dummy copies of once vital bankers like the Medicis. Canto XII handles them in the same style as Baldy, with one considered difference: Because Quinn's bankers have more responsibility than Baldy Bacon, their hollowness is more pernicious. Consequently, Canto XII modulates its comic manner into something approaching satire by involving the bankers in Quinn's "tale," which happens to be an obscene story about sodomy. Pound, however, does not intend full satire, and does not spell out the obscene implications of the tale. Canto XII's treatment of the bankers and Baldy Bacon delimits that segment of the *Cantos* rhetoric which can be called comic.

Canto XIII defines the standard of an "illustrious" style with which the *Cantos* will treat examples of true virtue. Confucius is presented with unadorned, measured language and stately, graceful verse:

> "Anyone can run to excesses,
> It is easy to shoot past the mark,
> It is hard to stand firm in the middle."

The strictures of the *Cantos*' decorum extend beyond language and rhythm to metaphor. Canto XIII concludes with

an image which is as rigorously decorous as any figure of
Spenser's:

> The blossoms of the apricot
> > blow from the east to the west,
> And I have tried to keep them from falling."

Kung's words are an evocation of the "golden world" before
nature had fallen. To keep the blossoms of the apricot from
falling is to keep nature in a permanent vernal bounty. As in
this last figure of Canto XIII, the *Cantos* will continue to
render their civilized men with images of natural increase
and divine tranquility.

Cantos XIV-XVI develop that portion of the poem's
rhetoric on the underside of comic. As in Jonson's *Volpone*,
where Mosca and Volpone are treated more harshly than the
Would-be's, the Hell Cantos describe the most responsible
offenders against nature in language harsher than comedy.
The implied and laughable scatology in Canto XII's little
tale becomes graphic and disgusting as we progress from
bankers to prime ministers:

> The stench of wet coal, politicians
> > . . . . e and . . . . . n, their wrists bound to
> > their ankles.
> Standing bare-bum,
> Faces smeared on their rumps,
> > wide eye on flat buttock,
> Bush hanging for beard,
> > Addressing crowds through their arse-holes,

Pound here systematically utilizes the full range of classical
satire — vulgar language, prosy and unpleasant rhythms, and
images of polluted nature. By Canto XVI, the rhetorical conventions of the *Cantos* were established. Pound afterwards
composed no sequence more disgusting than the Hell Cantos,
nor any sequence of a more sustained grandeur than Canto
XIII.

On August 24, 1923, Pound wrote his father that he had "revised [the] earlier part of the poem."[92] Now that we have seen the gradual development of the poem from *Three Cantos*, there is no need for us to postulate any sudden and extraordinary reason for Pound's decision to change Cantos I, II, and III. The multiple decisions of 1917 to 1923 had rendered more and more of *Three Cantos* inadequate and inappropriate. As early as the *Lustra* revisions, the Browningesque characterization of the narrator in Canto I had become cumbersome. When Canto IV took up the techniques of rendering rather than describing mental activity, it was obvious that *Three Cantos I* would need major revision. The inevitable decision to scrap Canto I came soon after Pound wrote Canto VIII (now Canto II). He realized that he had inadvertently repeated the action — the divine epiphany — of his first Canto, and repeated it with all the subtlety of his post-1919 style. With the exordium of Canto I obsolescent and its action redundant, there was no longer any good reason to justify keeping it. Pound moved Canto VIII to Canto II and scrapped *Three Cantos I*.

Pound also decided that *Three Cantos II* would not fit in with the improved compression of the rest of the sequence. The *Future* "excerpts" had convinced him that a few episodes could be more effective than many. He therefore wrote the new Canto III to supersede it. The characters of *Three Cantos II* had been presented as lost *nel mezzo del cammin di nostra vita*. He wanted to portray characters in the same situation, but decided that he would use just two radicals for the revised Canto. Because *Three Cantos I* and most of the traces of his narrative persona were gone, he chose *Three Canto I*'s image of the young E. P. languishing in Venice as one of the radicals. He thus made sure that the reader would have some sense of the poem's narrative correspondence with *The Divine Comedy*. As the other radical, he chose "Myo Cid," in part because the Cid's misfortunes were — like those

[92] Slatin, p. 191.

of E. P. — due to economic injustice. Pound refashioned both radicals for Canto III. The story of the Cid required only minor alteration. He added an explicit reference to the Cid's pawnbrokers to bring out the story's element of economic disorder. However, he made considerable changes in the segment dealing with E. P. Since those changes make an interesting commentary on the way the *Cantos* had changed, I wish to consider them at some length.

Three Cantos I had suggested E. P.'s haplessness by rather straightforward narrative devices. It used whimpering rhythms to depict E. P.'s immature vision, and then quickly modulated into skepticism:

> Your "palace step"?
> My stone seat was the Dogana's curb,
> And there were not "those girls," there was one flare, one
> face.
> 'Twas all I ever saw, but it was real. . . .
> And I can no more say what shape it was . . .
> But she was young, too young.
> True, it was Venice,
> And at Florian's and under the north arcade
> I have seen other faces, and had my rolls for breakfast, for
> that matter;
> So, for what it's worth, I have the background.

The revised version condensed the passage, and used indirect devices to suggest E. P.'s inadequacy:

> I sat on the Dogana's steps
> For the gondolas cost too much, that year,
> And there were not "those girls", there was one face,
> And the Buccentoro twenty yards off, howling "Stretti",
> And the lit cross-beams, that year, in the Morosini,
> And peacocks in Koré's house, or there may have been.

The changes in the revised version testify to the intervention of Joyce and Eliot. Pound remembered the way *Portrait* had deflated Stephen's Icarus-like soaring with distant cries

of "O, cripes, I'm drownded." He also remembered the way
the voice of *The Waste Land* had used the tune "the moon
shone bright" to puncture a bit of literary posturing. In a
similar fashion Pound used surrounding detail to comment
on E. P.'s amorous passion. An incongruous juxtaposition of
the Buccentoro's vulgar love songs ("Stretti" means embraced
in Italian, and comes from a rather crude popular ballad)[93]
tells us all we need to know about the quality of young
Pound's spiritual vision. Pound added two other details in
the revision to suggest indirectly other facets of E. P.'s plight:
(1) The line, "For the gondolas cost too much that year,"
interjects the theme of the economic disorder of the surrounding world; and (2) the line, "And peacocks in Koré's
house, or there may have been," catches E. P.'s deficient vision at an important angle. The line illustrates that E. P. is
unable clearly to perceive Persephone, one of the poem's
hierophants, who could enlighten him and help him out of
his difficulties.

One section of Canto III remains to be explained. Lines
7-19, beginning with "Gods float" and ending with "under
the cedars," do not fit in with the schema that Canto III
adapted from *Three Cantos II*. Pound retained these lines
from *Three Cantos I* for other reasons. When Pound decided
to revise the beginning of the poem, he realized that the significance of parts of Canto IV depended on the *Cantos* he
was going to cut, especially on motifs in *Three Cantos I*.
Pound set aside part of Canto III to reintroduce these
motifs. Lines 7-19 were included for that purpose. However,
Pound's flawed sense of how much he could condense old
material seems to have betrayed him once again. Lines 7-19 of
Canto III do not retain enough detail to clarify Canto IV.
Pound included the "grey steps" of *Three Cantos I*, for example, but he did not include the circumjacent detail that had
informed us that the grey steps led up to a teakwood temple
of the Japanese goddess Kwannon. In order to make sense of

[93] See E. M. Glenn's annotation in *The Analyst*, xxv (April 1969),
pp. 4-5.

the resonance of the water lotus (line 76) the reader must be introduced to more than an enigmatic detail like "grey steps"; he must have access, as he originally did, to the information that the water lotus is an image of Kwannon, goddess of mercy. The unfortunate effect of Pound's 1923 revisions was to obscure Canto IV forever. The divine presences of that Canto should be a lantern to guide the reader through the darkness of Cantos V-VIII. Instead, they now puzzle as much as they illuminate.

Pound's decision to begin the revised *Cantos* with Odysseus' visit to Hades has perhaps been given too much emphasis. We have seen that he isolated the passage in the 1918 *Future* Cantos without any intention to revise the architecture of the poem. In *Three Cantos* (1917), Odysseus' confrontation with the chthonic forces of the primitive past had been a parallel to that passage of Canto I in which the narrator confronted the ancient spirits of Sirmio in a once-pagan temple. In 1918, Pound decided that the Nekyia was the more effective episode and highlighted it accordingly. By 1923, he had become convinced that the *Cantos* would be more powerful were the Nekyia given still greater emphasis, and so he moved it from Canto III to Canto I.

The *Odyssey* had always been a major analogue of the narrator's spiritual journey. But Pound regarded the *Odyssey* as an epic journey of spiritual purification that had been assimilated and refined by *The Divine Comedy*. The critics have overstressed the Homeric, adventurous aspect of the early Cantos at the expense of their Dantesque vision. In the fourteenth century, Dante had incorporated the Nekyia into his *Inferno*. In the twentieth, Pound decided to retain it, and to underline once more its infernal perspective.

Appendix 1

Hugh Selwyn Mauberley: Realism Reprised

DURING 1917-1919, when Pound composed *Homage to Sextus Propertius* and Cantos IV-VII, he was ambivalent about the place of realism in his poetry. He was critically committed to supporting realist literature and had written numerous satirical sketches, but he continued to be unhappy when portraying sensibilities less sophisticated than his own. Only after editing *The Waste Land* and reappraising *Ulysses* in 1922 did he manage to incorporate realism's "tones of mind" into a *modus operandi* for the *Cantos* that did not offend his sense of the difference between prose and epic poetry.[94]

Between composing *Propertius* and reading *The Waste Land*, Pound worked on a sequence that would conform to his rather special idea of "the prose tradition." Although often cited, his remark that *Hugh Selwyn Mauberley* was "an attempt to condense the James novel" (L, 180) cannot be bettered as an account of that much-discussed work. In *Mauberley* and especially in its second movement, *Mauberley 1920*, Pound's aim was to fashion poetic equivalents for the devices habitually used by modern fiction. To see how he succeeded, we have only to compare a section of *Mauberley* to a passage from one of Pound's realist masters. I have chosen the following excerpt from *A Portrait of the Artist as a Young Man* (which Pound read as a realist rather than a symbolist work) because, despite *Mauberley's* exploitation of a Jamesian situation, the hardness of its approach resembles Joyce's "metallic cleanness" (P/J, 134) more than anything in James:

[94] In his *Little Review* essay on Henry James, Pound wrote that "most good prose arises . . . from an instinct of negation . . . [an] analysis of something detestable," while "Poetry is the assertion of a positive . . . [of] emotional values" (LE, 324).

Every part of his day, divided by what he regarded now as the duties of his station in life, circled about its own centre of spiritual energy. His life seemed to have drawn near to eternity; every thought, word and deed, every instance of consciousness could be made to revibrate radiantly in heaven: and at times his sense of such immediate repercussion was so lively that he seemed to feel his soul in devotion pressing like fingers the keyboard of a great cash register and to see the amount of his purchase start forth immediately in heaven, not as a number but as a frail column of incense or as a slender flower.[95]

Written in the third person, the paragraph nevertheless gives us Stephen through his own "tone of mind." The rising enthusiasm of the first sentence is Stephen's and not Joyce's, and the magniloquence of such phrases as "centre of spiritual energy" only becomes ironic when we distance ourselves from Stephen's point of view. We are forced to distance ourselves by the way Joyce adjusts the elements of Stephen's awareness: without being false to Stephen's *façon de voir*, particles of his thought unmistakably deflate each other. Hence the bathos of "he seemed to feel his soul in devotion pressing like fingers the keyboard of a great cash register. . . ."

Pound's procedures in the poem which opens *Mauberley* 1920 are strictly comparable:

> Turned from the "eau-forte
> Par Jaquemart"
> To the strait head
> of Messalina:
>
> "His true Penelope
> Was Flaubert,"
> And his tool
> The engraver's.

[95] James Joyce, A *Portrait of the Artist as a Young Man*, ed. by Chester G. Anderson (New York, 1968), p. 148.

Firmness,
Not the full smile,
His art, but an art
In profile;

Colourless
Pier Francesca,
Pisanello lacking the skill
To forge Achaia.

There can be no question of a narrative persona here. The point of view as given by the shading of phrases is Mauberley's, but Pound's use of the third person is as impersonal as Joyce's own. Pound, though, extends the deflationary possibilities of Joyce's prose by marshaling his rhythms, couplets, and quatrains into intricate patterns of enthusiasm and irony. In the first three stanzas there is an habitual incongruity, a rising and falling, both between each line of a couplet and each couplet of a quatrain. The simplicity of "strait head" underlines by contrast the "exact social tone" of the French locution "eau-forte" in an Englishman's speech; the closing reference to lascivious Messalina deflates the pretensions of a sensibility that would search out her strait head; and so on. We read *Mauberley 1920* with an expectation that each rise will have a fall and that each expression of Mauberley's passion will be punctured by a recognition of its effeteness. In the suite's culmination we see Venus Anadyomene emerging in Mauberley's song and, in the rising rhythms, anticipate her opening sexuality — only to find, of course, that she appears as an antiquarian's dusty photograph, "opening" in the "Pages of Reinach."

Unlike the straightforwardness of *Mauberley 1920*, Pound's narrative method in the first movement of *Hugh Selwyn Mauberley* is so problematic that critics have been unable to agree on whether the speaker (several poems are cast in the first person) is Pound, E. P., Mauberley, or a shifting mask in the manner of *The Waste Land*.[96] The last cannot be disproved, of course, but seems unlikely since there is little overt characterization to differentiate one speaker from another. To my view, the most pursuasive argument to date has been William Spanos', who reasons that it is Mauberley's voice we hear before the "envoi," and that "Pound's own voice is never heard directly in the sequence; it is always implicit in the varied ironies that are sounded by Mauberley. It is identical with Mauberley's when the latter is least private, that is, when he is attacking the age; it is ambivalent in the 'I' poems, identifiable with Mauberley's insofar as the latter sympathizes with the victims of the age, but distinct insofar as Mauberley tends to identify himself personally with them; it is totally distinct from Mauberley's when the latter is most private, that is, when he is completely absorbed in himself."[97]

It seems inconceivable that Pound, who wrote that "An 'idea' has little value apart from the modality of the mind which receives it," would have allowed half of his novelistic treatment of literary London to remain without a dramatic point of view. The persona Mauberley, whom Pound called a "surface" (L, 180) might best be conceived as one of the "registers or 'reflectors' " which in the preface to *The Wings of the Dove* James said authentically reflect their environment because they are "burnished . . . by the intelligence, the curiosity, the passion, the force of the moment . . . directing them."[98] In the first section of Pound's sequence, the persuasiveness of Mauberley's observations derives precisely from the "passion" of a writer whose aesthetic has been repudiated and from the "force of the moment" in which he perceives himself out of step.

[96] A summary of the controversy is provided in William V. Spanos, "The Modulating Voice of Hugh Selwyn Mauberley," *Wisconsin Studies in Contemporary Literature*, 6, 1 (Winter-Spring 1965), pp. 73-96.

[97] Spanos, pp. 77-78.

[98] *The Art of the Novel: Critical Prefaces by Henry James*, ed. with an introduction by R. P. Blackmur (New York, 1962), pp. 300-301.

Bolstering the argument for a dramatic speaker in the first section of the suite is the matter of *Mauberley*'s Odyssean correspondences. As Hugh Witemeyer has pointed out, the sequence assimilates "a number of historical and pseudohistorical figures to the archetypal patterns of . . . Homer's *Odyssey*. . . . The opening 'Ode' sets up the fundamental equation of the poet-as-Odysseus, engaged in an arduous quest for his true ideal (Penelope), but mortally tempted by a false ideal (Circe and the Sirens). . . . The failed minor artists of the poem . . . are, like the crewmen of Odysseus, diverted from their quest and destroyed along the way. . . . At best, these Elpenors may leave their oars . . . to commemorate their struggles."[99] The speeches in the first section of *Mauberley*, therefore, are intended to display a persona who lacks awareness of the Odyssean echoes and of Pound's mature sensibility as well. Although Witemeyer assumes the obtuse speaker in part one to be E. P. ("a pilgrim, an observer, a recorder, a buffoon, who is used to present the *periplum* of literary London"),[100] it is more reasonable not to insist on such prominence for E. P., a figure Pound said was "buried" by Mauberley "in the first poem."[101] The obtuse speaker of part one is Mauberley himself, and in his speech Pound gives us a less mannered, more youthfully vigorous version of the restless, abstracted voice rendered in *Mauberley 1920*.

Witemeyer's argument that the use of mythic correspondences in *Mauberley* led to Pound's 1923 reorganization of *Three Cantos* merits consideration. Certainly *Mauberley* reflects many of the revised Cantos' post-symbolist techniques. Both *A Draft of XVI Cantos* and *Hugh Selwyn Mauberley* rely on the modernists' "mythic method" to order and value events in the present. Both depend for their organization on

[99] Hugh Witemeyer, *The Poetry of Ezra Pound: Forms and Renewal, 1908-1920* (Berkeley and Los Angeles, 1969), pp. 163-164.

[100] Witemeyer, p. 163.

[101] See Thomas E. Connolly, "Further Notes on Mauberley," *Accent*, XVI, 1 (Winter 1956), p. 59.

an internal stitching of recurrent motifs.[102] Both use radically truncated allusions to call up cultural equations out of the past. We even find analogous metamorphic formations in both sequences, such as the changes undergone by what Canto XXIX would call "our mulberry leaf," the eternal female. In the first volume of Cantos, the feminine archetype appears in the shape of Aphrodite, Circe, Tyro, Helen, and Eleanor, all figures who suggest the unformed energies of desire and creation. *Mauberley* contains a comparable catalogue of women,[103] and, as in the *Cantos*, displays them in polarized aspects. To suggest bypassed vitality, *Mauberley*'s Elizabeth Siddal languishes in London just as Canto VII's Eleanor of Aquitaine "spoiled in a British climate." To represent the darker consequences of neglected instinctuality, Mauberley's end is attended by Venus Anadyomene, presiding over the doom of a man who misdirected her power as she presides in the early Cantos over the misdirected energies of an entire culture.

Hugh Selwyn Mauberley, however, was not so much a forerunner of the revised Cantos as a parallel sequence that utilized already developed techniques for different ends. As this study has demonstrated, Pound's use of mythic ordering, his structural methods, his reliance on allusion, and his inclination to exploit archetypes became part of the *Cantos* before (and for the most part long before) the composition

---

[102] In *Ezra Pound's Mauberley* (Berkeley and Los Angeles, 1955), John Espey called attention to the suite's "underlying musical structure" and outlined the development of several of *Mauberley*'s themes. See p. 75 and *passim*.

[103] Circe, Penelope, the Sirens, and the Muses in I, i; Sappho in I, iii (by ironic analogy); Helen in I, v; Elizabeth Siddal in I, vi; the harlots of I, vii; the "uneducated mistress" in I, x; the young woman of I, xi; Daphne and Lady Valentine in I, xii, the singer of the "envoi"; Messalina and Penelope in II, i; Aphrodite ("Nuktis 'Agalma") and the she of "her phantasmagoria" in II, ii; Aphrodite ("The Cytheraean") in II, iii; the ghostly presence of Elpenor's Circe in II, iv; and Aphrodite Anadyomene in "Medallion."

of *Mauberley* in 1919-1920. The development that prompted Pound's refashioning of the *Cantos* in 1923 had to do with the poem's enlarged decorum. And although there is no denying that *Mauberley* increased Pound's skill at rhythmic syncopation,[104] ironic control of material,[105] and realistic modeling of voices, in the *Cantos* those skills were applied to a meditative mode and to a long poetic line that have no parallel in *Hugh Selwyn Mauberley*. Nor did *Mauberley*'s discordant effects, even in the war poems, predict Pound's scatalogical liberties in Cantos XIV and XV.

Pound wrote *Mauberley* while the *Cantos* were on the back burner in order to compete, for once, with the novelists on their own terms. After a decade of wondering whether his fate would be to "sulk and leave the word to novelists" (*Three Cantos I*), he had achieved a major poem in the purest traditions of prose realism. The result as far as the *Cantos* was concerned was liberating: *Mauberley*'s impact was not an influx of satirical idiosyncrasies but rather a new flexibility in his willingness to mix realism with other modes. The power of *Mauberley* comes from the force of its certitude and its concentrated disgust for the "detestable," which Pound said was the true object of prose (LE, 324). The suite forgoes the *Cantos*' meditative posture and chiaroscuro for an unblinking analysis of English letters. Unlike the *Cantos*, where incidents are drawn out in the consciousness of a slightly puzzled raconteur and where even misdirected voices are allowed their lyrical moments, the elements of *Mauberley* are pared down and welded together by an assured judgment that prevails from the first poem to the last. We can see the difference clearly in the treatment of Victor Plarr. In Canto XVI, Plarr is allowed a personal cadence, and the effect of his honesty is balanced by a faintly disconcerting quaintness that we sense in his choice of words. Plarr is presented so

---

[104] Pound wrote that "The metre in *Mauberley* is Gautier and Bion's 'Adonis'; or at least those are the two grafts I was trying to flavour it with. Syncopation from the Greek . . ." (L, 181).

[105] For discussion, see Espey, pp. 106ff.

ambiguously, in fact, that we must seek the point of his monologue in its relation to the other voices that surround his own. But in the seventh poem (*"Siena Mi Fe'; Disfecemi Maremma"*) of *Hugh Selwyn Mauberley*, Plarr is presented not for his personal tone but as a diagnostic tool by which Pound's analysis of London is forwarded. Here Plarr exists by virtue of his family tree, his status as a survivor of the nineties, the tastes revealed by what he chooses to remember, his treatment by contemporary society and by Mauberley, and other details that have nothing to do with his style of speech. Like all the figures in *Mauberley*, he points beyond himself to the quality of his culture — exactly as he would, of course, had he appeared as a minor figure in *Madame Bovary* or *The Ambassadors* or *A Portrait of the Artist as a Young Man*.

CHAPTER VI

"MURMUR OF OLD MEN'S VOICES"

In *Three Cantos'* first theophany, the poem's speaker undergoes a shining moment of reverie and revelation. A "flare" starts his speculative progress from the dead surface of a Christian ritual back to the living presence of "some old god" hidden in the pagan origins of the feast of Corpus Christi. The speaker pauses over *loci* in Arnaut Daniel and Catullus, and ends finally amidst the luminousness of an embedded Latin word, *apricus* (drenched with sunlight). It is a magic moment to which Pound had often returned in his early poetry, and one that corresponded to the "delightful psychic experience" he had written about in 1912: "I believe in a sort of permanent basis in humanity, that is to say, I believe that Greek myth arose when someone having passed through delightful psychic experience tried to communicate it to others. . . ." (SR, p. 92).

By 1923, however, when Pound revised the beginning of his epic, the aura of "delightful psychic experience" in *Three Cantos* had all but disappeared. If we compare the revelation of the speaker in *Three Cantos* to the first theophany of *A Draft of XVI Cantos*, we are struck by how dark the poem has become. Canto II presents us not an unworried mental reverie but a medley of disturbing mythological stories — Menelaus facing Eidothea and Proteus, the Trojan elders facing Helen, Tyro facing Poseidon. The type of these stories is Jacob's struggle with the angel: In each, and in the longer story of Dionysus and the sailors that follows, we discover divinities that do not merely appear but must be wrestled with. Canto II seems to be defining revelation not as a moment of reverie but as an encounter with a dangerous force, an encounter whose consequence is not enlightenment but either mastery or disaster.

Furthermore, unlike anything in *Three Cantos*, Pound imbues the story of Dionysus with resonances of contemporary history. Taking his subject from the Cadmeiad of *Metamorphoses* III.1-IV.603, his episode is less personal testament than cultural tableau. In the Cadmeiad, a tale of the Theban tribe and its degeneration, Ovid used the episode of the impious sailors to mark a stage of cultural decay. With a minute's reflection we realize that Pound's intentions in Canto II are not dissimilar. Dionysus represents not only the nemesis of Thebes but one of the presiding deities of Western culture since Nietzsche, and in Canto II Pound wrote a parable of the shape of divine revelation in the late stages of his own civilization. In the sailors, "mad for a little slave money," he presented the debased state of modern sensitivity to the ecstasy and the buried energies of nature. In the sailors' plight, he introduced the type of circumstance that would send character after character in Cantos I-XXX crashing into collision with the gods. The sailors are mythological representations of the citizens of postwar Europe, about whom Pound wrote in 1920: "Perspicacity is not given to all men, and many have in abuleia gone to their doom" (*Selected Prose*, p. 182).

The *Cantos'* increasing exploitation of contemporary overtones in its choice of subjects was paralleled in the work of Eliot, Lawrence, Mann, and other modernist writers. To give only one salient example, at about the time when the mythology of the *Cantos* was becoming less "delightful," W. B. Yeats gave up the last vestiges of his aversion to political topics and developed the mythologized cultural history of *A Vision*. According to Yeats, it was in 1918 that his spiritual visitants "drew their first symbolical map of that history, and marked upon it the principal years of crisis."[1] And it was in 1919 that Yeats wrote quite close equivalents to

[1] W. B. Yeats, *A Vision* (New York, 1938), p. 11.

Canto II's picture of imperceptive modern society wrecked against the forces of the unconscious: Both "Nineteen Hundred and Nineteen" and "The Second Coming" enact *A Vision*'s prophecy that "myth and fact, united until the exhaustion of the Renaissance have now fallen so far apart that man understands for the first time the rigidity of fact, and calls up, by that very recognition, myth — the *Mask* — which now but gropes its way out of the mind's dark but will shortly pursue and terrify."[2]

It might be illuminating to consider in greater depth how the preoccupations and motifs of Pound's revised Cantos were echoed in his more widely read contemporaries. Literary analogues, however, can sometimes be traced to a common source in the popular imagination, and it is in their non-literary form that such figures are most informative. The vision of European decay that *A Draft of XVI Cantos* shares with *The Waste Land, Women in Love, Death in Venice,* or "Nineteen Hundred and Nineteen" was closely related to social myths that colored both the journalism of the period and also significant social criticism written by figures as diverse as John Maynard Keynes and Sigmund Freud. (For present purposes, Major C. H. Douglas should also be included.) In Chapter Five, I tried to make the post-war Cantos more accessible by briefly considering their literary sources. I demonstrated, for example, that Alessandro and the old men of Canto VII could be traced back to "Gerontion." Now I would like to pursue the provenance of the same old men beyond Pound's coterie to a broader segment of European culture. Even more than the episode of Dionysus and the sailors, the "old men's voices" of Canto II present Pound's elevation of a contemporary fact into a symbol of a state of mind. The full implications of the confrontation between the elders of Troy and Helen (impotence and enfeebled perception facing uncontrolled energy) express a pervasive European nightmare of 1919. By exploring one or two important

[2] This citation appears on p. 212 of the first (1925) version of the text.

266

versions of that nightmare, and by tracing the confrontation's growing importance in Pound's prose, I wish to create a context in which the darkened second opening of the *Cantos* may be understood and the imaginative gap between Pound's history and his mythology may be narrowed.

§

Several years before Eliot used a little old man as the paralyzed speaker of "Gerontion," the soldier poets of World War I pictured old folks safe behind the lines and youth dying at the front. As John Silkin has observed, the theme is taken up in Sassoon's *The Old Huntsman* and *Counter-Attack* and "is common to nearly every writer of the period concerned with the war. It occurs directly in Rosenberg's 'Dead Man's Dump,' and more especially in 'Daughters of the War'; it is the theme of F. S. Flint's fine 'Lament,' occurs in his 'Exposure,' in Blunden's 'War Autobiography,' Read's 'Kneeshaw Goes to War,' and in 'The Execution of Cornelius Vane.' It occurs in Sassoon's 'Suicide in the Trenches' and also 'The Death Bed.' "[3] It occurs especially (and perhaps most bitterly) in the work of Wilfred Owen.[4] In "Dulce and Decorum Est," Owen related loyalty to the state to filial loyalty, and damned both as "The old Lie." In other poems his bitter, emotional association of fathers and leaders was more explicit. In the prologue to "S.I.W.," Owen accused England's fathers of not wanting to know what the war was really like:

Patting good-bye, doubtless they told the lad
He'd always show the Hun a brave man's face;
Father would sooner him dead than in disgrace, —
Was proud to see him going, aye, and glad.

[3] John Silkin, *Out of Battle: The Poetry of the Great War* (London, 1972), p. 143.

[4] Owen's *Poems* were published by Sassoon in 1920 (Owen died in November 1918). For a discussion of the group of poems I am considering, see Gertrude White, *Wilfred Owen* (New York, 1969), pp. 71-81.

Perhaps his mother whimpered how she'd fret
Until he got a nice safe wound to nurse.
Sisters would wish girls too could shoot, charge, curse;
Brothers—would send his favourite cigarette.
Each week, month after month, they wrote the same,
Thinking him sheltered in some Y.M. Hut,
Because he said so, writing on his butt
Where once an hour a bullet missed its aim
And misses teased the hunger of his brain.
His eyes grew old with wincing, and his hand
Reckless with ague. Courage leaked, as sand
From the best sand-bags after years of rain.
But never leave, wound, fever, trench-foot, shock,
Untrapped the wretch. And death seemed still withheld
For torture of lying machinally shelled,
At the pleasure of this world's Powers who'd run amok.

He'd seen men shoot their hands, on night patrol.
Their people never knew. Yet they were vile.
"Death sooner than dishonour, that's the style!"
So father said.

Finally, in "The Parable of the Old Man and the Young,"
Owen telescoped both politician and father into one mythological figure:

So Abram rose, and clave the wood, and went,
And took the fire with him, and a knife.
And as they sojourned both of them together,
Isaac the first-born spake and said, My Father,
Behold the preparations, fire and iron,
But where the lamb for this burnt-offering?
Then Abram bound the youth with belts and straps,
And builded parapets and trenches there,
And stretched forth the knife to slay his son.
When lo! an angel called him out of heaven,
Saying, Lay not thy hand upon the lad,

268

Neither do anything to him. Behold,
A ram, caught in a thicket by its horns;
Offer the Ram of Pride instead of him.
But the old man would not so, but slew his son,
And half the seed of Europe, one by one.

In Owen's universe, Abraham, the universal patriarch, had become the quintessentially evil symbol of "this world's Power's who'd run amok." It is worth noting that, for Owen, modern fatherhood had reversed its traditional role of spreading seeds and now "slew" them, contradicting the laws of both God and nature.

Owen and his fellow poets, however, although they amplified the wartime motif of age and youth, could hardly be said to have invented it, even for their generation. They were utilizing a habit of putting things that already existed in the popular mind. Toward the end of the war, it was not unusual to find newspapermen using phrases similar to those of this correspondent at the Peace Conference:

> Some regard the Peace as wicked, some regard it as foolish, some, I believe, regard it as wise. But the one fact that must strike anybody who has been in Paris throughout these months is the decline of hope, and this is true of those who wanted this kind of Peace as of those who dreaded it. . . .
>
> What was wanted of the men who met in Paris was the imagination and the faith that the youth of the nation had shown in the war, for without the courage and the spirit of youth a new world could not be built. And it is the spirit and courage of youth that have been lacking in Paris, where the world has been in the hands of tired and exhausted men, resorting to old and discredited devices, under the spell of all the superstitions we denounced with such vigour four years ago. . . .[5]

[5] J. L. Hammond, special correspondent of the *Manchester Guardian* in Paris, writing in *The Nation*, Vol. 25 (June 7, 1919), pp. 286-288.

To a section of the English public it was commonplace to think of Europe's leaders as not only old, but also too blinded by convention to see a future different from the immediate past. As in the above, the old statesmen were considered "exhausted," lacking the creative "spirit" to recognize outworn conventions and build a new world. This notion of the old men at Paris became part of popular mythology, and lent itself to treatment by many writers in many fields.

❦

Following the armistice, England lived through a period of short-lived optimism followed by prolonged gloom. The negotiations at Paris began in October and November 1918, and the Treaty of Versailles was finally signed on June 28, 1919. For a year or two, while Ireland was being torn apart and Germany was gasping under economic chaos, England enjoyed boom conditions. In the late summer of 1920, however, the English economy succumbed to the post-war depression. The facts and resulting shift in mood are described by the historian Arthur Marwick, who renders the event in the catchwords of the period: "Unemployment, which averaged 3.1 per cent in the latter half of 1920, rose to 13.5 per cent in 1921 and 13.8 per cent in 1922. . . . Reconstruction turned to retrenchment, the land fit for heroes became the waste land."[6] The best description of the English state of mind, however, belongs not to Marwick but to a delegate at the Peace Conference who foresaw the depression and in good part fixed the terms through which it was understood. It is to John Maynard Keynes' *The Economic Consequences of the Peace* (1919) that we must turn for the nuances of the old man motif in its most complete English form.

In the preface to his work (dated November 1919), Keynes informed his readers that he had been the "official representa-

---

[6] Arthur Marwick, *The Deluge: British Society and the First World War* (New York, 1965), pp. 283-284.

tive" of the British Treasury at the Paris Peace Conference, and that he had resigned in June 1919 "when it became evident that hope could no longer be entertained of substantial modification in the draft Terms of the Peace." His introductory chapter presented a now-famous picture of the conditions of the conference, and explained why he had so vigorously desired "substantial modification" of its final conclusion. In that introduction, Keynes outlined the reasons why it was now particularly dangerous to allow the aged perceptions of established statesmen to control the fortunes of Europe. He warned of unseen economic dependencies and, to emphasize the point, he used the earth itself to figure economic reality. In Keynes' script, the leaders of Europe in their "insane delusion" had lost contact with the very ground on which they stood.

Very few of us realize with conviction the intensely unusual, unstable, complicated, unreliable, temporary nature of the economic organization by which Western Europe has lived for the last half century. We assume some of the most peculiar and temporary of our late advantages as natural, permanent, and to be depended on, and we lay our plans accordingly. On this sandy and false foundation we scheme for social improvement and dress our political platforms, pursue our animosities and particular ambitions, and feel ourselves with enough margin in hand to foster, not assuage, civil conflict in the European family. Moved by insane delusion and reckless self-regard, the German people overturned the foundations on which we all lived and built. But the spokesmen of the French and British peoples have run the risk of completing the ruin, which Germany began, by a Peace which, if it is carried into effect, must impair yet further, when it might have restored, the delicate, complicated organization. . . .[7]

[7] John Maynard Keynes, *The Economic Consequences of the Peace* (New York, 1920), pp. 3-4. The book's first English printing was in late 1919.

Keynes went on to extend his figure of the earth to an image of nature itself. The explosive power of economic forces, he suggested, was a kind of natural havoc of which only the English could "be so unconscious. In continental Europe the EARTH HEAVES [emphasis mine] and no one but is aware of the rumblings. There it is not just a matter of extravagance or 'labor troubles'; but of life and death, of starvation and existence, and of the fearful convulsions of a dying civilization" (p. 4). It was thus an "unconsciousness" of natural process that was about to bring forth "the fearful convulsions of a dying civilization." And so, in the act of conveying his economic message, Keynes molded the newspaper cliché of England's old men to the point where their essential characteristic appeared to be atrophied responsiveness to the forces of nature.

To Keynes, the perfect embodiments of the desiccation of European civilization were men around the conference table in Paris. He began his portrait gallery with Clemenceau — "by far the most eminent member of the Council of Four." He gestured at an appreciation of Clemenceau's wit and intelligence, but went on quickly to describe Clemenceau's dress: "he wore a square-tailored coat of very good, thick, black broadcloth, and on his hands, which were never uncovered, gray suede gloves. . . ." Despite Keynes' periodic bouts of faint praise, we understand Clemenceau to be only the shell of a man:

> He carried no papers and no portfolio, and was unattended by any personal secretary, though several French ministers appropriate to the particular matter at hand would be present round him. His walk, his hand, and his voice were not lacking in vigor, but he bore, nevertheless, especially after the attempt upon him, the aspect of a very old man conserving his strength for important occasions. He spoke seldom . . . he closed his eyes often . . . and the sudden outburst of words, often followed by a fit of deep coughing from the chest, produced their impression rather by force and surprise than by persuasion. (pp. 30-31)

Keynes' group portrait of Clemenceau, George, and Wilson was devastating:

> My last and most vivid impression is of . . . the President and the Prime Minister as the center of a surging mob and a babel of sound, a welter of eager, impromptu compromises and counter-compromises, all sound and fury signifying nothing, on what was an unreal question anyhow, the great issues of the morning's meeting forgotten and neglected; and Clemenceau silent and aloof on the outskirts — for nothing which touched the security of France was forward — throned, in his gray gloves, on the brocade chair, dry in soul and empty of hope, very old and tired, but surveying the scene with a cynical and almost impish air; and when at last silence was restored and the company had returned to their places, it was to discover that he had disappeared.[8]

Keynes applied the coup de grace with a sketch of Wilson that has clung to the President's reputation like a shadow. Having described a generation's shortsightedness, lack of integrity, dryness of soul, Chapter III ends with a Dickensian image of paralysis:

> If only the President had not been so conscientious, if only he had not concealed from himself what he had been doing, even at the last moment he was in a position to have recovered lost ground and to have achieved some very considerable successes. But the President was set. His arms and legs had been spliced by the surgeons to a certain posture, and they must be broken again before they could be altered. To his horror, Mr. Lloyd George, desiring at the

[8] Pp. 31-32. Keynes is very close to Pound when he gives his portraits symbolic resonance of the demonic. The Council of Four, no less than the builders of "babel" or the occupants of Dante's *Inferno* are constantly in motion but powerless to act. In a heroic decorum, they are comic figures—debased puppets of men controlled by negation and resembling the comic devils in the medieval cycle plays with their mysterious disappearances and "cynical and almost impish air."

last moment all the moderation he dared, discovered that he could not in five days persuade the President of error in what it had taken five months to prove to him to be just and right. After all, it was harder to de-bamboozle this old Presbyterian than it had been to bamboozle him; for the former involved his belief in and respect for himself.

Thus in the last act the President stood for stubbornness and a refusal of conciliations. (pp. 54-55)

Although I would like to postpone any application of this material to the *Cantos* until later in the chapter, certain things should be apparent by now. As early as 1915, Pound had condemned Wilson as "a man incapable of receiving ideas" and "a type of low vitality."[9] By 1919, when Canto VII was composed and *The Economic Consequences of the Peace* was published,[10] the image of Wilson and his colleagues as impotent and dangerously imperceptive old men had already become common property. Thus, when Pound wrote in Canto VII of "Thin husks I had known as men . . . speaking a shell of speech . . . Propped between chairs and table," he might well have been drawing on Gourmont, Eliot, and James,[11] but he was also enlarging a picture of the leaders of Europe that would have been familiar to his readers. And in 1922, when Pound wrote Canto XII, it was quite natural to describe more old men sitting around another table as Wilsonian "ranked presbyterians."

Three years before the Paris conference, Sigmund Freud looked at the experience of the soldier generation, and his

[9] See "This Super-Neutrality," *The New Age*, XVII, 25 (October 21, 1915), p. 595.

[10] Pound had read Keynes by 1920, when he mentioned him in a review of Douglas's *Economic Democracy*. See *Selected Prose*, pp. 177-179.

[11] I have discussed Canto VII in relation to Gourmont, James and Eliot in Chapter Five, pp. 220-21.

analysis took on a pattern similar to the *Economic Conse-quences of the Peace*. Although we do not know whether Keynes or Pound knew of Freud's speculations, they are well worth considering. By seeing how popular mythology could give a common shape to work in subjects as diverse as eco-nomics and psychology, we begin to understand some of the complicated functions of myth in the *Cantos*, where the abil-ity to suggest many levels of cultural reality is at the heart of Pound's mythic method.

Freud began his two-part essay "Thoughts for the Times on War and Death" with a lament about the difficulty of isolating a coherent etiology from the impressions of war: "Swept as we are," he wrote, "into the vortex of this wartime, our information one-sided, ourselves too near to focus the mighty transformations which have already taken place or are beginning to take place, and without a glimmering of the inchoate future, we are incapable of apprehending the sig-nificance of the thronging impressions, and know not what value to attach to the judgments we form."[12] The subject that Freud set himself was the attitude of horrified betrayal that the youthful generation had begun to take toward its elders. He attributed such "disillusionment" in part to the unnatural self-delusions of pre-war society. The refinement of society, about which the Victorians were so proud, "ex-acts good conduct and does not trouble itself about the im-pulses underlying it." Modern man in consequence has been forced to bear the "resulting strain" of an "unceasing sup-pression of instinct." Although the presumptions of civiliza-tion have been that instinctual demands can be eradicated, Freud wrote, "In reality there is no such thing as eradicating evil tendencies." Consequently, civilization has tended to become more and more hypocritical and at the same time more and more prone to subjection by its unrecognized baser instincts. Shifting his argument to individual nations, he declared that "Their interests serve them, at most, as ra-

[12] My citations are from the translation and collection of the essay in *Civilisation, War and Death* (London, 1915), edited by John Rickman.

tionalizations for their passions; they parade their interests as their justification for satisfying their passions." The disillusionment becomes greatest for those citizens who have internalized the professed ideals of their nations:

> The state exacts the utmost degree of obedience and sacrifice from its citizens, but at the same time treats them as children by maintaining an excess of secrecy, and a censorship of news and expressions of opinion that renders the spirits of those thus intellectually oppressed defenceless against every unfavourable turn of events and every sinister rumour. It absolves itself from the guarantees and contracts it had formed with other states, and makes unabashed confession of its rapacity and lust for power, which the private individual is then called upon to sanction in the name of patriotism.

Modern citizens were thus cast into the peculiar role of oppressed children. They must play the part of a mature son or daughter forced to suffer the whims of an irrational and hypocritical parent, whom they know to be blind to his own impulses. Freud ended the first part of his essay with a recommendation that his fellow citizens humor their nation states as they would humor a father who is passing through his second childhood: "the demands we make upon them ought to be far more modest. Perhaps they are reproducing the course of individual evolution, and still to-day represent very primitive phases in the organization and formation of higher unities."

Although he wrote about psychological forces rather than economic ones, it is not difficult to see that the outline of Freud's case study is similar to the contemporary work of Maynard Keynes. According to both, the delusions of Europe's wartime leaders had rendered them unconscious of currents that underlie human behavior. With only a debased perception of unseen forces, the aging leaders stumbled over trip wires that released natural havoc in various forms. There was an implicit warning, of course, in both Freud and Keynes that the imperceptive old men were still in control and could trigger, at any time, the explosion of Europe all over again.

§

Between 1917 and 1919 the author of the *Cantos* came to share with Keynes and Freud their vision of Europe helplessly unconscious of buried forces of disorder. The poem's new somberness reflected both the contemporary political situation and the cultural iconography we have been examining. But the strongest single influence on Pound's darkening palette proved to be neither the founder of modern economics nor the father of twentieth-century psychology. That distinction belongs to an unknown Jeremiah who combined an intuition for social and psychological dynamics with a program of radical solutions. Although the traditional explanations of Pound's interest in Major C. H. Douglas emphasize the economics of art,[13] a skeptical investigation suggests otherwise. Douglas' appreciation of the value of design was attractive, but far more attractive was his analysis of the explosiveness of modern society. He approached the effects of unchecked capitalism with what Pound called a humanist perspective, and his images of the European situation helped Pound to incorporate economic history into traditional epic iconography.

Pound encountered Douglas in 1918 discussing economics with Orage at the office of *The New Age,* and he must have sensed an immediate philosophic affinity. Having argued since 1915 against collectivism,[14] Pound was drawn to Douglas'

[13] The best explanation of how Douglas relates to the problems of the twentieth-century artist (and, for that matter, the best explanation of Douglas' economics in general) can be found in Hugh Kenner, *The Pound Era* (Berkeley and Los Angeles, 1971), pp. 301-317. But see also Earl Davis, *Vision Fugitive: Ezra Pound and Economics* (Lawrence, 1968), especially pp. 30-31 and Stock's *Life,* pp. 221ff.

[14] See above, pp. 155-56.

demand that the state allow each individual "in common with his fellows . . . [to] choose, with increasing freedom and complete independence, whether he will or will not assist in any project which may be placed before him."[15] Like Pound, Douglas saw arrayed against this eventuality a group of forces from Socialism to Prussianism, all growing in strength, and all ultimately making a "claim for the complete subjection of the individual to an objective which is externally imposed on him; which is not necessary or even desirable that he should understand in full; and the forging of a social, industrial and political organisation which will concentrate control of policy while making effective revolt completely impossible."[16] Whereas Pound had been satisfied with pointing out the cultural benefits of encouraging individualism, Douglas described the consequences of suppressing it. His *Economic Democracy* appeared in *The New Age* beginning June 5, 1919 — two weeks before the Treaty of Versailles was signed and a few months before the publication of *The Economic Consequences of the Peace*. In it, he combined economics with psychology and argued that Europe had sowed the dragon's tooth of collectivism, and had reaped the Great War as its first harvest.

The keynote of *Economic Democracy* was a jeremiad against the gathering forces of darkness. In the pattern of Freud and Keynes, Douglas warned against the "decaying" pediments of society, and pointed to the "play of forces" that had been made visible by the war:

> There has been a very strong tendency . . . to regard fidelity to one set of opinions as being something of which to be proud, and consistency in the superficial sense as a test of character. . . .
>
> It thus comes about that modification in the creed of the

[15] *The New Age*, xxv (1919), p. 97. I cite from the serial publication of *Economic Democracy*, which began on June 5, 1919, and continued until August 7 of the same year.
[16] *Ibid.*, p. 98.

orthodox is both difficult and conducive to exasperation; since because the form is commonly mistaken for the substance it is not clearly seen why a statement which has embodied a sound principle, may in course of time become a dangerous hindrance to progress. . . .

At various well-defined epochs in the history of civilisation there has occurred such a clash of apparently irreconcilable ideas as has at this time most definitely come upon us. Now, as then, from every quarter come the unmistakable signs of crumbling institutions and discredited formulae, while the widespread nature of the general unrest, together with the immense range of pretext alleged for it, is a clear indication that a general re-arrangement is imminent.

As a result of the conditions produced by the European War, the play of forces, usually only visible to expert observers, has become apparent to many who previously regarded none of these things. The very efforts made to conceal *the existence of springs of action* other than those publicly admitted, has riveted the attention of an awakened proletariat as no amount of positive propaganda would have done. A more or less conscious effort to refer the results of the social and political system to the Bar of individual requirement has, on the whole, quite definitely resulted in a verdict for the prosecution. . . .

Before proceeding to the consideration of the remedies proposed, it may be well to emphasise the more salient features of the indictment, and in doing this it is of the first consequence to make very sure of the code against which the alleged offenses have been committed. And here we are driven *right back to first principles — to an attempt to define the purposes, conscious or unconscious, which govern humanity* in its ceaseless struggle with environment.

To cover the whole of the ground is, of course, impossible. The infinite combinations into which the drive of evolution can assemble *the will, emotions, and desires,* are probably outside the scope of any form of words not too symbolical for everyday use.

But of the many attempts which have been made it is quite possible that the definition embodied in the majestic words of the American Declaration of Independence, "the inalienable right of man to life, liberty and the pursuit of happiness" is still unexcelled, although the promise of its birth is yet far from complete justification; and if words mean anything at all, these words are an assertion of the supremacy of the individual considered collectively, over any external interest. . . . It is suggested that the primary requisite is to obtain . . . such control of initiative that by its exercise every individual . . . in common with his fellows . . . can choose, with increasing freedom and complete independence, whether he will or will not assist in any project which may be placed before him.

The basis of independence of this character is most definitely economic. . . .

It seems clear that only by a recognition of this necessity can the foundations of society be so laid that no superstructure built upon them can fail, as the superstructure of capitalistic society is most unquestionably failing, because the pediments which should sustain it are honeycombed with decay.[17] (Emphasis mine)

These passages resemble Keynes' prophecy, but strike a more (Pound's word)[18] "humanistic" key. Keynes called attention only to the "forces" of international interdependence, but Douglas argued that a study of economics must go "back to first principles . . . conscious and unconscious," and must penetrate to the psychological "springs" of "will, emotion, and desires." European disregard of those "principles" has already begun to decay the "pediments" of society. And, Douglas went on, where the disregard has been most pronounced, the explosive side-effects have been obvious. Ger-

[17] *Ibid.,* p. 97.   [18] Below, p. 287.

many had been "completely altered in two generations," and "has become notorious for bestiality and inhumanity only offset by a slavish discipline. Its statistics of child suicide during the years preceding the war exceeded by many hundreds per cent those of any other country in the world, and were rising rapidly. Insanity and nervous breakdown were becoming by far the gravest problem of the German medical profession."[19]

Such, according to Douglas, were the psychological demons called up by collectivism. In every modern industrial state they are accompanied by equally destructive economic demons. Three centrifugal forces exist in modern capitalism that are on the verge of tearing the modern world apart: a constant artificial pressure to increase production; a rise in prices every time production increases; and a decrease in the standard of living every time prices rise. The combined effect, as Douglas saw it, is to produce an explosive situation of alarming proportions; and his charts (Fig. 1) constitute emblems of European dissolution no less frightening than Yeats's "widening gyre."

Douglas got to the meat of his argument in Chapters Four, Five, and Six, beginning with an analysis of what he called "super-production." The present system, he wrote, encourages production to multiply even when there is no real demand for new products. "If production stops, distribution stops, and, as a consequence, a clear incentive exists to produce useless or superfluous articles in order that useful commodities already existing may be distributed."[20] There is never enough money in circulation to pay for those commodities, however, and so the real determination over what will be produced comes not from consumer demand but from bankers' loan-credit. Since bankers wish merely to make the quickest possible return on their investment, loan-credit almost always flows into capital improvements rather than into improved consumer necessities:

[19] *The New Age*, xxv, p. 98.
[20] *Ibid.*, p. 161.

... loan-credit, that is to say purchasing power *created* by the banks on principles which are directed solely to the production of a positive financial result ... has become the great stimulus either to manufacture or to any financial or commercial operation which will result in a profit, that is to say, an inflation of figures. ...

... loan credit is never available to the consumer as such, because consumption as such has no commercial value.[21]

Thus, Douglas concluded, ever-increasing capital increments lead to a monstrous "super-production" that has nothing to do with society's real needs.

Douglas went on to point out that "super-production" is as harmful as it is needless. Every manufacture represents a decrease in society's total energy, and arbitrarily accelerating production decreases the wealth of the community at the same time as it "involves a continuous inflation of currency, a rise in prices, and a consequent dilution of purchasing power."[22] The result is a continuous borrowing on the future to keep up a system that makes whatever is convenient. The system is oiled by make-work and offensive advertising, and the consumer's constantly decreasing purchasing power is buffered only by a continual cheapening of goods.

At the end of Chapter Six, Douglas, usually dispassionate, threw up his hands in a gesture of Swiftian disgust:

All these and many other forms of avoidable waste take their rise in the *obsession of wealth defined in terms of money*; an obsession which even the steady fall in the purchasing power of the unit of currency seems powerless to dispel; which obscures the whole object and meaning of scientific progress and places the worker and the honest man in a permanently disadvantageous position in com-

[21] *Ibid.*, p. 147.

[22] *Ibid.* Douglas contends that the decrease in purchasing power is hidden by a complicated system of deceptive cost-accounting, and his points are well explicated by Hugh Kenner in *The Pound Era*, pp. 304-306.

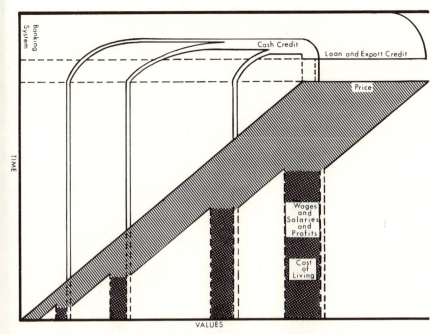

FIGURE 1. "The Inducement to Super-Production." Taken from *The New Age* XXV.22 (September 25, 1919), p. 356.

In the above diagram the shaded portion shows the growth of the cost of an article (or, equally, of the production of a community) under the bank-credit (so-called capitalistic) system, by the successive addition of all the sums paid out in all forms of remuneration, as shown in the vertical columns.

The cross-hatched portion of the vertical columns shows the money value of the cost of living of the persons amongst whom the remuneration is distributed; this represents over 90 per cent of the sums distributed as wages and salaries. In the case of large individual incomes, although considerable surplus purchasing power is available, there is no psychological demand, except for the purpose of "making money." There is consequently an increasing surplus production which must be met by credit.

If the above statements are correct for any industry chosen at random, they must be true for all industry. Consequently an increasing proportion of the product of industry must be appropriated by the financier and the entrepreneur who control credit, in contradistinction to the ultimate consumer who does not.

It should, of course, be borne in mind in connection with the above diagram that the economic system is dynamic, not static. All the components of it should be visualized as changing both in position, direction, and magnitude. A vector diagram could be constructed to represent the condition, but would not be generally intelligible.—C.H.D.

parison with the financier and the rogue.[23] (Emphasis mine)

In the last two chapters, he related the constantly expanding spiral of "super-production" to international relations, and extended the compass of his analysis until it was seen to include the forces that have caused the Great War, and that will cause another:

> We have already seen that a feature of the industrial economic organisation at present is the illusion of international competition, arising out of the failure of internal effective demand as an instrument by means of which production is distributed. This failure involves the necessity of an increasing export of manufactured goods to undeveloped countries, and this forced export, which is common to all highly developed capitalistic States, has to be paid for almost entirely by the raw material of further exports. Now, it is fairly clear that under a system of centralised control of finance such as that we are now considering, this forced competitive export becomes impossible; while at the same time the share of product consumed inside the League becomes increasingly dependent on a frenzied acceleration of the process.
>
> The increasing use of mechanical appliances, with its capitalisation of overhead charges into prices, renders the distribution of purchasing power, through the medium of wages in particular, more and more ineffective; and as a result individual discontent becomes daily a more formidable menace to the system. It must be evident therefore then an economic system involving forced extrusion of product from the community producing, as an integral component of the machinery for the distribution of purchasing power, is entirely incompatible with any effective League of Nations, because the logical and inevitable end of economic competition is war.[24]

[23] *Ibid.*, p. 161. [24] *Ibid.*, p. 243.

At the heart of Douglas' book is a tragic picture of useless waste and frustration; he described how first the individual will and then the social community are misdirected by capitalism toward inhuman purposes. He decried the redefinition of wealth in terms of money, and he saw modern economics as "a complete negation of all real progress," where progress is taken to mean something which serves "a definite, healthy, and sane human requirement."[25]

In passages like the following, Douglas recoiled from the "brutalising" substitution of artificial human satisfactions for real ones. And, to a mind like Pound's, saturated in Dante, what might have been merely conventional phrases took on new life:

> It is one of the most curious phenomena of the existing economic system that a large portion of the world's energy, both intellectual and physical, is directed to the *artificial stimulation* of the desire for luxuries by advertisement and otherwise, in order that the remainder may be absorbed in what is frequently toilsome, disagreeable and brutalising work; to the end that a device for the distribution of purchasing power may be maintained in existence. The irony of the situation is the greater since the perfecting of the organisation to carry on *this vicious circle* carries with it as we have just seen a complete negation of all real progress.[26] (Emphasis mine)

By depicting the course of industrialism as a "vicious circle," and by permitting the inference to be drawn (with the words "artificial stimulation") that perverted progress was equivalent to perverted sexuality, Douglas enabled modern life to be focused through the lens of the *Inferno*. In *Inferno* XI, Dante coupled the crime of usury, the perversion of wealth, with the crime of sodomy, the perversion of human reproductiveness; and Dante portrayed his sodomists "moving continually" in a vicious circle over a wasteland of hot

[25] *Ibid.*, p. 148.   [26] *Ibid.*

sand. In the same Canto, Virgil explained that usury was in its essence a perversion of the will of God, of nature itself, and of man's art:

"Force may be used against God, against oneself, against a neighbor. . . . Violence may be done to the Godhead by denying and blaspheming Him in the heart and by despising nature and her bounty, and therefore the smallest round [giron] stamps with its seal both Sodom and Cahors [usurers]. . . .

"Philosophy, for one who understands," he said to me, "notes, not in one place only, how nature takes her course from the divine mind and its art; and if thou note well thy *Physics* thou wilt find, not many pages on, that your art, as far as it can, follows nature as the pupil its master, so that your art is to God, as it were, a grandchild. By these two, if thou recall to mind *Genesis* near the beginning, it behoves mankind to gain their livelihood [*prender sua vita*: grasp one's life would be a better approximation, with an understanding of the spiritual overtones of *vita*] and their advancement [*avanzar la gente*: advance one's nation or folk], and because the usurer takes another way [*altra via tene*], he despises nature both in herself and in her follower [man, or more properly the pious arts of man], setting his hope elsewhere."

According to Douglas, economic institutions now force our entire society to try to gain a "livelihood" and build a "folk" on the sandy foundations of an "artificial" and unnatural "desire for luxuries." We carry on "this vicious circle," but it cannot go on forever. Unless we perceive the instability of our situation, we will experience the consequences of nature's disastrous revenge.

When Pound reviewed *Economic Democracy* in 1920, he responded precisely to the Dantesque aspect of Douglas' vision. In the *Athenaeum*, Pound remembered Douglas' remarks about our "brutalising" system, and wrote: "The author tries with undeniable honesty to solve the *vicious-circle*

286

riddle" (emphasis mine).[27] He praised Douglas' "humanism," and he handled in mythological terms Douglas' contention that modern economics has perverted the individual will. Douglas' reforms, he said, would assure us of "a much chastened Mammon"; but if we do not heed them we will expose ourselves to the "uniforming Death" within modern industrialism, which has already "encroached upon the purlieus of the living":

> The "button-moulder" of Ibsenian drama has long since passed from the supernatural to the mundane; uniforming Death has donned the robe of the social theorist, and, not content to wait extreme unctions, has encroached upon the purlieus of the living. Major Douglas' realism begins with a fundamental denial that man with his moods and hypostases is or can decently ever become a "unit"; in this underlying, implicit and hardly elaborated contention lies the philosophic value of his treatise. He is for a free exercise of the will, and his paragraphs arouse and rearouse one to a sense of how far we have given up our individual wills in all matters of economics. (*Selected Prose*, p. 177)

By this time Pound had absorbed Douglas' discussion of society's "obsession of wealth defined in terms of money,"[28] and it is clear that he had inserted it into the literary framework of something like Spenser's "garden of Mammon." It was not too long afterwards, we remember, that a combination of Douglas and the humanist tradition appeared in the *Cantos'* picture of usurious modern Venice as a "pleached arbour of stone" (Canto XVII).

Pound's reading of Douglas thus allowed him to incorporate Europe's historical situation into familiar iconographic terms. Douglas, by systematically analyzing the dynamics of postwar "decay," had articulated his own version of the myth

[27] From "Probari Ratio," first printed in *The Athenaeum*, xciv, 4, 692 (April 2, 1920), p. 45; and reprinted in *Selected Prose*, pp. 177-179.

[28] See above, p. 282.

of Europe's buried forces of dissolution that had so occupied writers as diverse as Keynes and Yeats. And in the postwar Cantos (with Douglas' Dantesque *façon de voir* paving the way), Pound coordinated the local iconography of that myth (the old men, the buried charges, the unexpected explosions) with the larger iconographic system of the *Commedia*. Late in 1919, for example, Pound depicted the infernal situation of Alessandro, who "in abuleia," "held his death for a doom" (Canto V). We understand a great deal more about the resonance of Alessandro's situation when we read in Pound's *Little Review* report on *Economic Democracy* that "Douglas' book offers an alternative to bloody and violent revolutions, and might on that account be more welcomed than it will be, but perspicacity is not given to all men, and many have in abuleia gone to their doom" (*Selected Prose*, p. 182). Alessandro is one of the old men of Europe who have allowed their smug self-delusion to blind them to the hidden forces of "bloody and violent revolution" that modern economics has called up by its perversion of God and nature.

We should approach the "economic themes"of the *Cantos* as we approach the astronomy of *Paradise Lost* or the politics of the *Divina Commedia*. Pound's *usura*, Milton's celestial spheres, Dante's Holy Roman Empire are all entities that cannot be completely defined outside the poems they inhabit because their full meaning exists only within the cosmography of the poems themselves. A knowledge of *Economic Democracy* will help us to understand why Pound characterized usury as he did; but it will prove ultimately misleading unless we understand it, as Pound did, in the light of the literary foundations of the *Cantos*.

The condemnation of usury in *Inferno* XI drew on a long history of special associations in the classical and Christian tradition. In his commentary on the *Inferno*, Charles Singleton points to the continuity between Aristotle and Aquinas on the subject, and cites Aquinas' remark that "a kind of birth takes place when money grows from [other] money. For this reason the acquisition of money is especially contrary to

Nature [*maxime praeter naturam*], because it is in accordance
with Nature that money should increase from natural goods
and not from money itself."[29] In the *Cantos*, Pound continues
the associations of that tradition. The usurers of Canto XIV
owe their identities to Douglas' historical analysis, but we can
trace their configurations (brutish monsters, swollen foetuses)
to *Inferno* XIV, where usurers squat "like dogs in summer that
ply, now snout, now paw, when they are bitten by fleas or
gnats or flies." In the end, we must acknowledge that Dante
combined with Douglas in Pound's mind to make usury not
just a contemporary problem but the *Cantos'* most important
emblem of the fall of the "green world" of natural bounty.
The *Cantos* condemn *usura*, the "obsession of wealth defined
in terms of money," not just because it interferes with an artist's creation ("Came not by usura Angelico"), but because
it perverts the bounty and sustenance of God's art, which is
nature.

We have seen that when Pound wrote about the power of
money in 1920 he mythologized it into the figure of "Mammon," and when he referred to the avenging demon of collectivism he called it "uniforming Death." It was Pound's
life-long habit, of course, to handle man's "moods and hypos-
tases" mythologically; and these two examples are characteristic of his search during 1918-1920 for figures that would
allow Europe's vision of impending chaos to be translated
into the medium of the *Cantos*. That search represented the
last major development in the genesis of A *Draft of* XVI
Cantos, and with an examination of it I shall end my study.

Pound's most explicit formulation of the "buried forces"
myth came in August 1918, almost immediately after he met
C. H. Douglas. Writing in the *Little Review* on Henry
James, Pound began one of his standard defenses of "realist"
literature. As he had done so often since 1915, he repeated
Flaubert's statement that the war of 1870 would never have
taken place had Europe read *Education Sentimentale*. Then,

[29] *The Divine Comedy*. Translated, with a commentary, by Charles S.
Singleton (Princeton, 1970). *Inferno*, Volume II, p. 182.

in praise of James, he started to consider the analytical value of James's portraits. But rather than proceeding in his normal, understated style, Pound took the unusual step of expressing his point with a mixed metaphor: "As Armageddon has only too clearly shown," he wrote, "national qualities are the *great gods of the present* and Henry James spent himself from the beginning in an analysis of these *potent chemicals*; trying to determine from the given microscope slide the nature of the Frenchness, Englishness, Germanness, Americanness, *which chemicals too little regarded, have in our time exploded for want of watching*" (emphasis mine). (LE, pp. 300-301)

Pound's description of the gods as "potent chemicals," so different from his 1913 statement that "A god is an eternal state of mind" (PD 2, p. 96), marks out his fellowship in the European nightmare of 1918-1919. Like Yeats and Lawrence, he based his understanding of "the great gods of the present" on powerful, natural forces. Like Keynes, who argued that England was "unconscious" of the "heaving earth," he contended that Europe had failed disastrously to perceive the power of those potent chemicals which "too little regarded, have in our time exploded for want of watching."

Pound wrote that James had uncovered the explosive force of "national qualities," but in the same essay he indicated that there were other more dangerous gods than these. Remarking that there were some areas that existed beyond James's reach, he cautioned his readers that James "sacrifices, or rather fails to attain, certain intensities" because he leaves out of his stories a dimension that Balzac, a lesser artist, achieved — a representation of characters "under the ἀνάγκη of modernity, cash necessity" (LE, p. 300). Pound, it seems, with Douglas and Dante at the back of his mind, had already begun to calculate the enormous power of "cash necessity" over modern life. He imagined that power in the Aeschylean terms of *anagke*,[30] and was starting to believe that the most

---

[30] I use Pound's transliteration in place of the usual *ananke*.

"intense" writing could not disregard it. Perhaps he had then connected the portrayal of "cash necessity" with the task of writing a modern epic. At any rate, we know he later wrote (in "Date Line, 1934") that "An epic is a poem including history. I don't see that anyone save a sap-head can now think he knows any history until he understands economics . . . Ariadne's thread . . . I am leaving my remark on *anagke* in the H. James notes" (LE, pp. 86-87).

We can trace Pound's exploration for materials to portray "the great gods of the present" from "the H. James notes" to the "Hellenist Series," which also began publication in August 1918.[31] Although the ostensible intention of the "Hellenist" articles was to compare the fidelity of Renaissance and modern translations to certain Greek texts, he took the occasion to compile a collection of passages relevant to his new concerns. In the two essays devoted to the translations of Hugues Salel, for example, Pound considered eight extended Homeric texts, and seven of them treated the enormous power of Homer's gods.[32] By examining their common preoccupations, we get a sense of the types of experience Pound was considering for his darkening inferno.

The passages cited in "Hugues Salel" can be divided into two parts according to the way they show men responding to the gods. One group treats the "explosions" of gods whose power has been "disregarded" by impious men, and includes the beginnings of both the *Iliad* and *Odyssey*, which tell us of the "ire" of Apollo and Neptune. A second group, com-

[31] The "Hellenist Series," reprinted in LE under the title "Translators of Greek: Early Translators of Homer," appeared monthly in *The Egoist* from August 1918 to April 1919. "Hugues Salel" comprised parts I and III of that series. The others were "Andreas Divus" (part II); "Sappho" (part IV); and "Translation of Aeschylus" (the section printed in LE, pp. 267-275, appeared as part V, and a sixth part considered *Prometheus Unbound*).

[32] The eight texts he considered were: *Iliad* III, 146-160; *Odyssey* I, 1-10; *Odyssey* II, 1-14; *Iliad* I, 1-5; *Iliad* III, 391-408; *Iliad* VI, 144-149; *Iliad* IX, 535-549; and *Iliad* X, 566-579. The exception is *Odyssey* II, 1-14, which treats the awakening of Telemachus.

posed of *Iliad* VI, 144-159 and *Iliad* X, 566-579, depicts the ritual piety of men who are anxious not to cross the god's power.[33] In the following, I wish to treat the implications of the first group at some length.

Iliad IX, 535-549 recounts the story of Oeneus and his son Meleagros, and tells how Oeneus brought down the anger of Artemis by failing to give her due sacrifice. In Lattimore's version of *Iliad* IX, Oeneus' negligence is accounted to two possibilities: "He had forgotten, or he had not thought, in his hard delusion" (IX, 537).[34] Pound, quoting Salel, renders it this way:

Calydon

En Calydon règnoit
Oenéus, ung bon Roy qui donnoit
De ses beaulx Fruictz chascun an les Primices
Aux Immortelz, leur faisant Sacrifices.
Or il aduint (ou bien par son uouloir.
Ou par oubly) qu'il meit à nonchalloir
Diane chaste, et ne luy feit offrande,
Dont elle print Indignation grande
Encontre luy, et pour bien le punir
Feit ung Sanglier dedans ses Champs. . . .[35]

---

[33] *Iliad* VI, 144-149, Glaukos' famous falling-leaves simile, comes in response to Diomedes' pious questioning. (Pound titles his citation "Glaucus Répond A Diomede.") Diomedes had explained that he does not wish to share the fate of Lykourgos, who unknowingly fought with Dionysus, and was striken blind.

In *Iliad* X, 566-579, Odysseus and Diomedes express a similar religious concern. The two heroes have just come back from their night raid, and Homer describes their ritual purification and homage to Athena. In Salel's version, they offer: "En faire ung jour à Pallas sacrifice, / Et luy offrir à jamais son seruice" (LE, p. 258).

[34] *The Iliad of Homer.* Translated and with an Introduction by Richmond Lattimore (Chicago, 1961), p. 212.

[35] See LE, p. 257. In Homer the story continues, describing how Meleagros killed the boar after it had done great damage. But Artemis, still angry, sends down a war. Again Meleagros begins to prevail, but again Artemis intervenes. She puts anger in his heart until he, Achilles-

In the *Iliad*, the Oeneus story is told by Phoenix as a warning to the recalcitrant Achilles, and is meant to represent a figure of the Trojan war. Pound, obviously interested in the content as well as the style of the passage, also included a citation that treated the *anagke* of the Trojan war directly. In *Iliad* III, 391ff, the pretense that the war has been caused by human interactions is suddenly dropped as we glimpse the power of an underlying supernatural compulsion. It is the moment that follows Paris' rescue from what would have been a disastrous (and culminating) encounter with Menelaus. Aphrodite, who rescued him, appears to Helen as a wool-dresser (a not unfitting occupation for one who prepares the loom of fate), and bids Helen come to Paris' vaulted room. It is at that point that Pound begins to quote Ogilby:

Helen

Who in this chamber, sumptuously adornd
Sits on your ivory bed, nor could you say,
By his rich habit, he had fought to-day:
A reveller or masker so comes drest,
From splendid sports returning to his rest.
Thus did love's Queen warmer desires prepare.
But when she saw her neck so heavenly faire.
Her lovely bosome and celestial eyes,
Amazed, to the Goddess, she replies:
Shy wilt thou happless me once more betray,
And to another wealthy town convey,
Where some new favourite must, as now at Troy
With utter loss of honour me enjoy. (LE, p. 256)

---

like, withdraws. When he finally reenters, it is too late, and Meleagros is denied his share of the gifts and honors. The story of the Aitolians is an emblem of the story of the Greeks at Troy, who become involved in the war (as Aeschylus reminds us in the *Agamemnon*) because they offended Diana, and who are unable to avoid their tragic destiny by victory alone. The picture of the ruined gardens at Calydon gave Pound an image of the consequences of affronting Diana, who becomes in the *Cantos* the goddess of natural bounty.

293

What happens then in the *Iliad* is one of the arresting moments of the poem. Aphrodite changes before our eyes from a honey-tongued persuader to a goddess at the full height of her awful power, a true Argicida. The goddess disabuses Helen of any thought that she, a mortal, can control her own fate, and the speech comes over in the poem as more of a revelation than a communication:

> Then in anger Aphrodite the shining spoke to her:
> 'Wretched girl, do not tease me lest in anger I forsake you
> and grow to hate you as much as now I terribly love you,
> lest I encompass you in hard hate, caught between both
> sides,
> Danaans and Trojans alike, and you wretchedly perish.'
>
> (Lattimore Translation, p. 111)

Aphrodite's speech tears away the fabric of human choice that the Trojans have been living with, and lets Helen (and through her, the reader) see behind the action to the forces that underlie choice. Helen is terrified, and submits quietly. From that moment on we know she is as much a god-controlled *Erinus* as a human character. The Trojans will be destroyed by the power of a goddess whom they do not understand, just as the Greeks will be decimated, and Agamemnon murdered, by the *anagke* that has entered the breasts of Agamemnon and Achilles. Immediately preceding *Iliad* III, 398-408, Pound alludes to Salel's translation of *Iliad* I, 1-5:

The Ire

Ie te supply Déesse gracieuse,
Vouloir chanter l'Ire pernicieuse,
Dont Achilles fut tellement espris,
Que par icelle, ung grand nombre d'espritz
Des Princes Grecs, par dangereux encombres,
Feit lors descente aux infernales Umbres.
Et leurs beaulx Corps privéz de Sépulture
Furent aux chiens et aux oiseulx pasture.

(LE, p. 256)

Aphrodite in Book III becomes just such a wrath, an angry god, a "chemical too little regarded" that has "exploded for want of watching."

The Greek text given most prominence in "Hugues Salel" took the notion of "Ire" one step further. In *Iliad* III, 146-60, Homer treated not only the destiny behind the war, but the Trojans' perception of that destiny. The story of the Trojan elders' response to Helen united the motif of hidden forces with the motif of atrophied consciousness. Pound would make it the keynote of Canto II and a token of the plight of Europe.

Pound gave no less than five translations of the episode — versions from Pope, Samuel Clark, Chapman, Rochefort, and Salel. The heart of the incident, of course, is the sudden impact of Helen on the aged counselors of Troy. These old men are well aware of her destructive power, and yet when they see her suddenly they are forced momentarily to endorse Paris' action. They experience an epiphany in which their knowledge of the goddess who moves through Helen is experienced as a brief sexual excitement. But they are dried-up old men, and the desire that might have developed into a true revelation of Aphrodite is insufficient. In Pope's words, they "like grasshoppers rejoice, / A bloodless race, that send a feeble voice."

In considering the various translations of the episode he had collected, Pound was most concerned with the "actual swing of words spoken," the "authentic cadence of speech" (LE, p. 250). It is through such cadences, according to him, that Homer or his translators are able to render "the old men's mental attitude" and capture their "reality" (LE, p. 254). We need only to relate these remarks to Pound's comments on realism to know what he means. Just as Flaubert was able to fix the immaturity of his characters by having them speak in clichés, so Pound sees Homer and Salel fixing the plight of the old men by realistically rendering their deficient vision in the "actual swing of words."

In the fifth part of the "Hellenist Series," Pound discussed a text that completed the metamorphosis of Helen from Homer's avatar of Aphrodite to a genuine historical force. It is an essay to which I have returned again and again in the course of this book, and it represents one of the most important contemporary sources for a study of the *Cantos*. It was in "Translation of Aeschylus" that Pound made his last gesture toward *Sordello*. It was in "Translation of Aeschylus" that he made his observations on "agglutinative" syntax. And it was in "Translation of Aeschylus" that he considered the tragic choruses that link the elders of Troy to the *anagke* of history.

The center of "Translations of Aeschylus" was an extended citation, mostly translated into Latin, of *Agamemnon*, 681-749. It is the choral ode that molds the pattern of the war into the pattern of the play. I present Smyth's "Loeb" version for convenient reference:

> Who can have given a name so altogether true — was it some power invisible guiding his tongue aright by forecasting of destiny? — who named that bride of the spear and source of strife with the name of Helen? For, true to her name, a Hell she proved to ships, Hell to men, Hell to city, when stepping forth from her delicate and costly-curtained bower, she sailed the sea before the breath of earthborn Zephyrus. And after her a goodly host of warrior huntsmen followed in pursuit on the oars' vanished track of a quarry that had beached its barque on Simois' leafy banks — in a strife to end in blood.
>
> To Ilium, its purpose fulfilling, Wrath brought a marriage rightly named a mourning, exacting in after-time requital for the dishonour done to hospitality and to Zeus, the partaker of the hearth, upon those who with loud voice celebrated the song in honour of the bride, even the bridegroom's kin to whom it fell that day to raise the marriage-hymn. But Priam's city hath learnt, in her old age, an altered strain, and now, I trow, waileth a loud song, even one of plenteous lamentation, calling Paris "evil-wed"; for

that she hath borne the burthen of a life fraught with desolation, a life of plenteous lamentation by reason of the wretched slaughter of her sons.

Even so a man reared in his house a lion's whelp, robbed of its mother's milk yet still desiring the breast. Gentle it was in the prelude of its life, kindly to children, and a delight to the old. Much did it get, held in arms like a nursling child, with its bright eye turned toward his hand, and fawning under compulsion of its belly's need.

But brought to full growth by time it showed forth the nature it had from its parents. Unbidden, in requital for its fostering, it prepared a feast with ruinous slaughter of the flocks; so that the house was defiled with blood, and they that dwelt therein could not control their anguish, and great was the carnage far and wide. A priest of ruin, by ordinance of God, was it reared in the house.

At first, methinks, there came to Ilium the spirit of un-ruffled calm, a delicate ornament of wealth, a darter of soft glances from the eye, love's flower that stingeth the heart. Then, swerving from her course, she made her marriage end in ruth, sped on to the children of Priam under escort of Zeus, the warder of host and guest, blasting with ruin by her sojourn and her companionship, a fiend ['Eρινύς]whose bridal was fraught with tears.

In this chorus, whose tangled syntax Pound says is meant to "remind the audience of the events of the Trojan war" (LE, p. 273), we see the past concentrated upon the present. A moment before Agamemnon arrives to be murdered by his own *Erinus* (Clytaemestra), the chorus recalls how the original offense of the Trojans against Zeus had called up Helen. Aeschylus thus uses dramatic irony to transfer the resonance of the disaster at Troy to the coming murder. The significance is not that Paris and Agamemnon are punished for what we would call sins, but rather that their impious self-delusions have put them so far out of touch with vital forces that they can no longer see the natural consequences of their actions. Impious blindness calls up necessity, *anagke*, and makes *Erines* out of first Helen, then Clytaemestra, then Electra.

In the *Agamemnon*, then, the events of the Trojan war are generalized into cultural history, and the figure of Helen becomes a true *anagke* or historical principle. In a panoramic canvas even larger than the *Iliad*'s, Aeschylus treats the impiety not of men but of "houses" and explores the mental attitudes of several generations. Once Pound had recognized the development between the Helen of *Iliad* III and the Helen who is the *Erinus* of *Agamemnon* 749, the techniques of the *Oresteia* became available for his own work. It is hardly accidental that, just as in the *Agamemnon* the role of *Erinus* is shared by Helen and Clytaemestra, in the *Cantos* the *anagke* of violated nature appears in the multiple guise of Helen, Eleanor, and Artemis. In Canto XXX it is "Madame ῩΛΗ" — Nature herself — who turns from bountiful goddess into nemesis when men disregard her rituals and her power.

"Translation of Aeschylus" was published in the January-February 1919 *Egoist*. In December of 1919, Pound wrote his father "done Cantos 5, 6, 7." In Canto VII, Pound used Aeschylus to combine Eleanor and Helen. The image of the desiccated old men had acquired its penultimate form:

> Eleanor (she spoiled in a British climate)
>   ῞Ελανδρος and ῾Ελέπτολις, and
>   poor old Homer blind,
>   blind as a bat,
> Ear, ear for the sea-surge;
>   rattle of old men's voices.

By the time Pound wrote the above, he no longer considered a modern experience of the gods to be primarily "delightful." The entire force of impious history and the late war rode behind his revised conception of myth. The *Cantos* would henceforth include Homer's perception of Helen as all the destructive energy of the sea, and Aeschylus' Helen, who, ἕλανδρος and ἑλέπτολις, embodied the nemesis of history. When Pound definitively revised the *Cantos* in 1923, he included an expanded version of the complex as a central motif in the prelude of what was now Canto II:

> And the wave runs in the beach-groove:
> "Eleanor, ἑλέναυς and ἑλέπτολις!"
> And poor old Homer blind, blind, as a bat,
> Ear, ear for the sea-surge, murmur of old men's voices;
> "Let her go back to the ships,
> Back among Grecian faces, lest evil come on our own,
> Evil and further evil, and a curse cursed on our children,
> Moves, yes she moves like a goddess
> And has the face of a god
>   and the voice of Schoeney's daughters,
> And doom goes with her in walking,
> Let her go back to the ships,
>   back among Grecian voices."

We can now see that the image of the old men included a vision of the wartime leaders and also of the paralysis to come. Unlike Wilson and Lloyd George and the prewar generation, Pound's old men have the sight to understand what is going to happen but not the will to stop it. They have enough of the old ritually inspired prophecy to peek under the "fact" and murmur an equivalent to Kurtz's "The horror! The horror!" In the final version of the *Cantos* their confrontation with Helen stands immediately after the appearance of Aphrodite Argicida, at the opening of Pound's journey into the inferno of modern life.

The *Odyssey*, the *Oresteia*, and the *Aeneid* turned upon the destruction of an impious world. The vision of the old men in Canto II and the image of "Troy but a heap of boundary stones" in Canto IV root Pound's epic in that ancient tradition. By his gesture toward Homer and Aeschylus, Pound was doing no more than Dante did in *Inferno* I, where Virgil was given leave to say:

Poeta fui, e cantai di quel giusto
figliuol d'Anchise che venne da Troia,
poi che 'l superbo Ilïòn fu combusto.
Ma tu, perchè ritorni a tanta noia?

I was a poet, and sang of that just son of Anchises who came from Troy after proud Ilium was burned. But thou, why art thou returning to such misery?

The *Cantos* comprise an epic like the *Aeneid* or the *Commedia*, which begins as the divine energies that are no longer harnessed by religious awareness sweep away an impious world. The poem proceeds through a hell of misdirected will, through a purgatorio where the old rituals are recaptured, to a paradise where "the shrine be again white with marble / . . . the stone eyes look again seaward." Like the *Commedia*, the *Cantos* begin by returning to the burning towers of Troy.

Appendix A

The *Future Cantos*

"Passages from the Opening Address in a Long Poem"

Ghosts move about me patched with histories.
You had your business: to set out so much thought,
So much emotion, and call the lot "Sordello."
Worth the evasion, the setting figures up
And breathing life upon them.
Has it a place in music? And your: "Appear Ve-
    rona!"?
                        I walk the airy street,
See the small cobbles flare with the poppy spoil.
'Tis your "Great Day," the Corpus Domini,
And all my chosen and peninsular village
Has spread this scarlet blaze upon its lane,
Oh, before I was up, — with poppy-flowers.
Mid-June, and up and out to the half ruined chapel,
Not the old place at the height of the rocks
But that splay barn-like church, the Renaissance
Had never quite got into trim again.
As well begin here, here began Catullus:
"Home to sweet rest, and to the waves deep laugh-
    ter,"
The laugh they wake amid the border rushes.
This is our home, the trees are full of laughter,
And the storms laugh loud, breaking the riven waves
On square-shaled rocks, and here the sunlight
Glints on the shaken waters, and the rain
Comes forth with delicate tread, walking from Isola
    Garda,
                Lo Soleils plovil.

301

It is the sun rains, and a spatter of fire
Darts from the "Lydian" ripples, *lacus undae,*
And the place is full of spirits, not *lemures,*
Not dark and shadow-wet ghosts, but ancient living,
Wood-white, smooth as the inner-bark, and firm of
    aspect
And all a-gleam with colour?
              Not a-gleam
But coloured like the lake and olive leaves,
GLAUKOPOS, clothed like the poppies, wearing
    golden greaves,
Light on the air. Are they Etruscan gods?
The air is solid sunlight, *apricus.*
Sun-fed we dwell there (we in England now)
For Sirmio serves my whim, better than Asolo,
Yours and unseen. Your palace step?
My stone seat was the Dogana's vulgarest curb
And there were not "those girls," there was one
    flare,
One face, 'twas all I ever saw, but it was real . . .
And I can no more say what shape it was . . .
But she was young, too young.
             True, it was Venice,
And at Florian's under the North arcade
I have seen other faces, and had my rolls for break-
    fast,
Drifted at night and seen the lit, gilt cross-beams
Glare from the Morosini.
            And for what it's worth
I have my background; and you had your back-
    ground,
Watched "the soul," Sordello's soul, flare up
And lap up life, and leap "to th' Empyrean";

          *   *   *   *   *

          Gods float in the azure air,
Bright gods and Tuscan, back before dew was shed;

It is a world like Puvis'?
                    Never so pale, my friend,
'Tis the first light — not half-light — Panisks
And oak-girls and the Maelids have all the wood;
                    Our olive Sirmio
Lies in its burnished mirror, and the Mounts Balde
     and Riva
Are alive with song, and all the leaves are full of
     voices.
"Non è fuggi."
                    "It is not gone." Metastasio
Is right, we have that world about us.
And the clouds bowe above the lake, and there are
     folk upon them
Going their windy ways, moving by Riva,
By the western shore, far as Lonato,
And the water is full of silvery almond-white swim-
     mers,
The silvery water glazes the upturned nipple.

"Images from the Second Canto of a Long Poem"

Send out your thought upon the Mantuan palace,
Drear waste, great halls; pigment flakes from the
     stone;
Forlorner quarter:
Silk tatters still in the frame, Gonzaga's splendour,
Where do we come upon the ancient people,
Or much or little,
Where do we come upon the ancient people?
"All that I know is that a certain star" —
All that I know of one, Joios, Tolosan,
Is that in middle May, going along
A scarce discerned path, turning aside
In "level poplar lands," he found a flower, and
     wept;

"Y a la primera flor," he wrote,
"Qu'ieu trobei, tornei em plor."
One stave of it, I've lost the copy I had of it in
    Paris,
Out of a blue and gilded manuscript:
Couci's rabbits, a slim fellow throwing dice,
Purported portraits serving in capitals.
Joios we have, by such a margent stream,
He strayed in the field, wept for a flare of colour
When Coeur de Lion was before Chalus;
Arnaut's a score of songs, a wry sestina;
The rose-leaf casts her dew on the ringing glass,
Dolmetsch will build our age in witching music,
Viols da Gamba, tabors, tympanons.
Yin-yo laps in the reeds, my guest departs,
The maple leaves blot up their shadows,
The sky is full of Autumn,
We drink our parting in saki.
Out of the night comes troubling lute music,
And we cry out, asking the singer's name,
And get this answer:
                  "Many a one
Brought me rich presents, my hair was full of jade,
And my slashed skirts were drenched in the secret
    dyes,
Well dipped in crimson, and sprinkled with rare
    wines;
I was well taught my arts at Ga-ma-rio
And then one year I faded out and married."
The lute-bowl hid her face. We heard her weeping.
Society, her sparrows, Venus' sparrows.
Catullus hung on the phrase (played with it as Mal-
    larmé
Played for a fan: "Rêveuse pour que je plonge");
Wrote out his crib from Sappho:
God's peer, yea and the very gods are under him
Facing thee, near thee; and my tongue is heavy,

And along my veins the fire; and the night is
Thrust down upon me.
That was one way of love, *flamma demanat*,
And in a year: "I love her as a father,"
And scarce a year, "Your words are written in
    water,"
And in ten moons: "O Caelius, Lesbia illa,
Caelius, Lesbia, our Lesbia, that Lesbia
Whom Catullus once loved more
Than his own soul and all his friends,
Is now the drab of every lousy Roman";
So much for him who puts his trust in woman.

Dordoigne! When I was there
There came a centaur, spying the land
And there were nymphs behind him;
Or procession on procession by Salisbury,
Ancient in various days, long years between them;
Ply over ply of life still wraps the earth here.
Catch at Dordoigne!

               Vicount St. Antoni —
"D'amor tug miei cossir" — hight Raimon Jordans
Of Land near Caortz. The Lady of Pena
"Gentle and highly prized."
And he was good at arms, and *bos trobaire*,
"Thou art the pool of worth, flood-land of pleasure,
And all my heart is bound about with love,
As rose in trellis that is bound over and over";
Thus were they taken in love beyond all measure.
But the Vicount Pena
Went making war into an hostile country,
And was sore wounded. The news held him dead,
"And at this news she had great grief and teen,"
And gave the church much wax for his recovery,
And he recovered,
"And at this news she had great grief and teen"
And fell a-moping, dismissed St. Antoni,

"Thus was there more than one in deep distress,"
So ends that novel. Here the blue Dordoigne
Placid between white cliffs, pale
As the background of a Leonardo. Elis of Mont-
    fort
Then sent him her invitations.

"An Interpolation taken from Third Canto of a Long Poem"

I've strained my ear for *-ensa, -ombra*, and *-ensa*,
And cracked my wit on delicate canzoni,
                Here's but rough meaning:
"And then went down to the ship, set keel to
    breakers,
Forth on the godly sea,
We set up mast and sail on the swart ship,
Sheep bore we aboard her, and our bodies also,
Heavy with weeping; and winds from sternward
Bore us out onward with bellying canvas,
Circe's this craft, the trim-coifed goddess.
Then sat we amidships — wind jamming the tiller —
Thus with stretched sail
                we went over sea till day's end.
Sun to his slumber, shadows o'er all the ocean,
Came we then to the bounds of deepest water,
To the Kimmerian lands and peopled cities
Covered with close-webbed mist, unpiercèd ever
With glitter of sun-rays,
Nor with stars stretched, nor looking back from
    heaven,
Swartest night stretched over wretched men there,
The ocean flowing backward, came we then to the
    place
Aforesaid by Circe.
Here did they rites, Perimedes and Eurylochus,
And drawing sword from my hip
I dug the ell-square pitkin,

Poured we libations unto each the dead,
First mead and then sweet wine, water mixed with
    white flour,
Then prayed I many a prayer to the sickly death's-
    heads,
As set in Ithaca, sterile bulls of the best
For sacrifice, heaping the pyre with goods.
Sheep, to Tiresias only; black and a bell sheep.
Dark blood flowed in the fosse,
Souls out of Erebus, cadaverous dead,
Of brides of youths, and of much-bearing old;
Virgins tender, souls stained with recent tears,
Many men mauled with bronze lance-heads,
Battle spoil, bearing yet dreary arms,
These many crowded about me,
With shouting, pallor upon me, cried to my men for
    more beasts.
Slaughtered the herds, sheep slain of bronze,
Poured ointment, cried to the gods,
To Pluto the strong, and praised Proserpine,
Unsheathed the narrow sword,
I sat to keep off the impetuous, impotent dead
Till I should hear Tiresias.
But first Elpenor came, our friend Elpenor,
Unburied, cast on the wide earth,
Limbs that we left in the house of Circe,
Unwept, unwrapped in sepulchre, since toils urged
    other.
Pitiful spirit, and I cried in hurried speech:
"Elpenor, how art thou come to this dark coast?
Cam'st thou a-foot, outstripping seamen?"
                    And he in heavy speech:
"Ill fate and abundant wine! I slept in Circe's
    ingle,
Going down the long ladder unguarded, I fell
    against the buttress,
Shattered the nape-nerve, the soul sought Avernus.

But thou, O King, I bid remember me, unwept, un-
    buried,
Heap up mine arms, be tomb by sea-board, and
    inscribed:
'A man of no fortune and with a name to come.'
And set my oar up, that I swung mid fellows."
Came then another ghost, whom I beat off, Anticlea,
And then Tiresias, Theban,
Holding his golden wand, knew me and spoke first:
"Man of ill hour, why come a second time,
Leaving the sunlight, facing the sunless dead, and
    this joyless region?
Stand from the fosse, move back, leave me my
    bloody bever,
And I will speak you true speeches."
                    And I stepped back,
Sheathing the yellow sword. Dark blood he drank
    then,
And spoke: "Lustrous Odysseus
Shalt return through spiteful Neptune, over dark
    seas,
Lose all companions." Foretold me the ways and
    the signs.
Came then Anticlea, to whom I answered:
"Fate drives me on through these deeps. I sought
    Tiresias,"
Told her the news of Troy. And thrice her shadow
                    Faded in my embrace."

Lie quiet Divus. Then had he news of many faded
    women,
Tyro, Alcmena, Chloris,
Heard out their tales by that dark fosse, and sailed
By sirens and thence outward and away,
And unto Circe. Buried Elpenor's corpse.
Lie quiet Divus, plucked from a Paris stall
With a certain Cretan's "Hymni Deorum";

The thin clear Tuscan stuff
      Gives away before the florid mellow phrase,
Take we the goddess, Venerandam
Auream coronam habentem, pulchram. . . .
Cypri munimenta sortita est, maritime,
Light on the foam, breathed on by Zephyrs
And air-tending Hours, mirthful, orichalci, with
      golden
Girdles and breast bands, thou with dark eyelids,
Bearing the golden bough of Argicida.

The above Passages from the Odyssey, done into an approximation of the metre of the Anglo-Saxon "Sea-farer."

Canto VI as it originally appeared
in A *Draft of XVI Cantos*

The Sixth Canto

THE tale of thy deeds, Odysseus!" and Tolosan
Ground rents, sold by Guillaume,
                    ninth duke of Aquitaine;
Till Louis is wed with Eleanor; the wheel . . .
("Conrad, the wheel turns
                    and in the end turns ill")
And Acre and boy's love . . . for her uncle was
Commandant at Acre, she was pleased with him;
And Louis, French King, was jealous
                    of days unshared
This pair had had together in years gone;
And he drives on for Zion, as "God wills"
To find, in six weeks time, the Queen's scarf is
Twisted atop the casque of Saladin.
"For Sandbrueil's ransom."
                    But the pouch-mouths add,
"She went out hunting there, the tuft-top palms
"Give spot of shade, she rode back rather late,
"Late, latish, yet perhaps it was not too late."
Then France again, and to be rid of her
And brush his antlers: Aquitaine, Poictiers!
Buckle off the lot! And Adelaide Castilla wears the crown.
Eleanor down water-butt, dethroned, debased, unqueen'd,
                    For five rare months.
Frazzle-top, the sand-red face, the pitching gait,
Harry Plantagenet, the sputter in place of speech,
But King about to be, King Louis, takes a queen.

"E quand li reis Louis lo entendit mout er fasché."
And yet Gisors, in six years thence, was Marguerite's. And
Harry *joven*
In pledge for all his life and life of all his heirs
Shall have Gisors and Vexis and Neauphal, Neufchastel;
But if no issue, Gisors shall revert
And Vexis and Neufchastel and Neauphal to the French
crown.
A song: *Si tuit li dol el plor el marrimen*
Del mon were set together they would seem but light
Against the death of the young English King,
Harry the Young is dead and all men mourn,
Mourn all good courtiers, fighters, cantadors.
And still Old Harry keeps grip on Gisors
And Neufchastel and Neauphal and Vexis;
And two years war, and never two years go by
but come new forays, and "The wheel
"Turns, Conrad, turns, and in the end toward ill."
And Richard and Alix span the gap, Gisors,
And Eleanor and Richard face the King,
For the fourth family time Plantagenet
Faces his dam and whelps, . . . and holds Gisors,
Now Alix' dowry, against Philippe-Auguste
(Louis' by Adelaide, wood-lost, then crowned at Etampe)
And never two year sans war.
And Zion still
Bleating away to Eastward, the lost lamb,
Damned city (was only Frederic knew
The true worth, and patched with Malek Kamel
The sane and sensible peace to bait the world
And set all camps disgruntled with all leaders.
"Damn'd atheists!" alike Mahomet growls,
And Christ grutches more sullen for Sicilian sense
Than does Mahound on Malek.)
The bright coat
Is more to the era, and in Messina's beach-way

Des Barres and Richard split the reed-lances
And the coat is torn.
> (Moving in heavy air: Henry and Saladin.
The serpent coils in the crowd.)
The letters run: Tancred to Richard:
> That the French King is
> More against thee, than is his will to me
> Good and in faith; and moves against your safety.

Richard to Tancred:
> That our pact stands firm,
> And, for these slanders, that I think you lie.

Proofs, and in writing:
> And if Bourgogne say they were not
> Deliver'd by hand and his,
> Let him move sword against me and my word.

Richard to Philip: silence, with a tone.
Richard to Flanders: the subjoined and precedent.
Philip a silence; and then, "Lies and turned lies
"For that he will fail Alix
"Affianced, and Sister to Ourself."
Richard: "My father's bed-piece! A Plantagenet
"Mewls on the covers, with a nose like his already."
Then:

In the Name
Of Father and of Son Triune and Indivisible
Philip of France by Goddes Grace

To all men presents that our noble brother
Richard of England engaged by our mutual oath
> (a sacred covenant applicable to both)
Need *not* wed Alix but whomso he choose
We cede him Gisors, Neauphal and Vexis
And to the heirs male of his house

Cahors and Querci Richard's   The abbeys ours
Of Figeac and Souillac And St. Gilles left still in peace
Alix returns to France.

Made in Messina in
The year 1190 of the Incarnation of the Word.

Reed lances broken, a cloak torn by Des Barres
Do turn King Richard from the holy wars.
                    And "God aid Conrad
"For man's aid comes slow," Aye tarries upon the road,
En Bertrans cantat.
                    And before all this
By Correze, Malemort
A young man walks, at church with galleried porch
By river-marsh, a sad man, pacing
Come from Ventadorn; and Eleanor turning on thirty years,
Domna jauzionda, and then Bernart saying:
                    "My lady of Ventadorn
"Is shut by Eblis in, and will not hawk nor hunt
"Nor get her free in the air,
                    nor watch fish rise to bait
"Nor the glare-wing'd flies alight in the creek's edge
"Save in my absence, Madame.
                    'Que la lauzeta mover,'
"Send word, I ask you, to Eblis,
                    you have seen that maker
"And finder of songs, so far afield as this
"That he may free her,
                    who sheds such light in the air."

313

GENERAL INDEX

Index

Index

Fry, Roger, 30
Frye, Northrop, 73-74
Futurism, 30, 31, 36

Gallup, Donald, 98n., 207n.,
 209n., 225n., 233n.
Gardner, Helen, 228n., 234,
 234n., 236, 237n.
Gaudier-Brzeska, Henri, 87, 90-
 91, 137, 140, 232
Gautier, Théophile, 206, 207,
 208, 243, 244, 262n.
"Gerontion" (Eliot), 3, 208,
 209-211, 209n., 216-217, 218-
 219, 220, 221, 222, 224, 225,
 228, 228n., 240, 266, 267;
 and *Ulysses*, 210; P.'s annotations, 210-211; and Cantos
 V-VII, 210-211, 216-219, 222-
 224
Glenn, E. M., 254n.
Golden Bough (Frazer), 114,
 114n., 121
Golding, Arthur, 158
Goncourt, Edmond de, 148,
 196n.
Gonzaga, 118, 191
Gourmont, Remy de, 7, 87, 144,
 147, 152-161, 155n., 156n.,
 163n., 167-168, 169, 170, 171,
 172, 173, 174, 175, 177, 180n.,
 195-196, 196n., 198, 202, 220,
 220n., 226, 235, 274, 274n.;
 as spokesman of modern
 thought, 156-158; as model
 for the Cantos, 159-161; and
 "Homage to Sextus Propertius,"
 175
Gregory, Lady Augusta, 103
"Grey Rock, The," (Yeats), 103-
 104

H.D. (Hilda Doolittle), 181

Hamilton College, 22
Hamlet (Shakespeare), 110
Hammond, J. L., 269, 269n.
Harrison, Jane, 88, 125, 126-128,
 126n., 131; *Myths of the
 Odyssey*, 126-127; *Prolegomena
 to the Study of Greek Religion*,
 127, 131; *Themis: A Study of
 the Social Origins of Greek
 Religion*, 127-128
Helen, 132, 182, 220, 261, 261n.,
 264, 266, 293-294, 295, 296,
 297, 298
Hermes, 133-134
Hermes Trismegistus, 137
Heydon, John, 86
Hogarth, William, 152
Hollow Men, The (Eliot), 222-
 223
Homer, 16, 75, 121, 123, 125,
 126, 128, 131, 132, 133, 181,
 246, 255, 260, 291-295, 292n.,
 299
Homeric Hymns, 124, 133, 141
Hueffer, Ford Madox, 146, 147
Hugo, Victor, 170
Hulme, T. E., 36-37, 89-90
Hutchins, Patricia, 146n.
Hynes, Gladys, 29n.

Ibsen, Henrik, 153, 154, 155, 287
ideogrammic method, 4, 10-14,
 21, 49, 178, 183, 197, 245n.;
 late formulation of, 10-14
Ignez da Castro, xi, 123-124, 191,
 191-192n.
Iliad, 128, 291-295, 292-293n.,
 298
Imagism, 4, 21, 23, 24, 48, 49,
 107, 145, 172n.
Impressionism, 31
Ithaca, 117, 134
Itow, Miscio, 160

318

Index

Jackson, Thomas, 29n., 88n.
Jacob, 264
James, Henry, 10, 142, 144, 148,
149-153, 158, 176-180, 202,
203, 204-205, 207, 213, 220,
220-221n., 225, 225n., 229,
230, 231, 235, 238, 241, 256,
259, 263, 274, 274n., 289-291;
realism in, 149-153; impact of
late style on the *Cantos*, 176-
180, 204-205; Jamesian "registers," 179, 229, 259; and
"Hugh Selwyn Mauberley,"
256, 259, 263
Job, 210
Johnson, Lionel, 74n., 158
Johnson, Samuel, 237
Joios, 118, 191, 200
Jonson, Ben, 175, 175n., 251
Joyce, James, 5, 83n., 95, 96,
104n., 125, 130, 131, 131n.,
144, 148-151, 153-154, 161,
193-197, 194n., 198, 200, 202,
206, 210, 216, 224, 230n., 232,
233, 242, 243-244, 245n., 253,
256-258. *See also* individual
works
Jung, Carl, 88
Juvenal, 244

Kandinsky, Wassily, 31-35, 38,
42, 49-50
Keats, John, 22
Kemper, C., 78n.
Kenner, Hugh, 15-16, 23n., 30n.,
125, 142, 142-143n., 149n.,
174, 204n., 209n., 228n., 234n.,
237n., 240n., 277n., 282n.
Keynes, John Maynard, 266,
270-274, 273n., 274n., 275,
276-277, 278, 280, 288, 290
Kurtz, 299
Kwannon, 138, 254-255

"La Figlia che Piange" (Eliot),
168
Laforgue, Jules, 161, 167, 168
(*bis*), 169-174, 170n., 172n.,
174, 196, 198, 205, 206
Lamartine, Alphonse de, 170
Landor, Walter Savage, 158, 162,
162n.
Lattimore, Richmond, 292, 294
Lawrence, D. H., 88, 265, 266,
290
Leighton, Frederick, 95
Leo X (Pope), 247 (*bis*)
Leonardo da Vinci, 138
Lewis, Percy Wyndham, 8, 24,
29-37, 39-48, 50, 51, 87, 166-
167, 167n., 171; impact on
Pound, 45-49; and the expanded
decorum of modernist art, 50.
See also individual works
Litz, A. Walton, 209n., 225n.,
228n., 234n., 237n., 238, 239
Lloyd George, 246, 273-274, 299
logopeia, 172, 172n., 173, 243,
246n.
Longus, 11
Lope de Vega, 122n., 123
Lorenzaccio, 213-214, 214n.,
217, 219, 222
Louis VIII, 213
Louis XIV, 212
"Love Song of J. Alfred Prufrock,
The" (Eliot), 140, 168, 206,
216, 227

Machiavelli, Niccolo, 217n.
Madame Bovary (Flaubert), 263
Malatesta, Sigismundo, 86, 222,
246, 248, 249
Mallarmé, Stéphane de, 136
"Manet and the Post-Impression-
ists" (exhibition organized by
Roger Fry), 30

Index

323

INDEX OF POUND'S WORKS

Index

327

Library of Congress Cataloging in Publication Data

Bush, Ronald.
   The genesis of Ezra Pound's Cantos.

   Includes index.
   1. Pound, Ezra Loomis, 1885-1972. The cantos. I. Title.
PS3531.082C293   811'.5'2   76-3245
ISBN 0-691-06308-7